Accounting Services, the Islamic Middle East, and the Global Economy

Accounting Services, the Islamic Middle East, and the Global Economy

David L. McKee
Don E. Garner
Yosra AbuAmara McKee

QUORUM BOOKS
Westport, Connecticut • London

Library of Congress Cataloging-in-Publication Data

McKee, David L.
  Accounting services, the Islamic Middle East, and the Global
economy / David L. McKee, Don E. Garner, Yosra AbuAmara McKee.
    p.   cm.
  Includes bibliographical references and index.
  ISBN 1–56720–139–3 (alk. paper)
  1. Accounting firms—Middle East.   2. Middle East—Economic
conditions.   3. Islam—Middle East.   I. Garner, Don E., 1935–   .
II. McKee, Yosra AbuAmara, 1948–   .   III. Title
HF5616.M628M39   1999
338.7'61657'0917671—dc21   98–30540

British Library Cataloguing in Publication Data is available.

Library of Congress Catalog Card Number: 98–30540
ISBN: 1–56720–139–3

First published in 1999

Quorum Books, 88 Post Road West, Westport, CT 06881
An imprint of Greenwood Publishing Group, Inc.
www.quorumbooks.com

Printed in the United States of America

The paper used in this book complies with the
Permanent Paper Standard issued by the National
Information Standards Organization (Z39.48–1984).

10 9 8 7 6 5 4 3 2 1

Contents

Acknowledgments

In the course of this work the authors benefited from the help and support of various individuals. Ross K. Baldwin of Arthur Andersen & Co. SC and Vincent King of Deloitte & Touche LLP provided invaluable materials concerning their respective firms.

The Library of California State University, Stanislaus was very helpful in the persons of Paula J. Crawford, Librarian–OnLine Research; and Julie A. Reuben, Librarian–Interlibrary loan specialist.

The research underlying the project was funded in part by a research, scholarship, and creative activity grant awarded by California State University, Stanislaus. Assistance was also provided in the form of a research sabbatical granted by Kent State University. The Department of Economics and the Graduate School of Management of that institution were generous in providing financial support for research travel.

Part One

The General Frame of Reference

Chapter One

A Preliminary Overview

The second half of the twentieth century has brought many changes to the region of the world known as the Middle East. During that period Israel has emerged as a regional superpower. The Arab jurisdictions of the region have become independent nations, free of varying degrees of colonial linkage to European powers. Iran has experienced a revolution and has curtailed its association with the United States. Turkey, a non-Arab state that is frequently considered to be a part of the region, continues to sustain a working relationship with its Arab neighbors, while at the same time attempting to clarify its position with respect to Europe.

The demise of the Soviet Union as a superpower has had repercussions within the region, notably the adjustments that have been made in the international posture of various nearby nations who had displayed varying degrees of cooperation with the former Soviet Union. The post–Cold War situation has also brought about adjustments in the nature and degree of U.S. involvement in the region.

Of course, the United States has been perceived by various Arab nations as a major supporter of Israel. Despite varying interpretations of the relationship between Israel and the United States, the latter nation appears to have taken on the role of a regional policeman in the Middle East. In that role, it has not been uniformly appreciated by the nations of the region.

Virtual libraries have been written concerning the issues referred to above. The present volume is not intended as an addition to those libraries. While acknowledging the obvious importance of such issues, the authors are concerned with other aspects of the circumstances facing the region, more specifically with a subset of business and economic concerns facing the region. Among such concerns are the developmental prospects of various individual nations and the role of international linkages in those prospects.

Beyond those concerns, the investigation is aimed at understanding the role that the major international accounting firms can or do play in facilitating business and economic operations in selected nations in the region and between those nations and the global economy. Events in the region have had a part in determining the nations to be discussed, notably events that have led to the exclusion of certain nations. Among those excluded are Iran and Iraq, as well as Jordan, Lebanon, and Syria. Israel has been excluded as well, since the project is aimed at investigating the issues described as they pertain to Islamic nations.

This volume builds upon earlier research regarding the role of major international accounting firms (McKee and Garner 1992, 1996; McKee, Garner, and AbuAmara McKee 1998). Though its organizational features do resemble to some extent those of the earlier investigations, the nature of the region has necessitated significant departures from earlier practices. Specifically, two factors appear to impact economic and business circumstances throughout the nations of the region. One is the impact of oil, which appears to be pervasive in many of the nations to be discussed. The other concerns Islam, which is the religion of the vast majority of the residents of the region and consequently impacts all aspects of human existence.

In pursuit of the goals set out, the volume is divided into four major sections. Part I attempts to present certain background information designed to assist in the understanding of what is to follow. In the chapter following this presentation an overview of international services is presented. Since the present authors have recently published an overview of the facilitative functions performed by business-related services in the global economy (1998, 3–11) the discussion in Chapter 2 is intended more as an addition to that work rather than a more historically complete treatment of the subject.

The exposition of services and their functions is followed in the ensuing chapter by an overview of Islam, since that religion has a major impact upon conditions and events in the region. In that context, an attempt is made to acquaint the reader with the basic tenets of the Muslim faith and the manner in which its practice impacts political, social, and economic considerations in the region.

No attempt is made to compare Islam to any other belief system, nor are judgmental stands adopted with respect to any Islamic beliefs or practices. Since the authors are not theologians, it is hoped that readers will accept their exposition as a good faith effort to provide information relevant to those contemplating conducting business in the region. Beyond that, it seems pertinent to suggest that the prospects of the region can only be assessed against a backdrop of the faith that governs the actions of its residents.

Part II presents overviews of the economies selected for discussion, their international linkages, and the parts played by major international accounting firms. This section of the volume is divided into four chapters. Chapter 4, which launches the section, provides a discussion of the situation in Egypt, and is followed by chapters which supply similar treatments of Saudi Arabia and Turkey.

Part II concludes with a review of the economies of the smaller jurisdictions of the Gulf Cooperation Council, and of course the role played by the major accounting firms in them. Specifically the chapter deals with Bahrain, Kuwait, Qatar, the United Arab Emirates, and Oman. This chapter completes the geographical menu of the volume. It is hoped that the nations selected for inclusion will serve to provide some understanding of business and economic concerns, and of course the role of the major international accounting firms in the Islamic Middle East.

In Part III, the emphasis is on a description of the legal and institutional parameters facing business operations, and the accounting field in the region. The organizational structure of this section resembles that of the preceding one. Separate chapters are devoted to detailing the business and accounting environments of Egypt, Saudi Arabia, and Turkey. The final chapter of the section deals with Bahrain, Qatar, and the United Arab Emirates. Kuwait and Oman are not discussed since the involvement of the major accounting firms in those nations has not been extensive.

The final section of the volume reviews the legal and institutional specifics that were discussed earlier and assesses the consequent implications for growth and change in the region. In this context, the real and potential impacts of the accounting firms are discussed. The objective is to draw the diverse elements of the project together in order to better understand the conditions facing the region and the real and potential policy implications of the actions of the accounting firms. In the final chapter of the volume certain economic aspects of Islam are emphasized once again with an eye to understanding their impact.

Chapter Two

The Role of International Services

Though the economies of most developed nations have long since been service oriented, there appears to be lingering confusion concerning the meaning of that phenomenon. The belief that the ascendancy of services has been at the expense of more robust manufacturing endeavors still appears to be prevalent, and that it signals weakness in the economies concerned. The chagrin engendered from the loss of assembly-line jobs seems to have obscured the positive impacts that are emerging in economies experiencing a service ascendancy. That chagrin rests on no stronger a foundation than the similar chagrin of work forces facing economies emerging from a base in agriculture or primary industry.

Despite ongoing interest on the part of economists, ambivalence and incomplete understandings still prevail concerning the role of services in advanced economies. Some of the confusion rests with the extensive cadres of service activities that are still expanding in those economies. Economists who have never exhibited much concern over explanations of the division of labor dating back to Adam Smith do not always accept the current divisions of labor that seem to be exporting manufacturing jobs to less developed nations.

Very visible consumer services, some paying minimum wages, draw attention away from more sophisticated services, many of which are geared to facilitating various other economic and business activities. Some such services are to be found in the transportation and communications fields. It has been services in those fields that have made a global economy feasible. Some of those services have made the migration of segments of production processes to less fortunate material settings possible. Those are the service groups that have assisted in guaranteeing acceptable quality in goods produced in the new settings, and having succeeded in that, have made a global market for the goods in question feasible. The sometimes quiet emergence of such services has permitted a division of labor on an international scale.

These service cadres are facilitators of activities in the global economy, activities that in turn expand employment opportunities in areas previously unlinked to global production chains. Beyond the spheres of transportation and communications, other business facilitators have emerged, which deal with engineering and construction, not to mention finance and business practices, while simultaneously becoming more specialized. It appears as though Adam Smith's division of labor has arrived in the service sector, and presumably is rendering both that sector and its business clients more efficient and better able to take advantage of opportunities for profit.

It cannot be concluded that because they have emerged and are continuing to proliferate, their effectiveness is assured. Discovering what such services do, much less measuring their impacts, can be a rather difficult task. Writing in 1995, Patrick N. O'Farrell and Lindsay A. R. Moffat suggested that although knowledge-intensive services are important to economic development at the national, regional, and firm level, there is "scant evidence as to their effectiveness" (1995, 111). Those authors, speaking of the United Kingdom, pointed out that the expansion of employment and number of firms between 1979 and 1989 showed a long-term expanding demand for strategic business services, which was not just the result of the contracting out of previously internalized services (112).

O'Farrell and Moffat were focusing on services that offered strategic information and expertise of a relatively intangible nature, yet potentially durable in its effects. Such information was concerned with "problem solving and policy making" and not simply with routine administration (112). Among services studied, the authors included market research, advertising and marketing, product design, research and development, export advice, and production planning. They also included quality control, production engineering, computer software–MIS services, CAD–CAM services, and the provision of training (112). In assessing the effectiveness of such services the authors also acknowledge the possibility that at times "business services are purchased by managers either to confirm pre-existing views or information, or possibly to improve individual or group 'political' positions within the organization" (118).

In a recent article, it was suggested that "The pursuit of growth and development through encouraging the emergence of certain service subsectors is a relatively recent phenomenon and indeed may not have found broad acceptance among those concerned with expansionary processes" (McKee, Amara, and Garner 1995, 258). It has not been long since the conventional views of development seriously understated the importance of services in economic expansion (1995, 258; see also Enderwick 1991, 292). Enderwick saw the most widely held view as believing an expanding service sector to be the result of development, rather than one of its causes. In contrast to that position, he saw services performing an enabling role in development. Indeed, he was of the opinion that the enabling function alone does not do justice to the importance of services (294).

   The Enderwick position is supported by the reality that seems to be facing emerging nations in the global economy. The importance of services in small emerging nations has been elaborated (Amara 1994a, 1994b). Amara suggested that a mix of primary, secondary, and tertiary activities are needed for success-ful development, and that tertiary activities are very important in that mix.

   The principal goal of emerging nations is economic development. This is often embodied with aspirations for economic and political autonomy from the in-dustrial countries. Hence, development strategy links developing countries to the international economy, yet the desire for independence involves reducing their dependence on the industrial countries. The strategy of most developing countries today appears to be aimed at developing modern industrial sectors to serve their domestic and the international markets. This has been done by in-troducing import substitution and export-oriented industry to generate employ-ment and to earn the foreign exchange needed to pay for their imports and to service their loans.

   Hence, industrial development projects are considered to be foundations in any aim to industrialize and sustain long-term development. Policy makers expect those projects not only to create prompt results by increasing production and employment, but also to become the basis for additional growth. They view the adoption of advanced methods as vital. Therefore, in heavy industry, the sector which is often granted priority, the use of advanced techniques is usually es-sential. For example, in the Arab countries, there is a tendency to import for-eign technology. While this is obviously more advanced than what is available in the Arab world, it uses less labor, costs more, is difficult to use, and usually requires a great deal of maintenance. It has been suggested that the methods used are generally taught by foreign consultants or by engineers trained abroad. They create very few jobs and may lead to a significant loss of employment in tradi-tional sectors of the economy (for an example, see Bouhdiba 1979, 181).

   The techniques of production are often devised in developed countries where unskilled labor is relatively expensive. Most developed countries boast reasonably large populations and incomes. Traditionally, production techniques in such settings tended to embody an optimal scale of operation large enough to meet industrial countries' demand, but too large relative to the capacity of markets available to developing countries, since many of those are either small in popu-lation, in income, or in both. This is not to suggest that economies of scale are functions of population or country size but rather a function of the scale of out-put. Hence, the extent to which a country can exploit such economies of scale in any given industry depends on the extent of the market. The extent of the do-mestic market depends on the size of the population and the level of per capita income.

   Furthermore, for industries to flourish, there should be an interplay in all three economic agents, namely agriculture, manufacturing, and services. Internation-alization of production demands a healthy and literate work force, administrative and management skills, marketing, legal and accounting services, a well-developed financial market, as well as advanced transportation, communications, and construction service sectors. Agriculture and manufacturing will continue to be as important as in the past, but services will facilitate the mobility of goods, information, and labor.

Comparing the rates of growth in exports and imports for various developing countries (with the possible exception of newly industrialized countries and the Persian Gulf oil producers), suggests that the developing countries' share of the exports has stagnated or even dropped in real terms in the last decade. This created balance of payments deficits and foreign-exchange problems. Historically, the prices of primary commodities have declined relative to manufactured goods. For developing countries, as exporters of the former and importers of the latter, export prices declined relative to import prices. Hence, developing countries' terms of trade tended to deteriorate over time. This being the case, developing countries have to sell more of their export products and employ more of their scarce productive resources merely to secure the same level of imported goods that they purchased in previous years. In other words, the real or social opportunity costs of a unit of imports will rise for a country when its export prices decline relative to its import prices.

Thereupon, most developing countries may not be able to sustain an international competitive position because they cannot exploit economies of scale as fully as developed countries, and their markets are unlikely to grow rapidly due to continuous adverse terms of trade effects. Then, industrialization cannot be geared to the home markets. As such, the only feasible development strategy in developing countries with limited natural resources lies in the creation of export-oriented industries or services. However, because manufacturing is usually more capital intensive than most other activities (e.g., farming, banking, or tourism), economies of scale and factor indivisibilities tend to be more important. It follows that countries with small domestic markets caused by small populations or small incomes are generally at a disadvantage, compared with larger countries, in undertaking manufacturing activities. Therefore, the existing international trade system disfavors the developing countries and virtually guarantees an export market for the major industrial countries' manufactured goods with their high degree of value added, and it will be very difficult for the developing countries to break the barriers of sustained economic growth.

Under these circumstances, it is likely that only sectors like services that are not generally subject to increasing returns to scale can provide a long-term escape route for developing countries that have limited resources. Services facilitate extractive and manufacturing activities, though value added occurs primarily in services. Therefore, every functioning economy must have an effective service sector. Economic efficiency depends on the interlinkages between the different production activities, not only on the activities themselves. Thus, given the incorporation of a continuously growing number of services needed for the industrial sector, service industries are a primary source of economic growth.

Enderwick has suggested that "services are typically characterized by significant economic linkages and the generation of externalities" (1991, 294). Such properties are recognizable in services relating to infrastructure, education, and health (McKee, Garner, and AbuAmara McKee 1998, 6), but, as Enderwick suggests, are equally important in various producer services such as insurance and finance (294). Enderwick points out that with respect to insurance, the pooling of risks and premiums provides not only a widening and deepening of financial markets, but also stimulates savings, credit facilitation, and the promotion of new economic activities (294).

It would certainly seem as though the major international accounting firms can be expected to generate the types of linkages and externalities referred to by Enderwick. He saw a role for service multinationals that are able to supply valuable expertise through superior technology, managerial skills, and quality standards (294). Certainly the accounting firms can be expected to exhibit these qualities. Enderwick saw multinational service firms providing "both a competitive and complementary role in stimulating through competition, the quality of service provision and in complementing the indigenous service offerings with those targeted at new market segments" (295).

O'Farrell, Moffat, and P. A. Wood have suggested that services have certain unique characteristics which must be considered in any attempt to analyze the international or interregional behavior of firms. Among such concerns is the fact that the difference between trade and investment is not as clear in the case of services as it is in manufacturing. Another concern is that "most business services require a greater degree of customization for the client than manufactured products" (1995, 693).

This would certainly be the case with the services offered by the major international accounting firms in the global economy. In the Middle East, those firms have responsibilities towards multinational clients wishing to conduct business within specific nations or between those nations and other parts of the globe. Specifically the customized package needed by multinational clients must surely include the means to facilitate their operations in an Islamic business environment. When the firms have Middle Eastern government agencies or private enterprises as clients they must be able to facilitate the operations of those clients in the international market economy.

Building upon their first two concerns, O'Farrell and his colleagues suggest that "Both customization of business services and the need in many services for simultaneous production and consumption (location boundedness) means that the establishment of affiliates in host markets . . . is necessary for most business service companies." Certainly their contention appears to apply to the operations of the major accounting firms in varying international environments. The authors under discussion explain that for such overseas offices, trade discrimination can be seen primarily when host countries accord preferential treatment to domestic firms. O'Farrell and colleagues suggest that "Physical presence in the market is often a sine qua non condition for international trade in business services" (684).

Writing on his own, O'Farrell points out that the "rise of flexible forms of production has changed the spatial organization of economic activity." His investigation was concerned with Scotland and southeast England, but it seems clear that his insights may easily apply to a much wider canvas. Speaking of interregional considerations, he suggests that the range of feasible locations has been extended significantly "resulting in the international restructuring of industrial regions formed in earlier phases of investment and the expansion of production activity into 'new industrial spaces'" (1994, 526).

It has occurred to the current investigators that what O'Farrell has said has implications for the global economy and for components of it that are either developed or hoping to develop. Flexible production suggests individual production units have a far wider menu of potential host settings to choose from. All that appears to be required is a sound linkage of the component units of production processes, wherever they emerge, so that firms and industries can effectively manufacture and market their products.

It seems clear that what has made such flexibility feasible internationally has been improvements and major innovations in the transportation and communications infrastructure. In emerging nations, such changes have made it theoretically possible for components of production to locate where previously that would not have been possible. Certainly components of internationalized processes can locate in smaller, poorer economies, where domestic markets could hardly purchase what is being produced. In the new transportation environment, components or presumably finished products can be marketed internationally in a global economy. Communications assist in insuring that production chains are efficiently linked. Beyond transportation and communications infrastructure, expanding ranges of facilitative business services are emerging, geared to insuring the efficiency of international operations.

O'Farrell saw new growth areas emerging in Scotland and southeast England that are "either socially or geographically isolated from the main loci of earlier Fordist industrialization." Students of business services have generally presumed that their expansion follows the needs of their clients. O'Farrell sees a different dynamic process occurring: "Rather than following manufacturing into new industrial spaces, business services have generally remained concentrated in large metropolitan areas" (526). Internationally various business services may follow their clients locationally, but they may also be able to service clients by means of improved communications from settings such as those alluded to by O'Farrell. A third possibility exists as well. New concentrations of business services may emerge in developed nations or in entirely new locations aimed at servicing clients in the global economy. The most visible example of the last pattern may be represented by offshore banking centers.

In a recent article, B. Warf explains that increased recent attention to trade in services is understandable, since producer services account for roughly 20 percent of all international trade. Warf was investigating engineering services, which he explained are increasingly seeking clients on a global basis as are other business services. Beyond obviously engineering related services Warf sees engineering firms offering "a diversity of services, including preinvestment studies, design of production projects, management advice and consultation." He suggests that the nature of such functions is often ambiguous and specific to the idiosyncratic requirements of particular clients (1996, 667, 668).

Warf saw the international pattern of demand for engineering services as reflective of such things as rates of growth in GNP, corporate income, private and public levels of construction and investment and "because engineering services are frequently bundled to commodities such as automobiles, global trade in many types of goods" (668). Of course, many of the variables cited here are relevant to the patterns of expansion and incidence of various other business services. Warf sees the petroleum industry as a major user of engineering services, and the Middle East as a relatively significant market for such services.

It is hardly surprising that business service firms have become multinational operations in their own right as they seek to facilitate the operations of their clients. As has been recognized, "A sophisticated cadre of international services has developed to accommodate the needs of the international business community" (McKee 1988, 115). The present investigation is directed toward a better understanding of how the major accounting firms are impacting economic and business potential in the Islamic nations of the areas indicated. Wherever possible, the actions of major accounting firms will be considered with an eye to identifying the real and potential impacts that such firms may be having upon the domestic economies of the nations in question, as well as upon the international economic and business linkages that the nations are experiencing.

Of course, the firms in question have been offering a variety of services on a worldwide basis. The potential impact of their offerings, assuming their success, can be seen in their own promotional releases. For example, KPMG sees their local expertise as invaluable to clients considering an entry into new and unfamiliar markets. The firm suggests that their established presence gives clients the necessary contacts with authorities and business figures. The firm "shares a knowledge of local business practices, of the intricacies of local legislation and the finer points of doing business in each particular culture" (KPMG International 1997d). It would seem that this statement provides a general understanding of what any potential client of the major international accounting firms may be seeking beyond traditional accounting services.

KPMG points to the efficiency of their international network, which uses the same approach and methods throughout the world as one of their essential strengths. The firm sees their key areas of functional expertise as accounting and auditing, tax management consultancy, and corporate finance (1997d). They provide services in more than 900 cities in 150 countries.

According to the firm, their expertise covers a wide range of industry and activity groupings. They maintain international industry groups specializing in

banking and finance, insurance, and transportation. They also have groups
equipped to consult in the building and construction field, retail, and consumer
products, and in industrial products. They can assist in information, communications, and entertainment, and in energy and natural resources, not to mention health
care and life sciences. Beyond such private-sector subcategories they also stand
ready to assist government units. In the Middle East, the firm maintains offices
or contact partners in Bahrain, Egypt, Jordan, Kuwait, Lebanon, Libia, Oman,
Palestine, Qatar, Saudi Arabia, the United Arab Emirates, and Yemen.

Prior to merging with Coopers & Lybrand, Price Waterhouse had a long history as an international provider of a wide range of business services. Among
its audit and business advisory offerings are actuarial and attestation services
and audit methodology and technology services. The firm also provides assistance in matters of business, and financial risks and control review services. Corporate financial services, employment, and environmental services are also among
its offerings, as are financial advisory services and strategic analytics, and shareholder value analysis and enhancement. Beyond the services listed, the firm offers
help with information systems, risk management, internal audits, and joint venture
services.

In the area of corporate finance, Price Waterhouse assists business leaders
in the purchase and sale of companies. Price Waterhouse personnel act as business advisors to corporations, financial investors, and lenders. They assist companies in identifying acquisition and divestiture targets, aid in actual negotiations,
and supply post-transaction services. They also assist with tax issues and help
to identify problems associated with mergers, acquisitions, investitures, joint
ventures, spinoffs, and strategic alliances. The firm's corporate finance specialists
are experienced in both domestic and cross-border transactions.

In the area of strategic change, the firm can assist corporate managers in their
responses to complicated issues in a multidimensional environment. In the area
of organizational change, the firm focuses on three main themes—organizational
design and development, cultural change, and technological assimilation. Speaking of process change, the firm identifies the bottom line as "fast, flexible, re-
sponsive, efficient, and technology-enabled processes . . . as the bedrock of
superior business performance" (Price Waterhouse 1997f). In the Middle East,
the firm has offices in Bahrain, Egypt, Oman, Qatar, Saudi Arabia, Turkey, and
the United Arab Emirates.

It may not be constructive to detail all of the services offered by each member of the Big Six due to significant congruencies. However, in reviewing the
offerings of the Middle East practice of Ernst & Young, significant business
community training courses were noted (1997a). That firm sponsors a program
of training courses in accounting, auditing, information technology, and related
areas. To facilitate these activities, the firm maintains fully equipped training
centers in various offices in the region. Their offerings exceed twenty courses.
One of their course offerings is designed to prepare students to sit for the U.S.
certified public accountants qualification.

Beyond such offerings, the firm has established specific training programs for a wide range of organizations. They also offer half-day and one-day seminars on various issues. Some of the firm's instructors are fluent in Arabic, and some of the courses offered have been translated into that language; thus, they are able to reach members of the business community who may not be fluent in other languages. Certainly the educational endeavors referred to here have the potential for rather broad impacts in the economies hosting them.

The Ernst & Young practice in the Middle East dates from 1923, and boasts fifteen offices in eleven countries. Host jurisdictions include the United Arab Emirates, Saudi Arabia, Jordan, Bahrain, Lebanon, Egypt, Qatar, Kuwait, and Oman.

Chapter Three

Islam and Its Impact

Since this book deals with Islamic countries, some explanation and clarification of the Islamic religion and the role it plays in those countries' economies is warranted. This chapter explores the role of Islam in shaping the cultures, and in turn, the economies of the countries under study. As a faith, Islam governs every aspect of conduct and advocates a complete code of human behavior. Moreover, it contains some detailed rules concerning business, law, administrative affairs, economics, and politics. Therefore, any examination of Islamic economy requires shedding some light on the Islamic faith.

The Muslim holy book, the Qur'án, is considered by Muslims to be the exact words of revelation from God to Prophet Muhammad and forms the basis of the Islamic belief system. It is considered to be the masterpiece of Arabic literature and is indeed the basic reference of the Arabic language. There is no doubt that the Qur'án is central to the Islamic belief system, and indeed, all devout Muslims rely upon it in shaping the direction of their day-to-day activities. Many Muslims and Arabic scholars even memorize it entirely. Its importance goes well beyond the boundaries of the Arab world, since the Islamic faith is embraced by 1.2 billion people. Thus, hundreds of millions of Muslims are not Arabs, and not all Arabs are Muslims. Clearly, the importance of Islam on a worldwide basis can hardly be denied, and any understanding of the economies of Islamic nations and their international linkages requires one to have some idea of Islam as a faith and of the practices that shape Muslim societies.

The Qur'án is the Muslim's holy book. The Hadeeth, or Traditions, is the Islamic teaching and the Qur'ánic interpretation of the Prophet. In a sense, Islam has no theology, as it is understood in other religions. The principles governing the system (known as usul) are to be found in the Qur'án which explains the revealed Word of God, and in the Hadeeth. These principles constitute the Islamic Shari'a' (law), and devout Muslims are expected to follow them under all circumstances (Gambling and Abdel Karim 1991, 22–28). In the present context, references will be drawn from only Islamic sources: the Qur'án and the Traditions. These are the sources of the Islamic theory from which all Muslim teachings and laws, modes of worship, and work emanate. Islam as a faith lays down the nature of the relation between the Creator and His creation, the nature of man's relation to the universe and to the world, and of man's relation to his soul. It also lays down the relation between the individual and society, between different societies, for mankind as a whole, and the relation between one nation and another.

Muslims believe in the absolute oneness of God. There exists one eternal and unchanging power that has no beginning and no comprehensible end. To that power belongs the government of the world of mankind and of all life. It is the power of God (Allah). The Qur'án is believed to be the divine guidance; it has specific laws that are immutable and general principles from which further laws can be deduced. The true Muslim believes in a clear distinction between the Qur'án and the Traditions of Muhammad, in that the Traditions are the practical interpretations of the Qur'án. The role of Muhammad was to convey the Qur'án as he received it from God, to interpret it, and to act upon it fully. His applications and actions formed what is known as the Traditions. These must be in complete harmony with the Qur'án. If there is any contradiction or inconsistency between any of the Hadeeth and the Qur'án, the Muslim must adhere to the Qur'án alone, regarding everything else as questionable, because no genuine Hadeeth of Muhammad can ever disagree with the Qur'án or be opposed to it (Abdalati 1993, 21).

Muslims are commanded to believe in God, His angels, His books (including the Tora, the Bible, and the Qur'án), His prophets, and in the day of judgment. Because Islam means submission to the will of God and obedience to His law, and because this is the essence of the message of all God-chosen messengers, Muslims accept all the prophets previous to Muhammad without discrimination. They believe in the existence of Islamic religion throughout a sequence of prophets; in other words, that all those prophets of God and their true followers were Muslims. For Muslims, there is just one revelation, of the only religion, Islam—it was made again and again through successive prophets. Muhammad's was the final prophecy; however, his was not more Islamic than that of Abraham, Moses, or Jesus. Muhammad was the last, not the only prophet, who reinforced and immortalized the eternal message of God to mankind. This message was revealed by God to many prophets of different nations at different times, including Abraham, Ishmael, Isaac, David, Moses, Jesus, and Muhammad. What is more important is that the Muslims are required not to make any discrimination among any of the prophets.

In Islam, the Qur'án is the final word of God up to the day of judgment. Its applications, as practiced in the life of the final messenger of God, Muhammad, and as recorded in the Traditions, forms the basis of Muslim behavior. The Qur'án provides principles from which further laws can be deduced. The Hadeeth, which shows how the Qur'án should be interpreted in life according to the recorded sayings, deeds, and approvals or disapprovals of the Prophet, is considered to be the second source of law in Islam. The Shari'a' should be viewed as the source of all laws, and all other laws should be derived from it. The Shari'a' cannot provide detailed rules for every possible event, and the Muslim should strive (make ijtihad) to arrive to the truth. Ibrahim thinks this is to allow for changes in the conditions and requirements of various societies and various times. He suggests that reason and sense perception should be used in the acquisition of knowledge in Islam. Allah endowed man with knowledge and freedom of action. Hence, the Shari'a' has expanded, through a process of analogy, consensus, and consideration of customs, blocking the evil, reasoning, and public interest (Ibrahim 1997, 15). Since the purpose of the Shari'a' is to promote the welfare of the people, which lies in safeguarding their faith, their life, their intellect, their property, and their wealth, this application has resulted in different opinions.

THE PILLARS OF ISLAM

The principles of Islam are sometimes stated as positive commitments that must be fulfilled, and sometimes as negative deeds that must be avoided. Among other things, the most important positive requirements are the five Pillars of Islam. Throughout the Qur'án there is resonant insistence on the oneness and unity of God. This is the very foundation of the Muslim belief. The subject is so vital that it is no accident that the Shahadat, or Muslim profession of faith, proclaims, "There is no god but Allah, and Muhammad is the Messenger of Allah." Thereupon, the Shahadat is the first Pillar of Islamic faith. As a consequence of this uncompromising monotheism, the greatest heresy in Muslim belief is associating other beings or partners with God. Prayer constitutes the second Pillar, done five times a day and on a timely basis. Zakat, or alms, is the third Pillar, and it is different from charity in the sense that it is obligatory. It is considered to be the right of the poor from the rich. Fasting is the fourth Pillar. Muslims are required to fast in the lunar month of Ramadan, and this is a duty of every healthy Muslim. The final Pillar in Islam is the Hajj (pilgrimage) to Mecca. The performance of the Hajj is obligatory upon every Muslim who is physically and financially able at least once in a lifetime.

ISLAM AND SOCIETY

The objective of an Islamic society is to establish a just one "We sent aforetime Our messengers with clear signs and sent down with them the Book and the Balance (of right and wrong), that men may stand forth in justice" (Qur'án, Al Hadeed 57:25). One basic element in the value system of Islam is the principle of equality. Differences of race, color, or social status have no bearing on the true stature of the person. There is no super race, nationality, color, or language, and there is no chosen people or chosen race. Man, in the eyes of God, is judged only by his piety and his deeds. Humankind will be rewarded in the hereafter for living in accordance with divine precepts and punished for breaking the command-ments, but with the possibility of forgiveness and repentance of sins in this life. This is an article of faith that is in the Qur'án and the Traditions. All humans came from the same source, namely Adam and Eve: "O mankind, We created you from a single (pair) of a male and a female, and made you into nations and tribes, that ye may know each other. Verily the most honored of you in the sight of Allah is (he who is) the most righteous of you" (Qur'án, Al Hujurat 49:13).

To Muslims, equality does not mean sameness. People are equal in the sight of God, but they are not identical. There are differences in potential and abili-ties. Yet, none of these differences establishes superiority of one person over another. There is no priesthood and no intermediary between the creature and the Creator. Therefore, the Muslim administrator cannot derive his authority from Heaven, but he derives it solely from the Muslim community. Thus, he derives his principles of administration from the Shari'a'.

The adherent to Islam cannot be a true Muslim without practicing his or her faith in social, legal, and economic relationships. It follows that a society cannot be Islamic if it does not practice the Shari'a'. One of the most important charac-teristic of this faith is that it is an essential unity. It is at once worship and work; religious law and theological beliefs are meshed with secular life and customs. Thus, prayer in Islam entails submission to none save to Allah. Islam does not prescribe worship as the only basis of its beliefs; rather it reckons all the activi-ties of life as comprehending worship in themselves, as long as they are within the bounds of conscience, goodness, and honesty (Kotb 1970, 9). Hence, it is clear that there can be no separation between the religious and the secular world.

Community in Islam is not founded on race, nationality, kinship, a name of a country or a leader, or any special interest. It is founded on the principle of submission to the will of God and the obedience to His law. What is required of the community as a whole is likewise required of every individual member. This is best described in the Traditions: "Whoever of you sees something wrong must correct it by his own hands (actions or deeds), if he cannot, he should try to change it by words, if he cannot, then in his heart (object it), and this is the least amount of faith" (AlMuntheri 1987, 16). The range and dimension of morality in Islam is comprehensive and far reaching. It combines at once faith in God, religious rites, spiritual observances, social conduct, decision making, intellectual pursuits, habits of consumption, manners of speech, and all other aspects of human life (Abdalati 1993, 43). Muslims should not associate them-selves with the power of the state or with the power of wealth, and thus keep the workers and lower classes complaisant by means of religion.

ISLAM AND SOCIAL JUSTICE

The Islamic belief is that humanity is an essential unity, and its scattered el-ements must be brought together, its diversity must give place to uniformity, and its variety of creeds must in the end be brought into one. Justice in Islam is a human equality, considering the adjustment of all values, of which the economic is but one. Values in this religion are very broad and composite to the point that justice must include all of them; therefore, Islam does not demand a compulsory economic equality in a narrow literal sense of the term. This is against nature, and it conflicts with the essential fact, which is that of the different endowments of individuals. Islam demands that rank, upbringing, origin, or class should not be obstacles in the way of any individual. As long as human justice is upheld by the provision of equal opportunity for all individuals, absolute justice permits that men's rewards be different, and thus some will always have more than others due to their endowments.

However, individuals are expected to inform themselves on matters of faith and morals in keeping with their intelligence and educational attainments and to act accordingly. Islamic faith does not depend for its proof on wonders or miracles, but rather it relies on the examination and scrutiny of the evidence of life itself and its facts. However, tolerance is required in this religion that associates learning with piety, making the former the path to the knowledge and reverence to Allah. "Those truly fear Allah, among His servants, who have knowledge" (Qur'án, Sura Fatir 35:28). Hence, those who have the inner knowledge that comes through their acquaintance with the spiritual world are considered to be above those who do not seek that knowledge, in the eyes of Allah. "Say: Are those equal, those who know and those who do not know?" (Qur'án, Sura Al Zumar 39:9). Moreover, Islam urges men to stand up for their rights. It warns those who abdicate their natural rights that they will be punished in the hereafter, and it calls them "self -oppressors" (Qur'án, Sura Al Nisa 4:97). Islam establishes the claim of the poor to the wealth of the rich. It lays down a principle for power and for money, and therefore has no need to condition the minds of people and summon them to neglect their earthly rights in favor of their expectations in Heaven.

The leader of the Islamic community is best described as one who makes an analogy between him and the Imam (one that leads the Muslims' prayer). Sayyid Abul A'la Mawdudi found striking parallels between the leader of the prayer and the head of the state. An Imam must be the best in character, piety, and righteousness (1992, 171). He must have greater knowledge of Islam (the Qur'án and the Traditions) than others. He also should be liked and respected by the majority of the congregation, and he should not lead the prayer against their wishes.

Here is an important principle for electing a leader. The elected should lead the prayer in such a way that no trouble is caused to other people. For example, he should not make lengthy recitations that may not suit the old, the sick, the children, or those who do not have the time. In other words, the leader should be kind and compassionate. However, if the Imam realized that he broke one or more of the requirements for prayer, he should immediately hand the leadership to one of the men behind. Here, one can conclude that if the nation's leader is unable to carry out his duties, he should resign.

One other aspect of the prayer is that the leader must be strictly followed. However, strictly followed does not mean blindly followed. If an Imam makes a mistake during prayer, he must be corrected by other people. For example, he may make a mistake in reciting the Qur'án; then, any member of the Jama'ah (congregation) who recognizes the correct recitation must correct him. However, if the mistake was intentional, such as the Imam knowingly changing the direction of the prayer, or commits any sin during the prayer, then it is incumbent on the members of the congregation to break away immediately and leave him alone. Here one can compare the relationship between the Imam and his congregation with that of the head of the state and the citizens (Mawdudi 1992, 171–174).

POLITICS, ECONOMICS, AND FINANCE IN ISLAM

Islam is a comprehensive religion, such that it is difficult to separate what is politics, what is economics, what is law, and what is worship. To be a true Muslim, all aspects of life have to be conducted according to the rules of Islam. Further, all aspects of the Muslim state have to be conducted according to Islamic principles, and it is the duty of the Muslim to oppose what is wrong. Gambling and Abdel Karim see that Islam does not value conservatism for its own sake. As a fundamental principle of Islam, anybody can express his or her opinion on the interpretation of the Shari'a'. Nevertheless, the extent to which this right should be exercised by a lay person is a matter of challenge these days. Every Muslim is left to exercise ijtihad (discretion) over how best to implement the general terms of Islamic teaching as they are in the Qur'án and the Traditions. However, this is not a matter of personal choice—its criteria and purpose must always be the public interest of the whole community (Gambling and Abdel Karim 1991, 28–29). This flexibility enables Muslims to adapt to changing conditions and environments. Islam has always had a body of jurists (ulama) whose sole mission is to derive application from the Islamic law that can fit different times and different environments. Due to the complexities of the Shari'a', a lay person often finds it more realistic to refer to their opinion than to his own.

The countries in the Middle East are no longer as isolated as they were in the past. Their populations are bound to be influenced by events elsewhere in the region, if not in the world. Though they differ in some respects, none of them appear to apply Islamic rules to their political or economic activities. Abi-Aad and Grenon describe the autocratic nature of governments in the Middle East as a long-term insecurity. They see a growing demand for more representation in governments in this region. This representation is likely to threaten regimes and to become a major source of instability. Among the countries under study, only Turkey has enjoyed a liberal electoral policy for a sustained period of time (1997, 13). However, Fuller sees that the secular reforms of Ataturk had their negative impacts in suppressing the long cultural legacy of Turkey as the center of the Caliphate and of Sunni Islam. Fuller suggests that since the Ottoman empire represents some of the most glorious pages in the history of Islamic Turkey, there will be growing public interest in the Muslim heritage of Turkey (1997, 48). Islamists have shown openness of agendas and adaptability to the political cultures of their country. In Turkey, the parliament is naturally the place for struggle, where the Islamic party often had to compromise in order to seek a role and subsequently maintain its participation in government (Mottahedeh and Fandy 1997, 304).

Egypt has been seen by some as duplicating the authoritarian socialist regime to some extent. Those authors concede that there have been some changes of government, but suggest that there is no real democracy with multiple parties. Generally speaking, the regime is governed by one ruler supported by a single party. The ruling party allows other parties to operate but only under its endorsement. The ruling party retains the majority of seats in parliament and nominates the candidate for the presidency, who historically has been the incumbent. Under this regime, the president has absolute power and is the pivot of a small circle of people, mainly the chiefs of state security and the military who uphold the regime, ensuring its stability and its very existence. (Abi-Aad and Grenon 1997, 13–37).

The remainder of the countries under study are governed by kings, princes, and sheikhs. Though these rulers have fostered economic systems differing from those of the authoritarian socialist, they are no less autocratic. Each of those countries is ruled by hereditary monarchies that govern by decree. Where advisory councils of ministers exist, they are generally composed of members of the monarch's immediate or extended family. In fact, members of the ruler's family in these countries usually take over the key ministries of finance, security, defense, and sometimes oil and foreign affairs, but almost always inter-Arab relations (Abi-Aad and Grenon 1997, 13–37).

In such an environment, where political parties, labor unions, and any form of democratic activity is prohibited, the Islamists find a fertile and rich soil for underground activities. They acquire the support of the population, not only due to their religious influence, but also as an alternative to other democratic parties that could not survive. In recent years, Muslim societies have seen the re-emergence of Islamic movements.

This is not surprising in view of the fact that historically, there was no separation between religion and secular life. However, the colonial powers divided the Middle Eastern countries by artificial political boundaries. Gary G. Sick and Lawrence G. Potter acknowledges that "with the exception of Iran and Oman, the Persian Gulf states are all creations of the twentieth century, and their boundaries were largely imposed by imperial powers. Resistance to these borders has cropped up repeatedly and has even led to wars, such as those between Iran and Iraq, and between Iraq and Kuwait" (Sick and Potter 1997, 7).

The political and economic systems that were introduced as substitutes for Islam were alien to the region and were introduced without the consent of the populations. The so-called post-independent states in the Arab world are still governed either as socialist republics or as absolute monarchies. Even after thirty years since the British withdrawal from the Arab states in the Gulf region (1971), the states are still ruled by the same families under the same political, social, and economic systems and within virtually the same borders that were imposed by the British. Sick suggests that the tribal monarchies proved their ability to translate oil revenues into political legitimacy and staying power. So, by the mid-1990s, the small states of the Gulf (the monarchies) were seen as stable and reliably pro-Western (Sick and Potter 1997, 12).

The rulers may fear that introducing any kind of participation in government would hasten their demise and that any change would ultimately mean opposition. In fact, the aim of decision makers in those Middle Eastern countries is to maintain regime security rather than simply state security. The leaders of those governments want to avoid intensifying the already growing demands for greater participation and representation. In the words of Salem, "The statist perspective is that held by the military, party, and/ or monarchist elites that sit atop the various Arab states. For those groups regime survival, security, and overall stability are virtually the sole motivating aims." Salem goes on to suggest that the interest of the rulers "lie in politics and how to preserve and protect the present political system from breakdown, coup, or revolution. Their interest in change is only tactical and is operative only when they are convinced that limited and controlled change is the only way to avoid graver risks and uncertainties" (Salem 1997, 29).

Though many Middle Eastern countries mention Islam and Shari'a' and advise their courts to fill gaps in Western-based codes using Islamic precepts, they generally ignore the persisting question that is most important to Muslims— whether such arrangements are truly Islamic. Moreover, Islamists are dissatisfied on religious grounds with the political status quo. They cite lack of democracy depicted in the form of restrictions on freedom of expression, forced exile, corruption, unemployment, and subjugation of the press to the government (Fakhro 1997, 181).

It is no secret that many Muslim countries have rather poor freedom and human rights violation records. With the exception of Turkey, all of the countries under study remain outside the circle of democratic states. As it is, populations in those countries, both Muslim and non-Muslim, often view the situation unfavorably for not altogether different reasons. The reason that the Islamist critique is so persuasive is that it rings true. According to Norton, the rank and file supporters of the Islamist movements are remarkably mobile in terms of granting or withdrawing their compliance. More important, compliance to one or another Islamist organization often has much less to do with questions of piety or religiosity than with the organization's demonstrated efficacy and integrity (1997, 13). Virtually all existing Muslim regimes face political opposition on both secular and Islamic grounds. Hence, Islamists share at least that secular part with the non-Muslim oppositions. Perhaps one could explain the growth of the Islamist movements in the countries concerned on the grounds of the inherent appeal of Islam compared to secular ideologies. But equally important is the failure of the Islamic governments to implement democracy. Islamists often criticize governments for not implementing the Shari'a', which they view as a condition for installing democracy. Islamists believe that the failure to ground modern political institutions on Islamic foundations is one of the major causes of political radicalization in the Islamic World. As a consequence, the results are startlingly poor. Islamic law is impressively endowed with political ideas, many of them surprisingly modern in their connotations.

Support for popular participation in governments can be found in Islamic scriptures. The Qur'án speaks of the conduct of affairs by mutual consultation (shura) (Qur'án, Sura Al-Shura 42:38). Under Islam, the social contract requires the consent of the governed (baya'); the rule of law (the sovereignty of God and of the Shari'a'); the right to petition for restitution of grievance (nasiha or mazalim); the sanctity of individual life; liberty, and property and their protection from state interference; equality of all before the law; office as public trust (amana); and the prohibition of embezzlement (ghulul). In the words of Abi-Aad and Grenon, "In theory, Islam is an inherently political religion. Classically, the state's legitimacy depends on its role as protector of the Islamic community (Umma) and the preservation of the divine law (shari'a') by 'enjoying the good and forbidding the evil.'" Those authors go on to suggest that "present regimes do not seem to offer a way forward, only more of the same" (1997, 24). Islam views tyranny, intolerance, corruption, and the denial of human rights as evil.

Muslims see contradictions between what their governments are practicing and what they are claiming to be. In other words, while the governments are not following Islamic values, they still claim to be Islamic states. This allows many Muslims to distance themselves from their governments and seek the Islamist organizations. In general, members of those organizations are highly educated, sophisticated, and well organized. No organizations in the societies in question could rival the Islamists in terms of the depth and breadth of support. For many, the organization is not just the Islamist party, it is a credible opposing voice to a ruling party that had failed to promote rapid and fair economic development, to accommodate political participation, to preserve the culture, to generate social values, or to prevent excessive Westernization. Hence, Islamist movements stem largely from the suffering of government repression and the absence of any other means of discharging frustration, or of participation in the political process.

Islamists have the support of the pious and the not-so-pious because both sides believe in the necessity of political reform, lifting government repression, ensuring basic liberties of speech, and establishing full democracies. Fuller describes this situation as if it is a normal cause and effect. Fuller feels that it is not surprising that Islamist politics are growing in the region, feeding off illiberal, unelected, often incompetent and failing regimes, whose social and economic problems strengthen the Islamist appeal to frustrated societies (1997, 55).

Salem also mentioned some reasons for the rapid growth of the Islamist movement. He sees it as the revolutionary expression of a rising generation that rejects the status quo and seeks to challenge the power of the previous generation through radical religious politics. He sees it as a gradual reaction to the many failures of the modern Arab states and as the direct approach to Islamic revival that had the most appeal to the masses (1997, 25–27).

In the view of Salem, there are some reasons for the rapid growth of the Islamist politics. First, politicized Islam has an accessible and understanding audience, so that once enough members of the intelligentsia moved toward it as a political option, it was fairly easy to mobilize a mass support. Second, the ideologies of liberal nationalism and revolutionary secular, pan-Arab nationalism, had lost their ideological appeal by the early 1970s after having failed to deliver. Islam was the only political ideology that had not yet been tried. Third, the defeat of 1967 and the failure of the post-independent states on virtually all of the economic and social development fronts brought the demise of public support. Fourth, as Arab regimes became more oppressive, most other political parties collapsed or disappeared (1997, 25–27).

Within the mosque system (which could not be closed down without mass criticism), the Islamist parties had access to a network to which they could retreat and preserve their thought and organizational ties. Moreover, since religious discourse was a type of discourse that could not be easily suppressed, in most Arab countries Islamic forms of political expression became the only forms open to those dissatisfied with the status quo. Finally, the main capitals that had developed and elaborated on secular thought (Cairo, Beirut, Damascus, and Baghdad), were virtually ineffective (1997, 23–29).

It is obvious that Islamists are gaining strength in rich countries as well as in poor ones. In Algeria, Egypt, Tunisia, and Saudi Arabia, governments hope to defeat Islamists through repression. Though experts outside those regimes do not expect this strategy to succeed, those countries have declared war on Islamists. Inside many nations of the Muslim world, governments oppose Islamists with arrests, torture, and killings. Those regimes usually tolerate Islamic innovation or experimentation only in the most innocuous and controlled ways, fearing opportunism or encouragement of radical Islamism. However, many experts fear that violent repression will radicalize the Islamist movement and solidify it even further (1997, 23–42).

Beyond politics, Islam offers grounds for reforms in economics and finance. Islam has developed modes of investment and banking that are unfamiliar to Western systems. Those modes can be adopted only by mutual agreements, and requires some government regulations and laws. Since such measures have very little effect on political stability, change is possible in those civil areas. What drives Islamic economics and finance are three major religious principles: namely, the prohibition of interest, zakat (alms), and the distribution of inheritance.

As mentioned earlier, the Shari'a' is a collection of the interpretation of the Qur'án and the practices of the Prophet. The expansion of the Shari'a' was successful for about a thousand years. In this period, the Ulama (Muslim jurists) were active in deriving laws from the Qur'án and the Hadeeth. They had to practice ijtihad (the process of seeking the truth through the Shari'a') in every case presented to them, even if that case had a precedent. In doing so, they were pursuing the Islamic regulations. After that, changes in the political system (the conversion from consultative leadership to monarch, and the division of Muslim lands by the Mongol, and later by the Western colonial powers) and, accordingly, social factors caused a retreat in the ijtihad process. This regression reached its peak after the Western colonization of Muslim countries and the separation between religion and politics. Islam was not only removed from law and social life, but there were also restrictions on the application of Islamic business principles in economics and finance. Western interest-based banking systems were implemented, and alien, unfamiliar business laws were introduced as substitutes to Islamic business laws. At present, with the Islamic resurgence, Muslim countries find it difficult to develop an Islamic business law that can cope with the complexity of the present situation.

The Qur'án emphasizes the prohibition of riba (usury), which is interpreted to mean interest on loans. This prohibition has resulted in Islamic banking. This involves the adherence to the exclusion of charging or receiving interest regardless of the purpose for which such loans are made, and regardless of the rates at which interest is charged. Hence, there was much pressure on Islamic governments to facilitate the development of Islamic banks. Some governments, such as Saudi Arabia, have resisted Islamic banking for political reasons. The assumption was that it symbolizes the openness to Islamist causes. Islamic banks are based on profit–loss sharing principals. Prohibition of interest stems from the idea that money should not generate money, but money should be created by taking risks in productive investments. One can suggest that the Islamic economic theory states that capital will share the value produced by it, to be determined as a percentage of the profits earned, rather than a percentage of the capital itself. Moreover, investments can be only in legal activities that are not prohibited in Islam. Prohibitions include gambling, any alcohol-related activity, pornography, and any activity that is considered harmful to society.

Currently, there is much pressure on Islamic governments to facilitate the development of Islamic finance, economics, and accounting standards. Bahrain is leading the competition as it anticipates its emergence as a new Islamic financial center. Several Islamic countries have financed development projects using Islamic techniques. Among them are Pakistan, Sudan, Jordan, and Malaysia. Despite its strongly Islamic population, Saudi Arabia has refused to let Islamic banks mention their intentions to comply with Islamic laws in their charters (Vogel 1997, 286–289). Al-Rajhi Bank was the only exception. This is based on the assumption that including the word "Islamic" might imply that all other banks are "non-Islamic," promoting demands to dissolve them. However, Saudi Arabia hosts several of the world's most important institutions for research on Islamic banking and is considering the possibilities of using Islamic techniques to attract private investors for development projects, reducing foreign borrowing and deficit financing (1997, 286–289). Islamic scholars are also searching for solutions for the fundamental economic problems. In this endeavor, the Ulama (Islamic jurists) have been joined by other experts such as bankers, economists, lawyers, and financiers.

The objective of the prohibition of interest may be better understood in combination with zakat (alms), which constitutes the second principle that governs the mode of Islamic business practices. Islam alleviates the existence of conflict and tension in society due to inequality in wealth by not making everybody equal, but by enforcing an equitable transfer of wealth through zakat. Islam does not object to the earning of millions, but makes it the duty of the state (through the enforcement of the zakat) to see to it that not a single individual is left unprovided with the elementary necessities of life in society. Technically, zakat is a poor tax—an obligatory claim on the property of the wealthy in favor of the poor. Zakat is not to be confused with regular taxes that the state imposes.

Zakat is to be distributed among certain groups mentioned in the Qur'án, such as the poor, the needy, those employed to administer it, those whose hearts have been reconciled, those in bondage, those in debt, those in the cause of God, and for the wayfarer. All Muslim jurists agree that zakat is a compulsory charity ordained by God. Muslims must pay it regardless of the enforcement of any other tax. Indeed, zakat is one of the pillars of Islam. In the Qur'án, zakat is mentioned along with the order to establish prayer. In his book, Ahmad stated that there are at least twenty-seven passages in the Qur'án where prayer and zakat are mentioned together. This excludes verses in which only charity is mentioned (Ahmad 1952, 104).

The word zakat in Islam literally means purification. In the moral sense, it is believed that zakat purifies the wealth and the soul. However, its purpose is to provide social justice and eradicate poverty. Zakat is different from any other charity in that it is considered as the right of the poor from the rich. What the wealthy are called to pay to the poor is what really belongs to the poor. The wealthy do not exclusively own the wealth that they possess. They share its ownership with the poor. At the end of every year, the share of the poor is to be calculated and returned to them.

Zakat is a certain share or percentage (nisab), specified in the Shari'a', charged against wealth such as cash, crops, cattle, gold, silver, jewelry, and anything that constitutes wealth. In general, it is assumed to be 2.5 percent of the value of the wealth that is kept lying unused for a year. It is believed that this system of wider distribution of spending power will improve the standard of living in general, and this in turn will increase the demand for goods. More important, zakat works against hoarding. In fact, hoarded wealth is the first item on which zakat is assessed. By combining the zakat giving with the absence of interest, it can be concluded that uninvested wealth will be used up over time. In Islam, wealth should be used in one of two ways: to be spent on the good things of life or invested in commerce and industry. This interplay between zakat and free interest encourages investment and hinders hoarding. There are verses in the Qur'án that encourage Muslims to direct their wealth toward these channels. Muslims are permitted to trade even while performing the Hajj. From an economic point of view, those two channels, spending and investment, are the driving force of the economy.

The third domain that affects doing business, according to the Islamic law, is the law of inheritance. The primary contribution of the Islamic law of inheritance to the economy is that it runs counter to the concentration of wealth in a few hands. Muslims can will away charity that shall not exceed one third of their property. The remainder must be shared among relatives as stated in some detail in the Qur'án. A deceased Muslim's wealth must be distributed, in specified amounts according to the Qur'án, among his or her relatives including all surviving children, a surviving spouse, and surviving parents. Under certain circumstances, brothers, sisters, and even more distant relatives can inherent a share. A Muslim cannot take away the right of any of his or her relatives by excluding them from the will. In other words, a Muslim cannot give away all his wealth to a single person, excluding the rest. Again this is a form of redistribution of wealth among many hands instead of one.

The application of the three laws discussed will certainly result in wider distribution of spending and investment power throughout an economy. Moreover, through these rules, Islam reflects that wealth should not be monopolized. From an economic point of view, it seems that Islam agrees with the capitalist system to a certain point. It grants full recognition of the independence of the individual and his private property, but at the same time it does not value monopoly.

ISLAM AND THE WEST

The West is influenced considerably by media depictions of Islam as fundamentalism, often related to terrorism. Some see the revival of the Islamist movement as backwardness, or more precisely as it was described by Mottahedeh and Fandy, "as a spring board of the emergence of an Islamintern: a coordinated conspiracy of single-minded fanatics who are addicted to violence and sworn to the hatred of America and the oppression of women." Those authors go on to suggest that many of the "autocratic regimes, hostile to an Islamic revival, know that, no matter how distasteful their policies might be, this is the button to press in order to get American support" for their regimes (1997, 297).

Western observers often assume that any call to Islam is enforceable and that pious Muslims will automatically answer it. It follows that if they do not support any call for the application of the Islamic law and the Islamic state, they have turned their backs on God. Such a position underestimates how Muslims understand their faith. In fact, according to Islam, no Muslim has the authority to judge the degree of faith of another Muslim, and no Muslim may be excommunicated.

If anything, Islamist movements in the Arab world draw their support from recognizable organizational efficacy and integrity. Changes in such perceptions will in turn foster changes in support. For example, in Lebanon, many Shiite Muslims have shifted from the Amal movement to Hizballah for the reason that Amal was perceived to be corrupt and inefficient, while Hizballah had demonstrated clean dealings and sensitivity towards the needs of its constituency. Vogel addressed this issue. He thought that Muslims in general seek civil rights and freedoms for both men and women, equal opportunities, fair distribution of wealth, and legitimate and honest government, and consider those to be Islamic values. However, many Muslims reject Islamist movements and consider them to be harsh, ideological, or violent. When the West fails to appreciate the range of religious attitudes toward Islamic movements, it generates an audience to amplify the short-term influence of Islamist politics and undermine the long-term legal, constitutional, and political importance of Islam (1997, 250). Even those who do not regard Islamic government as a priority believe that the application of Islamic norms in politics will guarantee democracy.

Islamic governments in the Arab countries gained their legitimacy through state-subsidized and affordable public services. Recent crises with respect to state budget deficits may sooner or later force the countries concerned to discontinue or reduce these services. This may lead to serious problems, especially in the political arena. Thus, it appears to be shortsighted to presume that Islamic norms are losing their relevance to public life. The relationship between the Islamic movements and their governments depends to a certain extent on the willingness of those governments to include the movements in political processes. For example, Kuwait has opted for limited admissibility. Bahrain excluded them completely from the political process, while Egypt has assumed an even more militant stance against them.

Whatever political situation may develop in the Arab countries, it seems unlikely that any of them will be able to exclude the concerns of Islam. In all the countries under consideration, the vast majority of the populations are Muslim, whether or not they support the Islamist movements. Typically, the members of those movements are relatively well educated and highly motivated and will not be dismissed lightly by the mainstream of the populations.

Part Two

The Major Accounting Firms and Development in Selected Islamic Jurisdictions

Chapter Four

The Egyptian Economy, International Linkages, and the Major Accounting Firms

This chapter deals with the situation in Egypt. It begins with a general overview in which the general political and economic situation facing the nation is discussed. Following that, some detail is supplied concerning the makeup of the Egyptian economy and its potential. The third section of the chapter discusses the role of major accounting firms in the nation's economy. The chapter concludes with an overall appraisal of the situation facing the nation as it becomes more involved with the global economy.

A PRELIMINARY OVERVIEW

Ibrahim M. Oweiss suggested that the background against which all current economic and political events should be analyzed is Egypt's strategic position (1982, 57). The intervening years have been kind to that assessment. The location of the nation in the northeastern corner of Africa insures its importance as a link between that continent and the nations of the Arabian Gulf.

As Oweiss has pointed out, Egypt has enjoyed a central position in the Arab world (57). With a population of nearly 58 million, it is the most populated nation in the Arab world (World Bank 1997, 215). With the Mediterranean to the north and the Red Sea to the east, not to mention the Suez Canal that links those two bodies of water, Egypt has an important role in trade in the region. "The combination of geography, population, and culture, then, has resulted in a long history in which Egypt's centrality to the region remains unquestioned" (Oweiss 1982, 58).

As the largest nation in the Arab world, Egypt did lose some credibility in that community based upon its rapprochement with Israel. However, the intervening years appear to have restored the nation's status to some extent. It has to be considered as an important participant in the process of voicing Arab concerns to the world at large. In that larger world, Egypt has always been considered to be an important presence in the region—witness the machinations of the United States and the former Soviet Union in their efforts to assert their influence in the Middle East through that country.

Oweiss has described U.S. interests in the Middle East as having been focused on three broad objectives: "resolution of the Arab–Israeli conflict, containment of the Soviet influence in the region, and assured access to Middle East oil" (1982, 59). Though concerns regarding Russia or the former Soviet Union have declined in significance in the region, concerns over Arab–Israeli relations are still pressing. The United States would appear to have a vested interest in maintaining a close and friendly relationship with Egypt. Of course, such a relationship will be strengthened by any expansion of ongoing business and economic dealings between the two nations.

Egypt, like various Arab nations in the Middle East, has an ongoing need for linkages with the world economy and with the non-Islamic world. While relying upon the world economy for its supply of various manufactured goods, it must pay for those goods with exports and at the same time must devise ways of conducting such operations within parameters that do not compromise its cultural and religious traditions. Real or perceived incursions upon domestic customs and traditions may cause domestic unrest and, in isolated cases, violent reactions. Visible breaches in value systems and religious principles may also generate suspicion among the nation's Arab neighbors.

At the time of the Oweiss article, oil revenues were increasing, as were remittances from Egyptian citizens working abroad. Both of those occurrences were helpful in supplying foreign exchange. The construction industry was booming and consistent increases in private sector activities were being realized. However Oweiss also drew attention to negative factors that he felt would have ongoing impacts upon the continuing course of development in Egypt. Among those were "lack of adequate housing, the recent downward trend in agricultural productivity, inefficiency in the public sector, the balance of payments deficit and the government subsidy policy" (78–79). Of course, such items are candidates for reassessment if the current situation in Egypt is to be understood.

In considering the task that confronts Egypt with respect to national development and increasing linkages to the global economy, it must be remembered that during the Nasser regime large segments of the nation's economy were socialized. As late as 1990, 7.3 percent of the population or 25.3 percent of the work force were in public employment (Ayubi 1997, 298). According to Ayubi, from 1962–1963 to 1970, the nation's national income grew by 68 percent, "resting on an increase in the labour force of no more that 20 percent." Parallel to those changes, "posts in the public bureaucracy had increased by 70 percent and salaries by 123 percent." Ayubi's comment on this seems telling—"Thus far the rate of bureaucratic growth had quite exceeded the rate of growth in population, employment and production" (299). Such data certainly suggest a very strong ideologic base for the economy, one that should surely require major efforts to adjust. Nonetheless, according to Ayubi, Egypt became the first Arab nation, with the partial exception of Tunisia, "to experiment with economic liberalization and privatization, from the mid-1970s onwards" (339).

Ayubi is critical of the pace of these policy shifts and suggests that "although domestic capital has welcomed the new policies, and while international capital has encouraged it, privatization in Egypt is still basically a public policy pursued by the state for its own purposes" (340). Handoussa and Kheir-El-Din are also critical of the state bureaucratic apparatus. Those authors have called for administrative reform, suggesting that "the Egyptian civil service hinders production and investment." They call for a reduction of the civil service from its current level of 3.5 million people, and a revision of the salary scale to bring it into line with realistic living standards and to minimize corruption. They also suggest that promotions and remuneration should be tied to performance, and call for training opportunities (1998, 59).

The positions of those authors and Ayubi notwithstanding, International Monetary Fund researchers see privatization proceeding successfully. "Majority divestitures of government shares have been completed for 42 companies, including in the industrial, agricultural, construction, retail and tourism sectors." Emphasizing their position they explain that "More than one-fourth of the state-owned enterprise sector is now in private hands" (El-Erain and Fennel 1997, 11).

THE EGYPTIAN ECONOMY

Though Egypt has a relatively important agricultural sector, it also gives high priority to industrialization. Consequently, the dependence on foreign sources to meet food requirements has substantially increased in recent years. Since consumer prices of main staples are heavily subsidized, increasing food demand resulted in an added leakage from the government budget. In Egypt, agricultural supply offers opportunities for successful agro-industry. The low labor wages can, at least for a time, add an element of comparative advantage. Its geographical location also gives it excellent accessibility to regional and international markets.

Throughout the latter half of the nineteenth century and during the first three decades of the twentieth century, the Egyptian economy was said to have been exhibiting "a classic Third World dependency syndrome, the essence of which was reliance on the export of a single, usually primary, commodity" (Library of Congress 1997a). In the case of Egypt, the staple in question was cotton. Of course few economists would suggest that crop as the basis for growth or prosperity in the economy of the upcoming millennium.

Nonetheless agriculture has been recognized in some circles as the nation's main source of growth. Those authors claim however that "More than three decades of pervasive government intervention in pricing, marketing, input delivery, crop area fixing, and crop rotation determination have had a detrimental impact upon agricultural performance." Those authors report agriculture as generating 15 percent of GDP, down from 30 percent in 1973 (Handoussa and Kheir-El-Din 1998, 63). It represents 12 percent of export proceeds, down from 50 percent in 1973. The authors are correct in pointing out that such statistical declines are partially explained by expansion in other sectors of the economy.

Agriculture has been described by the U.S. Department of Agriculture as one of the most "liberal and progressive" sectors in the nation's economy. However less than 4 percent of the nation's land area is arable. "Primary crops include rice, corn, a variety of vegetables, citrus and wheat." The historical importance of cotton has been alluded to earlier and that commodity remains Egypt's most important agricultural export (Arab World Online LLC 1997b).

Handoussa and Kheir-El-Din explain that the manufacturing sector has been at the center of the Egyptian growth strategy since the 1950s. It receives the "lion's share" of public investment by a government which has been emphasizing import substitution and diversification (1998, 65). Indeed the government "has established technology development as one of its basic tools for the overall development of the country." The intent behind establishing the Technology Development Program was to create an environment to assist in the expansion of the high technology, with an eye to raising living standards (Technology Development Program 1995).

The program aims at establishing a strategy for the development of high technology. It seeks to coordinate "all entities related to the development of the high technology, leading to a unified vision for the establishment of the basic foundation for high technology industries through preparing suitable environments, supplying the required information base and training with respect to cutting edge methods and techniques" (1998, 65).

According to Handoussa and Kheir-El-Din, growth rates in manufacturing attained an average of nearly 9 percent during the period from 1975 to 1992 (1998, 65). In spite of such a strong expansionary performance, the sector's share of GDP has remained at 17 percent. The authors attribute this to manufacturing growth having been superseded by the performance of petroleum, utilities, and services (65).

Though Egypt is hardly considered in the same light as certain other Middle Eastern nations with respect to oil production, "The oil and gas sector accounted for nearly 10% of Egypt's GDP in 1993/94." In that year, oil products accounted for more than 52 percent of total exports, however oil reserves "are expected to last only 14 years at the current output of 860,000 barrels per day" (Arab World Online LLC 1997b).

Faced with this reality, the government is turning to the country's natural gas reserves that have been estimated to be approximately 21 trillion cubic meters. The government had plans to build gas driven power plants and had hoped to raise the percentage of power plants relying on gas from 60 to 80 percent by 1997 (1997b). Plans are also in existence for the export of natural gas.

The industrial sector produces a wide variety of goods, including textiles, processed foods and beverages, building materials, fertilizers, chemicals, vehicles, electrical products, and engineering goods. The state monopoly over cotton and spinning and weaving suffers from ongoing inefficiencies (1997b). Of course, Egypt is still emerging from a rather heavily socialized economy, and it can be presumed that gains from the market economy and international linkages based upon that economy will not be fully enjoyed until privatization efforts are completed (Arab World Online LLC 1997b).

Arab World Online suggests that "The 90% private sector-owned ready-made garment sector has boomed, producing under international franchises such as Benetton." Since 1991 the government has been permitting foreign automobile producers to compete with the state owned monopoly, an action that appears to have revitalized the vehicle assembly sector. Cement output is expected to double in four years as a result of an anticipated boom in construction.

The Technology Development Program may have positive impacts upon the manufacturing sector. Among its many objectives, some of which have been mentioned above, is the elimination of major problems and obstacles in the path of technological development, as well as the selling of that form of change as the correct line of advance. The program seeks coordination and cooperation between the private sector and related government entities. The program establishes pilot projects, encourages coordination and cooperation, and private sector investment in the technology industry (Technology Development Program 1995).

"Acknowledging the importance of technology as the gateway to the twenty-first century the Cabinet . . . has included the Sinai Technology Valley (STV) . . . as one of the major boosting projects necessary for accelerating socioeconomic development in Egypt." The project is aimed at many facets of economic development and activities of the market both domestic and international.

The project seeks international investment in sectors such as information and communications technology, medical technology, and automation technology, as well as biotechnology and environmental technology. Indeed the project is aimed at the creation of a broad industrial base for Egypt. Major multinational firms will be offered the benefits of the location of the STV. The Sinai Technology Valley is an example of the type of undertakings determined by the Technology Development Project as essential for the establishment of a technological base for the nation's economy.

Egyptian technology is concentrated in a small number of major public sector companies and many small enterprises and industries. The government is hopeful that STV "will play a crucial role in the establishment of a competitive and booming technology industry and economy in Egypt" (Technology Development Program 1995).

Handoussa and Kheir-El-Din are of the opinion that manufacturing growth can be encouraged through exports. Their reasons include the fact that manufacturing enjoys a well-diversified production base "with substantial installed capacity in upstream processing along a wide horizontal spectrum." Beyond that, they point to abundant labor, experienced and willing to work at highly competitive wages. "Third, a wide range of labor-intensive industries is based on sales to a large and protected domestic market—and now shows signs of being profitable in export marketing, even if on a small scale." Those authors see certain strategies necessary for maximizing the potential of "both the large, formal manufacturing sector and the traditional small sector." They call for a shift in emphasis from an inward to an outward orientation in pursuit of more rapid expansion, able to employ existing capacities and accelerate in the direction of higher value added products, thus encouraging increased specialization among the producers of both goods and auxiliary services (1995, 65).

Beyond that the authors see the necessity for increasing the pace of incoming foreign direct investment. In connection with that, they call for strong links between domestic firms and multinational corporations with the hope of generating employment and encouraging the adoption of modern technology and managerial practices. They go beyond this to suggest that such reforms in trade, investment, and fiscal regimes should hopefully permit the nation "to serve as the locus of transnational industrial activities for European and Middle East markets" (65).

The same authors call for the development of high-tech industries with an eye to utilizing the nation's pool of engineers, technicians, and other professionals. Potential target industries included microelectronics, telecommunications, and computers. They also recommend that the traditional microenterprises, comprising 211,000 manufacturing establishments, with fewer than fifty employees, should be developed so as to integrate with the modern industrial complex (66).

As an incentive to investment by foreign interests, the government permits 100 percent foreign ownership of companies and guarantees the owners the right to repatriate capital and income earned in the country. Such companies are regulated by the General Authority for Investment and Free Zones, and are protected from nationalization or confiscation without compensation (Arab World Online LLC 1997b).

The nation has established seven free trade zones, which are "located in Cairo (Nasr City), Alexandria, Suez, Ismailiya, Port Said, Damietta, and Sohag." These zones are open to any type of sectoral investment, and participating companies are exempt from standard Egyptian taxes and fees. Instead, "An annual fee equal to one percent of the value of commodities traded or revenue generated in a business is collected." Firms with exports amounting to 80 percent or more of output are permitted to operate in foreign currency. Goods from free zones that are sold in Egypt are treated as imports and thus are subject to existing duties and regulations. Egyptian personnel must account for 75 percent of the work force in the free trade zones (1997b).

The major impediments to Egypt's industrial development can be summarized in shortages in finance and foreign exchange, competition between industry and agriculture for scarce resources, poor standards of production and productivity, excessive control, and destructive bureaucracy. A network of complementary infrastructural facilities must be built up in the areas of technical education and training, transportation and communications, ports, construction, energy supply, and distributional and storage facilities. However, since industrial growth is inherently conditioned by flexibility and efficiency, the issue of bureaucracy has to be resolved as one of the first preconditions for increased productivity and growth in Egypt.

Those issues can be facilitated through a better regional integration with the rest of the Arab world. The key issues here are the pressing need for financial capital, the restructuring of economic policies in the long run, administrative and institutional reform, and expansion and redirection of exports. Integration with the Arab world is very crucial to Egypt, considering its need for financial cooperation and the relative shortage in raw materials. Arab industrial strategy should aim at a structural reform, not just marginal growth. This would reduce the problems of economies of scale and comparative advantage. Adequate capital and absorptive markets can be obtained more expeditiously through economic integration among Arab nations.

The integrated area would offer better opportunities for establishing a wide range of optimal-size industrial firms—ones that can take advantage of scale economies, efficient use of resources, and large domestic markets that gain bargaining power in the international market. Furthermore, efficient use of resources would encourage domestic and foreign investments.

Very little has been accomplished so far in the actual implementation of Arab integration. In the absence of that, Egypt may be able to improve its development prospects through its service industries (e.g., tourism, banking, insurance, and accounting). The following section will examine the impacts of the services provided by the international accounting firms on Egypt's economy.

ACCOUNTING SERVICES AS FACILITATORS

Vinod Bavishi has reported the number of partners of the leading international accounting firms who are resident in various nations worldwide (1991, Appendix B). In 1991, he reported Egypt as having a total of fifty-four partners in major international accounting firms, of whom forty-one were associated with members of the Big Six. Cairo harbored forty-nine partners, while the remaining five were divided between Alexandria and Heliopolis. Clearly if the firms can be expected to generate major impacts upon the Egyptian economy, Cairo would appear to be the focal point for such impacts.

Egypt presents an interesting case. Despite a lengthy and storied history, it has been subjected over the years to various foreign invasions and occupations. Its location at the northeastern corner of the African continent has given it a historical position as a land bridge between that continent and what was called Asia Minor and beyond. Of course, the Suez Canal has been called "the gateway to the markets of Asia and the Far East and Europe" (Deloitte Touche Tohmatsu International 1994a, 1).

Given its positioning and historical involvement, one might expect Egypt to be a focus of international business and international linkages. Whether that is actually the case must be considered against the nation's history in the post–World War II era. The Egypt of the late 1990s must be considered against the background of events in the Middle East. To understand the economic potential of the nation necessitates an understanding of its role in the Arab World and how its culture and traditions mesh with economic and business linkages to the world at large. Certainly its international linkages may well be facilitated or encouraged by the involvement's of the major international accounting firms.

Problems with foreign linkages may be a lingering legacy of colonial experience. The nation's development strategy has been described as having moved through several different phases. "During the 1940s and early 1950s the development process witnessed an industrial entrepreneurial class, modern corporate structures, and an infant stock market." Unfortunately the entrepreneurial class was frequently seen as having "stronger links to colonial powers than to the well-being of Egyptians" (1994a, 1). Whether true or false, such a perception seems hardly supportive of substantial international business and economic linkages.

Since 1991, public policy in Egypt has been aimed at a comprehensive program of structural adjustment "under the auspices of the International Monetary Fund and the World Bank." The nation is moving in a gradual fashion toward a market-oriented economy. The Public Enterprise Office was established in November of 1991 and with help from private consultants is overseeing the valuation of firms "in preparation of decisions to privatize or restructure" (2).

It would appear as though the major accounting firms may have much to offer in such an environment. However, based on Bavishi's reporting of partners, their involvement seems less than pervasive. Shawki & Co., the Egyptian member of Deloitte Touche Tohmatsu International, has offices in Cairo and Alexandria and boasts a staff of four hundred. That firm "provides a full range of financial and management consultancy, audit, accounting, executive recruitment, social insurance, and tax and business advisory services to international and national business enterprises and government institutions." It is a market leader in developing viable and efficient privatized organizations and is well experienced in the assessment of public sector companies (70).

Another member of the Big Six active in Egypt is Price Waterhouse. In coordination with its associated firm, A. H. Shakawi & Co., it offers accounting and auditing, tax, and management consulting services to a wide range of domestic and international organizations. One of its main concerns is supplying the needs of foreign multinational firms in Egypt, "including those operating in the oil and gas industry." It boasts a staff with a wide range of experience in international auditing, accounting, and taxation, not to mention an extensive understanding of conducting business in Egypt (Price Waterhouse 1995, 107, 108).

The firm also serves many smaller customers. It employs an expatriate audit staff of CPAs, as well as several licensed Egyptian accountants. Price Waterhouse in Egypt and its local Egyptian associated firm have the capability to provide a full range of services that includes audit, business advisory, tax, and management consulting services (108).

In the areas of audit and business advisory services, the firms act as independent auditors and "at a minimum provide an audit service that satisfies the statutory requirements of Egyptian law." They see their auditing function as more than a statutory necessity—indeed, "as a constructive and cost-effective aid to management in the task of managing the enterprise" (108). This of course speaks to their awareness of the depth of their potential for impacting business.

Their audits include reviews of the adequacy of their customers' systems of internal accounting controls. They also review the effectiveness of accounting procedures and supply suggestions for strengthening both systems and procedures. They also conduct various types of reviews and agreed-upon procedures and provide various business advisory services. Their business advisory services include consultation on company and branch formation, familiarization with local statutory and regulatory requirements, and staff recruitment (108).

In the area of taxation, the firm provides routine assistance for clients and represents them in negotiations with the Egyptian Tax Department. They provide tax planning and compliance advice. Their management consulting menu covers most business functions. They help in putting together economic plans and strategies and provide management assessments and operations reviews. They design, review, and fine tune accounting financial systems and do organization studies. As parts of the worldwide network of their parent firm, they are able to supplement the skills of their domestic consultants with those of more specialized consultants when needed (109).

A FINAL OVERVIEW

In assessing the situation with Egypt and its relationship to the global economy, various circumstances that may be at cross-purposes must be considered. As the most populated nation in the Arab world, Egypt's relationship to that world in general as well as to its neighbors must be considered. Of course, that relationship was complicated by the rivalry between the United States and the former Soviet Union and more recently by the Egyptian accord with Israel.

Beyond its role in the Arab world, Egypt has had an ongoing relationship with the world at large. As the locus of the Suez Canal it has been a strategic link in East–West trade. Of course, it is also a link between Asia and the African continent. Beyond such linkage functions, it has been a supplier of cotton and, more recently, oil to world markets.

Recently it has been emerging from a period during which large segments of its economy were essentially socialistic. It may be premature to make definitive judgments concerning the nation's efforts at privatization or its search for foreign investment, except to suggest that both objectives appear to be necessary.

Economic growth through industrialization will hardly be accomplished without them. With a growing population, the nation is in need of expanding employment opportunities if sustained development is to be realized.

For economic success, Egypt must build linkages with its Middle Eastern neighbors and also with the world at large. At the same time, it must find ways to strengthen and grow its domestic economy. In pursuit of such goals, a face-off between Islamic values and those of the global market economy seems to be inevitable. Islam and the global market are far from mutually exclusive. However, any interface between them will require sensitivity and understanding.

It appears to the present investigators that the major accounting firms may have much to offer in Egypt with regard to building understanding between the various parties who have a stake in the successful development of the economy. Assuming that those firms have or can acquire the needed understanding of the nation's domestic culture, together with both the secular and religious laws and operating procedures that support it, they should be in a strong position to advise potential foreign investors, domestic businesses, and public agencies concerning what appears to be needed in order to practice in the economic environment that is emerging in Egypt.

Chapter Five

Some Facilitators of Economic Expansion in Saudi Arabia

This chapter assesses the climate for economic development in Saudi Arabia. It hopes to supply some insights concerning the actual and potential roles of the oil industry and Islam in establishing the foundations of business and economic strength. Following that, it reviews public policy as it relates to external linkages and the importance of such linkages. The discussion then turns to the role of major international accounting firms in the facilitation of business. A concluding overview deals with the direction public policy should take if the nation is to sustain a positive climate for business.

Saudi Arabia holds considerable significance for the modern world due to the fact that it harbors major Islamic religious sites and in addition is a major supplier of petroleum products to the world at large. Religion and energy are sources of both strength and weakness in an economy in search of both stability and material advancement.

"Islam due to foreign perceptions concerning how it applies in the nation may be daunting to various foreign business interests that might otherwise find Saudi locations attractive" (McKee, Abu-Amara McKee, and Garner 1998). The Saudi setting may appear to be threatening to foreign interests who might well gain from the stability that Islamic morality can instill in a business environment. Thus, Saudi Arabia may be experiencing shortages of foreign investment and consequent impediments to economic development. It seems reasonable to assume that the energy base of the nation (oil) and good transportation and communications linkages with the global economy should provide adequate foundations for economic development. Beyond that, Saudi Arabia occupies a strategic geographical location and enjoys relatively easy access to Europe, Asia, and Africa.

THE ECONOMY OF SAUDI ARABIA

Oil was discovered in the Eastern Province of the nation in 1938, just six years after the unification of the country as the Kingdom of Saudi Arabia. "The process of building the state fortified by oil revenues distributed through the modern institutions of bureaucracy, worked to unify this economically diverse country" (Library of Congress 1997c). The emergence of the nation as a major source of petroleum products played a large part in its becoming of strategic interest to the Western World.

As early as the mid-1970s, the government elected to use its expanding oil revenues for developmental purposes, most notably industrialization. This led to investments in processing plants employing hydrocarbon resources. "It meant financing and building the gas-gathering systems, the pipelines for gas and crude oil to bring the raw material to the two chosen main industrial sites—Al Jubayl . . . and Yanbu al Bahr . . . and building the industrial sites themselves." Other development projects included airports, hospitals, roads, and ports. By the mid-1980s, such spending totaled U.S. $500 billion (1997c).

Funds spent on development are in large part aimed at promoting private sector investment. Beyond the infrastructure projects listed, this entailed assisting private firms in the supplying of electric power. It also meant improving water supply capabilities. "Telecommunications were quickly brought up to international standards, allowing Saudi Arabia to handle all its communications needs in local and international telephone, telegraph, maritime and television distribution services, via cable, satellite and terrestrial transmission systems" (1997c).

The thrust of major investment in the nation has been capital intensive, thus providing rather limited opportunities for manual or unskilled labor. The primary labor demands have been for highly skilled and qualified managerial and supervisory personnel. Egypt has been an ongoing source for such labor needs. The best opportunities for less skilled workers have rested within the service sector.

The use of oil revenues to import state-of-the-art modern technology has created relatively few employment opportunities for the nation's citizens. Indeed, the nature of imports has increased the pressure to expand capital imports, including spare parts and computerized equipment. Thus, the processes of labor absorption, so necessary for expanding development and accompanying improvements in human material conditions, has been slowed to some extent.

At this writing, there is as yet no solid foundation for a true economic development strategy designed to enable the nation to diversify its economy beyond a very heavy reliance on oil. The nation, though oil rich, remains relatively underdeveloped. Occupying roughly 80 percent of the Arab Peninsula it is known to possess considerable mineral wealth beyond oil, including deposits of gold, silver, copper, lead, iron, zinc, chromium, tungsten, titanium, and lithium. "There are also exportable amounts of fluorite, limestone, clay, phosphate, manganese, asbestos, pyrites, and gypsum" (Abdeen and Shook 1984, 5).

Agricultural potential is relatively sparse, with limited areas of the nation being suitable for cultivation. In spite of this, according to Bouhdiba, "Saudi Arabia has poured billions of dollars into high capital-intensive and costly food production projects although less than 2 percent of the country's land area is arable" (1979, 181). Agriculture has remained a relatively insignificant sector of the nation's economy.

Though the nation does possess some resources in addition to oil and boasts some industry, it is still far too dependent on oil. The inclusion of oil revenue in per capita income computations overstates the strength and stability of the economy. It seems evident that sustained growth and prosperity will require more economic diversification than oil can provide. The Saudi economy is faced with the need to accumulate enough productive resources in non-oil sectors to offset the depletion of energy resources over time. Present oil revenues can assist in the attainment of that end.

"In the industrial field, the Saudi private sector is involved in the production of . . . soft drinks, paper products, detergents, furniture, plastics and building products, and in textile manufactures and light metal industries." Ayubi points out that most private-sector industrial firms are small in size and "more concentrated in the area of rather similar consumer products." Most of those enterprises are private companies or partnerships. Private manufacturing firms are not very efficient and are run using "rather primitive managerial and accounting practices." Ayubi also suggests that private sector companies are heavily dependent upon subsidized borrowing from state financial bodies (Ayubi 1997, 377).

It appears as though Islam provides a strong and sustainable subsector for the Saudi economy. The impact that religion can make on the economy must be considered. As suggested earlier, the Muslim holy sites, aside from their religious significance, have generated a major economic impact. "The Hajj or pilgrimage to Mecca, occurs annually . . . and represents the culmination of the Muslims' spiritual life" (Library of Congress 1997c). Every adherent to Islamic belief is expected to make the pilgrimage at least once. With Islam boasting 1.2 billion adherents worldwide, it seems as though the numbers making the annual pilgrimage can be expected to increase. Currently, pilgrims number from 1.5 to 2 million annually.

Modern transportation and communications have already fostered substantial increases in foreign pilgrims for the Hajj. Though Hajj-related activities last little more than a week, they do generate a significant infusion of foreign exchange, as well as a number of full- and part-time employment opportunities. The economic importance of the Hajj is not always apparent as compared to its religious significance.

The Ministry of Pilgrimage Affairs and Religion Trusts is responsible for matters to do with the Hajj. Special pilgrimage visas are issued permitting visitors to visit Mecca and the Tomb of the prophet in Medina, though they require them to leave the country quickly. This practice illustrates the nation's insularity and may not be well received among non-Saudi Muslims.

Aside from insuring some religious access, the government has been protective of the nation's job markets and has taken steps to insure that pilgrims do not become job seekers. This is perhaps ironic in light of the numbers of jobs that are created by the pilgrimage. The Saudis have made rather massive adjustments in their transportation and communications infrastructure to accommodate the Hajj.

Certainly the Hajj generates a significant economic impact, but it does not offer a means for maximizing material benefits to the nation from the hosting of religious observances or the visitation to major Islamic sites. Beyond the Hajj, the sites are significant in their own right and are certainly capable of attracting numbers of Islamic visitors on an ongoing basis. Lesser pilgrimages and rituals, such as the Umra, attract visitors. The Umra is frequently carried out in conjunction with the Hajj.

The encouragement of religious visitors on an ongoing basis would have substantial positive economic effects. In fact, the economic overspill from religious tourism may be more predictable and long lasting than are the gains from the energy sector. Beyond the Middle East, oil may be considered to be the lifeblood of the Saudi economy. However, Islam may well be able to supply more permanent underpinnings for that economy. At a minimum, the religious foundation of the economy may supply a stable base from which various secondary and tertiary activities may emerge.

PUBLIC POLICY, FOREIGN LINKAGES, AND GROWTH POTENTIAL

Though the nation remains somewhat remote in the eyes of foreigners, particularly those from wealthy, non-Islamic nations, it seems clear that the nation's government understands the importance of foreign linkages. Saudi Arabia has been involved with OPEC for sometime, and its position in the Islamic world has necessitated various international arrangements as well.

Beyond these concerns, the government has displayed a willingness to entertain an escalating international involvement. Perhaps the roots of such involvement are visible through hindsight with the creation of the Gulf Cooperation Council as early as 1981. That was the arrangement through which the Saudis involved themselves as political partners with the smaller Arab jurisdictions of the Persian Gulf.

That involvement soon became economic as well as political. Perhaps the Saudis were assuming security responsibilities in the Gulf, which previously had been the preserve of the British earlier in this century. In return, certain small principalities were providing a window on the world for the Saudis. Indeed Bahrain and the United Arab Emirates have emerged as offshore financial centers that may well be facilitating Saudi international dealings to some extent. The freedom of movement that has emerged between members of the Gulf

Cooperation Council, including Saudi Arabia, represents a major movement on the part of the latter nation toward linkages with the global economy.

In the 1990s, the Saudis have appeared to be somewhat more willing to develop foreign business and economic linkages. Witness the formation of the U.S.–Saudi Arabian Business Council. Since its formation in 1993, that organization has maintained offices in Washington, D.C. and Riyadh. "The overall purpose of the Council is to become the focal point for the exchange of knowledge between the private sectors in the U.S. and Saudi Arabia" (U.S.–Saudi Arabian Business Council 1997a).

The council's goals seem geared towards economic growth in Saudi Arabia. For example, it encourages manufacturing related joint ventures between U.S. and Saudi Arabian firms. In addition, it attempts to supply information concerning opportunities available for smaller- and medium-sized U.S. firms. It also works to encourage a better knowledge and understanding of the business and cultural climates of both nations. Finally it is intended to "develop and strengthen working relationships between the Council and relevant private and government agencies and industry leaders in order to respond to business needs" (1997a). The success of this enterprise may require some time to assess. Of course, there are those who may be critical of a symbiosis of such proportions between the Saudi business community and that of one foreign country, especially the United States.

The Sixth National Development Plan was introduced in Saudi Arabia in 1995. Although it called for the further development of the technical skills of the Saudi populace and an increasing emphases on the role of the private sector (U.S.–Saudi Arabian Business Council 1997b, 4), there appears to be little mention of foreign linkages.

Among its specifics, the plan was intended to restrict government expenditures for development programs to actual revenues (5). Beyond that, it called for relating government loans and support to firms to the "implementation of Saudization commitments." The government intended to deepen the dialogue with the private sector. Thus, regular meetings with private sector representatives were to be arranged (4).

Private capital was to be more involved in financing government projects. The financial conditions facing small firms were to be improved and the activities of the Saudi Credit Banks were to be expanded. Methods to encourage small-scale industries were to be devised and an agency to facilitate that was to be created. Industrial parks were to be positioned in areas with expansionary potential. The plan also called for "meeting the rising demand for modern infrastructure facilities in addition to safeguarding existing facilities through routine maintenance" (4).

The plan was also cognizant of environmental needs and concerns. It called for bringing nonconventional water resources on line in an efficient fashion. In this regard, it mentioned desalinated water, treated waste water, and agricultural drainage water (4). It called for full privatization of electric utilities as a medium- to long-term goal. More specifically, geared to the environment, it called for instituting a national system for adopting environmental impact assessment, especially with regard to industrial, agricultural, and urban projects (4). Among various specific growth-oriented goals, the plan set an annual production sector expansion quota at 4.2 percent and a parallel expectation for services at 4.4 percent. Whether such goals can be attained, and if they are, what that may portend, remains to be seen.

Though the Sixth National Development Plan (1997) displays little that explicitly addresses foreign linkages, the Saudis have hardly abandoned interest in such linkages. In a report dating from 1996, Nando.net and Reuter Information Service refer to Saudi interest in joining the World Trade Organization, a move that they reported would "open international trade doors wider, but at the same time put pressure on the oil rich Kingdom to liberalize its economy" (1997).

Both domestic and foreign linkages are significant for the ongoing development of the economy. The U.S.–Saudi Arabian Business Council refers to the importance of air travel domestically, due to the distances separating Saudi cities (1997c, 19). The nation boasts three major modern international airports: "King Khalid International Airport in Riyadh, King Abdulaziz International Airport in Jeddah, and King Fahd International Airport in the Eastern Province" (19). The last mentioned facility was soon to be operational.

Beyond the major international airports, the nation boasts twenty-two regional and local airports. The nation's major cities and regions are well connected by roads. Major port facilities are located in Jeddah, Yanbu, Dammam, Jubail, Jizan, and Rabigh (19). The Council describes the Jeddah and Dammam ports as "state-of-the-art commercial ports" and Yanbu and Jubail ports as "state-of-the-art major industrial ports with modern bulk cargo and container handling capabilities" (19). On the gulf, Ras Tanura is among the world's largest oil terminals. Thus, it seems clear that the nation is reasonably endowed with both domestic and international transportation linkages.

The modern sectors of the economy appear to be housed in or accessible from major urban areas. The largest of the nation's cities is Riyadh, with a population in excess of 2 million. The city second in size to the capital is Jeddah, with a population of 1.5 million. Jeddah, situated on the Red Sea, is the nation's main port and the major gateway for foreign pilgrims. The largest urban area in the eastern region is Dammam, an important port on the Persian Gulf. That city has a population in excess of 1 million and is the site of the newly constructed King Fahd International Airport.

Clearly the nation has developed a fairly substantial network of urban areas. According to the U.S.–Saudi Arabian Business Council, "The two main roles of the Saudi government in its effort to diversify the industrial base are to provide the infrastructure and incentives to encourage industrial development and to generate industrial projects to take advantage of the Kingdom's oil resources" (1997c, 4). Though these are significant goals, it seems as though the nation must pay attention to forging more substantial international industrial and service ties beyond what oil has generated. The infrastructure that it has developed, coupled with its strategic geographical position, makes such a policy thrust feasible.

FACILITATORS OF BUSINESS EXPANSION

In another context, the current authors have suggested that "Careful strategic planning and implementing realistic goals are essential for the diversification of the Saudi Arabian economy" (Abu-Amara McKee, McKee, and Garner 1997). In the last twenty-five years, major groupings of international business service providers have emerged, whose clients include multinational corporations and various governmental agencies in settings throughout the world where the production units of the multinationals are housed. The business service firms in question have become expert in facilitating the operations of client corporations and have also displayed an ability to assist public agencies in nations hosting such jurisdictions (McKee 1988).

The major international accounting firms have become important elements in the service cadres in question. They appear to have significant potential for improving international linkages to the Saudi economy. Bavishi reported that the Big Six accounting firms had a significant presence in Saudi Arabia (1991). In 1991, the nation housed fifty-one partners in those firms; however, only three of the Big Six operated offices in the nation. Ernst & Young, Price Waterhouse, and Arthur Andersen were the firms in question. It is important to note that these firms are operating offices in Jeddah and Riyadh exclusively; other Saudi cities are not hosting local offices. Of course, any impacts from the firms should be expected to be most noticeable in the centers housing them. Any impacts beyond those locations remain to be seen.

Price Waterhouse operates through International Accounting Associates and Abdulaziz A. Al-Barrak Consulting Associates. Those firms offer a wide range of services to local and international clients (Price Waterhouse 1991, 138). A brief overview of services offered by the firm was provided in another context (Abu-Amara McKee, McKee, and Garner 1997, 35–39).

The firm can assist with audits and accountancy, Saudi taxation, international assignment tax services, training seminars and courses, and management consulting (Price Waterhouse 1991, 139). With respect to accounting, auditing and related services, the Price Waterhouse staff is knowledgeable in both international and local practices. In addition to traditional audits, they have conducted acquisition reviews, not to mention other business advisory services.

"The firm's tax practice works closely with the audit practice." According to the firm, "Virtually all business decisions are affected by Zakat and income taxes. A substantial portion of Saudi tax law is supported by custom instead of formal regulations." The firm keeps its clients alert to the Zakat and tax implications of their operations through periodic newsletters (139).

Through its office in Riyadh, the firm provides assistance for clients in the preparation of U.S. individual tax returns. They can also provide this service to persons requiring it in other areas of the Middle East. The firm can assist "with respect to the unique problems of other expatriate employees, including foreign nationals with U.S. filing requirements" (139).

The firm's international assignment tax consultants can assist in lowering the cost of international assignment programs and in helping assignees to meet their foreign tax filing obligations (139). The firm and its staff of United States, United Kingdom, and Middle East professionals "have developed and presented training courses on the subjects of accounting, data processing and internal auditing among others." Such courses have been developed for petrochemical companies, banks, hotels, and government agencies throughout the Middle East (140).

The firm offers an extensive selection of management consulting services. Its financial consultants for the most part are U.S. certified public accountants. They provide services aimed toward improving the financial operations of organizations. The firm can also assist in developing computerized information systems. With respect to strategic and organizational management, it can assist with expected changes, rapid growth, changing customer needs, and alterations. It can also deal with operating efficiency and the effectiveness of organizations (140). Clearly Price Waterhouse is capable of significant impacts in Saudi Arabia.

Details concerning the firm's offerings in the area of global energy, and more specifically oil, are worthy of consideration. The firm is quite active in the oil industry. It "is the auditor for six of the 10 largest integrated oil companies in North America and serves more than 1,500 other oil and gas companies around the world" (Price Waterhouse 1997b, 1). It has allocated more than 1,200 professionals to the PW World Petroleum Industry Group. Certainly this level of involvement renders the firm's strong presence in Saudi Arabia hardly surprising.

According to the firm, petroleum companies benefit from its network in various ways. It stands ready to share up-to-date knowledge of oil and gas taxation in both the operating jurisdictions and the home countries of its clients. It can also supply information on currency regulations, local content requirements, and employment practices (1).

The firm claims to have considerable contact with government petroleum regulators as well as with various oil and gas companies. It is prepared to assist clients in the conduct of various nonstrategic functions, including accounting, litigation assistance, information technology, the establishment of systems, and both the acquisition of operating facilities and their management (1).

"Price Waterhouse also helps its petroleum clients reengineer their systems and procedures to reduce costs with best-in-industry and best-across-all-industry benchmarking analysis" (4). As an example, they have developed a proprietary software program, for both mainframes and client–server environments, that is designed to catalogue the production, marketing, and distribution of both oil and gas. The program handles taxation as well, not to mention joint-interest ownership, and various other accounting and reporting requirements, with an eye for cutting costs and increasing the accuracy of information (4).

The cost-reduction services offered to the petroleum industry by the firm beyond what has been discussed are extensive. "They include asset and hydrocarbon reserve valuations—which often reveal clients have inaccurately valued their reserves for tax purposes." The firm provides expert assistance with acquisition, asset sales, production-sharing contracts, and the establishment of joint-operating agreements designed to save both money and time for its clients (5).

Certainly Price Warehouse has much expertise to offer regarding the energy sector of the nation's economy. Indeed, the petroleum expertise that it claims may also prove useful to public agencies concerned with the ongoing success of the oil industry. The extensive oil expertise of Price Waterhouse as described above should certainly contribute to the ongoing success of the energy sector of the Saudi economy.

It must be remembered that oil hardly represents the entire range of expertise offered by Price Waterhouse through its global network. Oil has been highlighted here to illustrate the depth of involvement that Price Waterhouse is willing to undertake in a specific industry. Parallel levels of involvement can be expected in other industries according to the needs of the firm's global clients. Through such involvements with clients, Price Waterhouse and other major accounting firms have become multinational firms in their own right.

The Saudi economy has potentially much to gain from the presence of major accounting firms. The firms can facilitate both domestic and foreign corporate operations, provide demonstration effects in the local economy, and facilitate economic linkages at all levels. Indeed, their potential for assisting government agencies should not be underestimated.

A FINAL OVERVIEW

It seems clear that the Saudi prosperity has been largely oil based. A more lasting prosperity should probably be sought through a more diverse economy. Presumably this is recognized in the most recent Saudi five-year plan, which calls for annual increases in both manufacturing and services in excess of 4 percent. Such a growth pattern can best be realized through a more vigorous pursuit of international linkages. These linkages will require the courting of a broader manufacturing sector and a year-round involvement in religious tourism. Evidently Saudi Arabia has developed adequate transportation and communications linkages. These linkages can only deliver positive impacts through use.

Certainly the major accounting firms can facilitate such involvements. They can assist foreign firms wishing to operate within the Kingdom. In addition, they may be able to advise both public and private entities on the mechanics of dealing with the global economy.

Chapter Six

The Turkish Economy, International Linkages, and the Major Accounting Firms

This chapter deals with the subject of Turkey. That nation shares religious ties to the Arab World that go back many centuries. At the same time it has historical linkages to the Western World through Europe that date from the days of the Eastern Roman Empire and before. In some ways, the two root systems referred to here are at cross-purposes in the Turkish setting. The nation is positioned geographically to sustain linkages to both the Middle East and Europe. In the economic sphere, both linkages have their attractions or advantages. It seems clear that Turkey can be stronger economically if it is successful in its foreign linkages.

It is the position of the current authors that international business services, notably those available through major multinational accounting firms, may have much to offer in facilitating Turkey's international economic linkages and thus the strength of its domestic economy. In clarifying that position, the present chapter gives a brief overview of religious and cultural issues. Following that, a survey of the nation's economy is presented. This sets the stage for some examples of what the major accounting firms have to offer. The chapter concludes with a summary and overview of the argument.

RELIGIOUS AND POLITICAL ISSUES

Any understanding of how Turkey relates to the world economy, not to mention the nation's potential for ongoing diversification and growth, requires knowledge of how the nation perceives its relationship with Europe and how religious and cultural factors influence that relationship. Writing in 1993, Sencer Ayata suggested that the "changing relationship between the state and religion is likely to constitute one of the most important debates in Turkey in the 1990s" (1993, 63).

Ayata explained that after coming to power in 1980, the military leaders were looking for a medium between religion and the secular state. Those leaders were aware of the growing significance of the Islamic Middle East as a trading partner, and this, coupled with a deterioration of relations with Western Europe, prompted a more favorable attitude towards the Islamic nations in the region (63). The military leaders were also cognizant of religion as a potential legitimizing support for their policies and as "an important instrument in the struggle against anarchy and terror" (64).

The post-1983 world saw what Ayata described as the unprecedented level of penetration of state institutions by neotraditionalist Islamic groups. "Many official departments became vehicles for the promotion of fundamentalist ideas and interests." Ayata predicted an increase in such developments (64). Thus, it would appear that Islamic concerns within Turkey, together with a strong rational for economic and political ties to the Islamic nations of the Middle East, are forces that must be factored into any policy initiatives aimed at economic development and increasing global linkages.

Ayata saw big business interests based in Istanbul as the most significant deterrent to religious fundamentalism. "This . . . bourgeoisie is pro-Western in its views, business ties, and lifestyle." Ayata suggested that the manner in which ethnicity, regionalism and demographic devisions in an Islamic nation are influenced by religiosity and fundamentalism is a very important issue (66). Of course, such an issue should be expected to have a major impact upon international economic linkages and thus upon the nature and extent of domestic development potential.

Recently, Turkish foreign policy toward the Middle East has changed dramatically. Turkish leaders became aware that they need to distinguish their country's interests in the Middle East independently from the United States in order to mend their country's relations with the Arab States.

Turkish–Arab relations are greatly influenced by Islamic ideology. Birol A. Yesilada has suggested that economic difficulties experienced by Turkey led to improved relations with the Arab World and an infusion of financial capital from Saudi Arabia and other oil-rich Arab states (1993, 175). The 1980s saw a joining of Turkish nationalism and Islam "as the only viable channel for creating a strong Turkey" (177).

This ideology embraced a union of religion and the state, and indeed a society built upon Islamic foundations. Beyond that, it saw a coalition between government and the military ruled by religious law (Shari'a'). The proponents of this philosophy saw various potential enemies who should be removed. Included were atheists, separatists, Western humanists, and followers of other religions (177).

Sharing space on the elimination list were "those who blame Islam for the collapse of the Ottoman Empire" and "leftist, elitist, and etatist intellectuals." Yesilada points out that these principles and goals of the Turkish–Islamic synthesis reflect the objectives of the International Shari'a' Congress held in Pakistan in 1976

(177). Clearly such an ideology, if espoused in government policy, can be expected to determine the direction and success of the nation's international and commercial relations.

That ideology became a crucial factor in Turkish political policy following the International Shari'a' Congress in Pakistan in 1976 (177). This laid the foundation for consequent entry of Saudi Arabian capital into Turkey. Moreover, the Islamic Development Bank, which heavily depends on Saudi Arabia's contributions, provided the necessary financial assistance for industrial, agricultural, transportation, energy, and communications projects.

Turkish foreign policy encouraged Saudi Arabian capital. For example, Faisal Finance and Al Barada Turkish Finance are provided with special exemptions from Turkish bankruptcy laws (186) and the Islamic Development Bank enjoys special tax exemptions. No other foreign company presently operating in Turkey enjoys such a wide range of exemptions from Turkish laws. Hence, Saudi Arabian and Iranian investments in Turkey increased significantly in the last decade. Among these investments, the most crucial are the Islamic finance houses that started an alternate form of banking, known as "interest-free banking" in Turkey (186). In the face of such changes, Turkey's commitment to Westernization has become weaker and Turkey's role in the Islamic conference and its ties with the Islamic world have increased. In 1981, Turkey assumed the chair of a standing Committee for Economic and Commercial Cooperation, established at the third summit meeting of the organization. The 1980s witnessed an increase in Turkey's trade with the Middle East, and in joint Turkish–Arab banks and trading companies especially involving Saudi Arabia (202–203).

THE TURKISH ECONOMY

The year 1980 appears to represent a turning point in the development of the Turkish economy, since it signals the beginning of a structural transformation. In that transformation, the economy began moving away from direct regulation and control by government to a more liberal posture relying on the workings of the market. The government has adopted "twin goals of stabilization and transformation with an ultimate goal of integration into the world economy" (MFA 1997a, 1).

The most significant factor among industrialization policies has been identified as the liberalization of foreign trade. By strengthening exports, foreign exchange rate policies and tax rebate practices, the integration of the nation into the world economy has been accelerated, and beyond that, the private sector has gained an increased share in the industrial sector (1).

With respect to structural adjustment, the liberalization of capital movements has been given special importance with an eye to increasing the competitive power of the economy. "The Turkish banking system has been made compatible with . . . universal banking" (2). An interbank money market was established as early as 1986 with an eye to unifying the money market and establishing a rational cash flow between financial institutions.

In keeping with the liberalization of the economy, the 1980s saw "continuous legal, structural and institutional changes and developments in the Turkish banking sector" (MFA 1997b, 2). A series of reforms were introduced designed to promote the development of financial markets. The main intent of the reforms was to increase the efficiency of the financial system by stimulating inter bank competition. Interest and foreign exchange rates were freed, new firms were permitted to enter the banking system and foreign banks were encouraged to enter the country.

The Turkish banks began doing business abroad by opening branches and representative offices as well as by purchasing foreign banks. The weakening of foreign exchange regulations increased foreign exchange transactions on the part of the banks. Beginning in the mid 1980s, special finance houses following Islamic banking principles emerged in the Turkish financial system. In 1986, unified accounting principles were adopted together with a standard reporting system. In the following year, banks began being audited by independent external auditors in keeping with internationally accepted accounting principles. The government introduced legal and institutional arrangements aimed at encouraging the development of capital markets (2).

Banks began performing other services. They negotiated security issues and traded in securities. They underwrote fund management and established mutual funds and financial consultation (2). The 1980s also saw the diversification of services and products offered, not to mention progress with respect to computerization and automation (3). Growth was stimulated through increasing the importance of training manpower (2).

The commercial banks in Turkey can operate legally in all financial markets. "The Turkish state, apart from its regulatory interventions in banking transactions, also controls the bulk of the Turkish banking system." Though there were only nine state banks by the end of September of 1995, those institutions represented 45 percent of the system. Most commercial banks have ownership linkages to nonfinancial institutions. Banks have no effective nonbank competition. The majority of insurance and leasing companies are affiliated with banks (3).

Near the end of 1995, Turkey boasted sixty-nine banks. With the exception of the central bank and thirteen investment and development banks, the remainder were commercial banks. Publicly owned banks included six commercial banks and three development and investment banks. There were twenty-two foreign banks in the country in the fall of 1995. Those institutions formed a significant element in the nation's banking system because of new concepts and practices they introduced. They have changed attitudes toward competition and dynamism in the banking system (3).

"Turkish banks have begun developing strategies to replace unprofitable services and activities, install new services and increase profitability and competitive strength through better control of operating costs" (3). Clearly their operations are suggestive of the impacts that various facilitative business services might have upon the economy.

Turkish banks are also operating abroad. By 1995, "There were 17 branches and 71 representative offices and 2 bureaux of Turkish banks abroad" and the number was on the increase (3). Such involvements can be assumed to be strengthening the foreign linkages enjoyed by the Turkish economy.

Beyond such linkages fostered by the operations of the banking sector, Turkey has shown an interest in foreign involvements. The nation's relations to the European Community date from the late 1950s, and it became an associate member of that organization on 12 September 1963. Since that time it has worked toward strengthening its linkages. In 1987, it applied for full membership in the community and related organizations and has moved toward meeting customs union obligations to the community. Turkey boasts membership in the International Monetary Fund (IMF), the International Bank for Reconstruction and Development (IBRD), and the Organization for Economic Cooperation and Development (OECD).

Turkey has considerable agricultural strength and is self-sufficient in food. As has been the case with many nations the agricultural sector was historically Turkey's largest employer and a major component in the nation's gross domestic product (GDP), export sector and industrial growth. With development, agriculture has declined in significance relative to expanding manufacturing and service sectors. In 1970, agriculture accounted for 35 percent of GDP, and by 1995 its share had fallen to 16.4 percent. Despite this decline in the relative importance of agriculture, "Turkey is still the largest producer and exporter of agricultural products in the Near East and North African region" (*Agriculture* 1997a, 1).

The Turkish government has a history of intervention in the agricultural sector. It has done so through price supports, input subsidies, import protection, marketing monopolies, export subsidies, and tax policies (10). The purpose was to increase self-sufficiency vis-à-vis food as well as to stimulate rural development. Other aims have included the stabilization of farm incomes, the provision of affordable food, and adequate nutrition, as well as export promotion (1).

Since 1980, Turkey has taken on a series of agricultural policy reforms with an eye to privatizing markets, reducing agricultural subsidies, and removing trade barriers. Such adjustments were aimed at integrating the nation into the global economy (10). "Turkey's proximity to Europe, the Middle East and North Africa gives it easy access to large markets through the Black Sea to the north, the Aegean Sea to the west and the Mediterranean Sea to the south" (6).

The domestic market for agricultural products has been strong due to a rising population and higher incomes (6). Though agriculture is experiencing a diminishing significance in the Turkish economy, it can be expected to play a continuing role parallel to manufacturing and service activities. Certainly ready markets for Turkish food products in the Arab world should insure an ongoing place in that market for the agricultural sector.

In recent years, manufacturing activities have been gaining in importance in the nation's economy. The manufacturing sector has achieved significant growth, registering "an annual average growth rate of 6% since 1990 and it accounted for 70.9% of total physical production in 1994" (MFA 1997e, 1). This success was attributed to several factors, including abundant natural resources, the geographical proximity to export markets, infrastructure development, the existence of a large domestic market and liberal economic policies (1). Among manufacturing subsectors, textiles and clothing have been the most prominent.

Summarizing developments in the industrial sphere during the 1980s, Oktar Turel saw the economy as becoming increasingly specialized in textiles, clothing, leather, glass, and to a smaller degree, food industries. Turel saw Turkey reducing import surpluses in iron and steel and actually emerging as an exporter of unsophisticated products in those subsectors. The nation was seen as continuing as a net importer in most process industries such as paper, chemicals, and nonferrous metals. It was also described as becoming an importer of engineering products, with the exception of metal products. Indeed, Turel saw the pace of such imports accelerating. Beyond those developments, Turel saw the nation as rapidly losing its position as a net exporter of tobacco because of rising imports of finished tobacco products. Turel described Turkey as marginally involved in trade in beverages, wood products, printing and publishing, rubber and plastics, oil products, and nonmetallic products, excluding glass (1993, 76).

Despite some of the weaknesses referred to, Turel saw the growth of output and productivity from 1980 to 1987 as fairly satisfactory, even measured by international standards. However, he attributed this to the utilization of idle capacity and bountiful balance of payments support. Indeed, he suggested that a very large fraction of the rise of productivity in manufacturing is attributable to improved capacity utilization, leaving a modest contribution from technological change and/or capital deepening (90).

Turel also pointed out that overall productivity per man in large establishments fell by nearly 20 percent from 1976 to 1985. He suggested that this productivity issue was not evident in the aggregate due to an ongoing structural transformation, which is raising the share of large-scale, high productivity units at the expense of smaller less productive units. The overall increase in productivity was seen as dependent upon individual sectoral performances, together with resource shifts away from low productivity pursuits. Turel was pessimistic since the trade orientation and the trend in capital accumulation are less than conducive to stimulating gains in productivity (90).

Despite the pessimism exhibited by Turel, manufacturing activities have a significant role to play in the Turkish economy. "The food industry, chemicals and plastics, glass, iron and steel, motor vehicles and parts, electrical non-electrical machinery, electronics and furniture are . . . well established sectors." Manufactured exports represented nearly 86 percent of the export total in 1994 (MFA 1997e, 1).

A sustainable export performance has been seen as dependent upon increasing competitiveness in international markets. Beyond prices, factors impacting competitiveness were seen as including closing technological gaps with developed countries, improving product quality, developing trademarks acceptable in international markets, producing environmentally friendly products, and diversifying both products and markets (1).

Among manufacturing products Turkey has been increasing its steel production. In 1981, steel output stood at 2.6 million tons, giving the nation a worldwide ranking of thirty-second (2). By the end of 1995 the nation was producing 12.7 million tons and had risen in the ranks of steel producing nations to twelfth. In 1996, Turkey entered an agreement with the European Coal and Steel Community to abolish customs duties on various steel exports and imports.

In the sphere of chemicals, Turkey enjoys a comparative advantage in boron due to the size of its reserves, the quality of its minerals, and its proximity to consumer markets. "The major export products of the Turkish chemical industry are petrochemicals (especially aromatics, ethylene glycol, dimethyl terephthelate, polyethylene, and synthetic fibres and yarns), boron chemicals, borax, pentahydrate, boric acid, sodium perborate and petroleum products (fuel oil, jet oil and HVGO)." Beyond such products are such things as fertilizers, chromium chemicals, soda, fatty acids, rose oil, soaps, detergents, and paints (3).

The nation's machinery industry includes the production of boilers and burners, building equipment, heavy industrial equipment, machine tools, lathes, and milling, drilling, cutting, and bending machines. Beyond such products, it includes woodworking machinery, pumps and compressors, hand tools, power turbines, and air conditioning units. Also included are textile machinery, food processing machinery, hoisting and conveying equipment, sewing machines, refrigerators and washing machines, valves, gears, and bearings. The industry is capable of supplying nearly all parts and accessories for the items listed above, in competitive qualities and at competitive prices (3). Machinery exports were on the increase in the early 1990s and in 1995 had reached approximately $691 million in value (6).

In the realm of electronics, significant capacity has been developed in consumer electronics and telecommunications. In 1995, exports of electronics reached a value of roughly $994 million (6). Thus, various technologically sophisticated manufacturing subsectors are joining more traditional production activities in a diversifying export sector.

BUSINESS SERVICES AND THE
MAJOR ACCOUNTING FIRMS

According to Deloitte Touche Tohmatsu International, "Since the 1920s Turkey has based its culture and economic development on Western principles. Links with Europe and the United States are strong" (1994b, 1). Bavishi has reported

Turkey as having fifty-seven partners in the major international accounting firms, thirty-five of whom were associated with the Big Six. The majority of the partners (forty-four) were located in Istanbul, the nation's largest city (1991, Appendix B). Ankara, the capitol, boasted nine partners, while the remaining four were based in Lefkosa (1991, Appendix B).

The nation holds an association agreement with the European Union and has signed a trade zone agreement with the European Free Trade Association. "On March 6, 1995, the Turkish–European Community Partnership Council approved Turkey's accession to the Customs Union with the European Union (EU)" (Arthur Andersen 1997c, 121). The actual union came into being on 1 January 1996. Technical aspects of the union include the free flow of goods, the harmonization of trade policies and legislation, arrangements with respect to agricultural goods, and the simplification of customs formalities (121).

"When the Customs Union became operational, duties on imports and exports, retaliatory taxes and measures, and quotas all ceased to exist." The agreement called for Turkey to adopt EU rules with respect to "measurement, calibration, quality, accreditation, testing, and documentation" over a five-year period of transition. Within that time span, no restrictions were to be applied to the importing of any product conforming to EU documentation requirements (121). Certainly these arrangements may alter the nation's economic relationships to other components of the global economy.

Foreign investors are said to find the nation attractive for a number of reasons. "The government maintains a liberal policy toward all forms of foreign investment" and "the political and social climate is stable." Beyond those considerations energy costs are attractively low and the nation boasts a rather large domestic market. Labor is plentiful and relatively inexpensive and the nation is well positioned geographically between Europe and Asia (Deloitte Touche Tohmatsu International 1994b, 1–2).

In order to stimulate its economy the nation introduced free trade zones as early as 1985. The purposes behind the zones included increasing investment in export-oriented production; accelerating the acquisition of foreign capital and technology; "providing inputs to the economy in an economical and orderly manner"; and raising the use of foreign trade opportunities as well as foreign financial instruments. The free trade zones are considered as outside Turkish boundaries for customs purposes. Thus "income and revenues generated . . . are exempt from income and corporate taxes . . . on condition that the transfer of such income and revenue into Turkey is realized pursuant to foreign exchange regulations." Beyond that, "Legislative provisions on taxes, levies, duties, customs and foreign exchange rulings are not in effect in the free trade zones" (Arthur Andersen 1997c, 125, 126).

If trade occurs between the zones and other areas of the nation, it is governed by the foreign trade regime (126). This means that transfers of goods between the zones and Turkey are treated as exports or imports. "For trade taking place between the free zones and other countries, free zones, the foreign trade regime is not applicable since the free trade zones are considered to be beyond the customs line of Turkey" (126). It seems clear that there are ample opportunities for the major accounting firms to offer their facultative services as Turkey increases its dealings in the global economy.

Among Big Six firms with offices in Turkey are Deloitte Touche Tohmatsu International and Price Waterhouse. Deloit & Touch, the Deloitte Touche Tohmatsu International member firm offers a full range of audit, accounting, management consulting, and tax services through its offices in Istanbul and Ankara. By its own estimate the firm "is the premier international professional service firm to operate from Turkey's key cities." It serves clients large and small, both domestic and international (59).

Price Waterhouse Turkey dates from 1984. Since then, "It has been mainly concerned with providing all types of accountancy services on a national and international level to clients in a wide variety of industries." The firm, which is internationally oriented, operates with a staff of one hundred (Price Waterhouse 1993, 169, 170).

According to the firm, most of the clients have international connections either because of extensive trading operations or because they are foreign parent companies. For its part, the firm has partners and staff, many of whom have dual qualifications and have served in other countries (170).

The firm offers services in three areas—auditing, taxation, and management consulting. "For audit purposes, the company was restructured, having all authorized auditors as partners and members of the board and carries on its activities under the name: Bards Serest Muhasebeci Mali Musavirlik Anima Circuit, a member of Price Warterhouse." Beyond the review and certification of financial statements, drawn up according to International Accounting Standards, Turkish legislation or other accounting principles, auditing extends to "acquisition, creditworthiness and similar examinations of other businesses" on behalf of their clients (170).

Tax services are the preserve of Baseman Yeminli Mali Musavirlik Ltd. Ste, a member of Price Waterhouse. Advisors from that firm are authorized to certify certain documents as stated in the laws and related legislation. The firm's tax services "include not only compliance work, including supporting clients during fiscal audits or other forms of negotiations with the tax authorities, but also concentrate to a large extent on foreign investment advice . . . strategic tax and business planning" (171).

Management consultancy services are the preserve of Price Waterhouse Yonetim Danismanligi A. S. They include "not only the design and implementation of accounting systems, but also advice and other assistance extended in connection with the establishment of a business, including locating and equipping premises and the selection of appropriate locally hired staff" (171). The operations of Price Waterhouse outlined, though firm specific, certainly suggest the types of facilitative services that accounting firms may offer in the jurisdictions that host them.

The firms are certainly well aware of the potential impacts of the services they offer. In the forward to a rather substantial recruitment publication, Saban Erdikler, the Country Managing Partner for Arthur Andersen in Turkey, describes his firm as the global multidisciplinary professional service firm. According to him, "The ability of institutions to focus the full weight of various resources and make them work together in a synergistic manner to solve problems and exploit opportunities will differentiate success and failure." He sees his firm as focused upon helping its clients to improve their performance through the application of knowledge, experience, and expertise acquired from worldwide business dealings over a long period of time. The firm assesses problems and assembles teams of experts to solve them (Arthur Andersen 1997b).

In addressing prospective recruits, Arthur Andersen provides insights concerning the type of business knowledge that its employees can gain, which of course is suggestive of the potential that the major accounting firms have as training grounds for those contemplating business careers in jurisdictions hosting the firms.

Speaking of Turkey, Arthur Andersen tells prospective employees that they will have to acquire whatever information may be necessary for understanding the business of their clients. Such information may concern markets as well as financial circumstances and objectives. The firm suggests that employees must understand the processes and systems as well as the operations of a wide range of businesses (1997b). Certainly the acquisition of such expertise would benefit the recipients regardless of whether they pursue ongoing careers with Arthur Andersen or in other directions within the Turkish economy. Such benefits would supply positive externalities to that economy as well.

In Turkey, Arthur Andersen offers a wide range of advisory services, including matters to do with corporate organization, the managing of business risks, and the setting up or improvement of internal audit functions. Beyond such matters, they offer treasury management advice, training, market position analysis surveys and help with projections and forecasting. Their services are aimed at strategic market sectors which include "financial markets, hospitality and leisure, consumer products, energy, manufacturing and construction" (1997b).

According to the firm, its consulting services are intended to help clients accomplish measurable improvements in performance, pace their information and business systems to their growth, and to put together and introduce "world class performance measurement and business control systems." Toward such aims, the firm assists with business process redesign and the management of change. In addition, it offers aid in total quality management, cost and productivity management, and performance measurement (1997b).

It can also advise on matters of revenue enhancement and market research. It engages in information and systems planning and in managing application software implementation. In the realm of taxation, the firm offers advice on tax laws, foreign investment legislation, and incentive legislation, as well as on foreign exchange legislation, social security law, banking law, and other financial and fiscal laws and regulations. The firm also offers international tax advisory services and help with tax planning and optimization. It can assist with tax litigation and reconciliation and with the structuring of business operations. It can provide "sworn fiscal consultancy services and reports required by Turkish tax authorities" (1997b).

Arthur Andersen is also very active in the country in the area of human capital services. With respect to executive searches, the firm can locate, interview, and select appropriate personnel for its clients. All levels of recruitment are offered, though the firm focuses mainly on senior and middle level executive positions. The firm can also assist with performance evaluation and reward systems. Beyond that it consults with respect to salary surveys, career management, job evaluation, as well as climate surveys and benchmarking (1997c).

The firm's "benchmarking analysis is based on a compilation of a variety of data on the organizational and business resources structures of the participating companies." It is designed to demonstrate similarities and differences in ratios and frequency distributions on matters such as employee ages, years of service, salaries, qualifications, functional areas, absenteeism, and turnover. The human resource services offered are intended to assist human resource professionals "to reinforce, revise and renew their direction and commitment" (1997c).

A FINAL OVERVIEW

It seems clear that Turkey is a nation with considerable economic potential. It is self-sufficient in agriculture and indeed is hardly taxing its capacity to produce foodstuffs. Although it has been attempting to diversify its economy away from or beyond primary products, it seems quite clear that such products may have a rather large potential market in the Middle East.

Though Turkey has been a member of NATO and the OECD, its political relations with Europe have not been problem free—witness the ongoing Cyprus situation for example. Attempts to draw closer to Europe have been met with indefinite fervor in various European circles and have generated a certain amount of suspicion among some of its Islamic neighbors.

The nation is predominantly Islamic, yet not an unquestioned participant in Middle Eastern affairs. It has long existing links with Europe and the Western World and yet is not accepted as an equal partner in that world. Geographically, it is positioned on the peripheries of both worlds. Its economic and political security seems to require a balance between those worlds.

Many nations have faced serious difficulties due to the encroachment of a global economic system that seems to threaten their customs and values. Turkey is stronger, larger, and in possession of more resources than many of those, yet it seems to face an interwoven maze of difficult issues in finding its way.

No one would suggest that multinational service firms can easily solve Turkey's dilemmas, yet it does seem that the mixture of local understanding and international savoi-faire possessed by the major accounting firms may be of some assistance. At least the firms contribute to the confidence of an international clientele wishing to conduct business in Turkey. Indeed, they may very well assist in forging sound international linkages that may lessen very obvious political flash points. Of course, they will only be able to assist in that manner by abiding with the parameters of Turkish culture.

Chapter Seven

The Smaller Jurisdictions of the Gulf Cooperation Council

This chapter is concerned with the economic situation facing the smaller nations that belong to the Gulf Cooperation Council. It begins with a general overview. Following that, it turns to the summarization of the economic circumstances of the nations concerned. Next, services offered by the major accounting firms in the region are reviewed on a selective basis. The chapter concludes with a final overview highlighting the economic circumstances of the nations concerned and the potential that the major accounting firms may have for assisting them.

A PRELIMINARY OVERVIEW

Ragasi El Mallakh described the emergence of the Gulf Cooperation Council (GCC) as "the most sweeping action to actualize economic and other benefits of regionalism in the Gulf and to expand and co-ordinate activities and programs already in place" (1981, 15). This arrangement dates from 1981 when Bahrain, Qatar, Kuwait, Oman, Saudi Arabia, and the United Arab Emirates formed a regional entity.

The organization was begun as a "security umbrella for these generally small but strategically significant Arab Gulf States but has also moved into the economic sphere." The original agreement called for the eventual economic, financial, and industrial integration of its participants for the free movement of goods, capital, and labor. It was also intended to facilitate the coordination of economic and financial policies (152).

In 1983, the scope of the agreement was expanded. Customs duties among the parties to the United Economic Agreement were abolished on all agricultural livestock and manufactured products originating in member states (153). Free access for GCC ships to ports belonging to the members was guaranteed, and both goods and passengers were exempted from taxes and fees. Vehicles registered in a member state could be driven by the nationals of member states throughout the states concerned without permits or taxes. Products of the individual states were to be free of taxes when transiting other member states.

Beyond such arrangements, "Citizens of one GCC state specializing in medicine, law, engineering, accounting and local consulting firms could function through other member countries without obtaining permits or paying taxes." The citizens of the individual states could establish businesses in others, provided that at least one-quarter of the shares are subscribed by the citizens of the states where the company is established (153–154).

The council has as its purpose to encourage relations and cooperation "on such matters as the economy, finance, defense, education, health, trade, travel, transport, customs, and legal matters." The United Economic Agreement (1981) was intended to establish a united economic system. A new tariff structure for imports from beyond the Gulf region has been put in place and "decisions have been made to give more freedom to the private sectors of the member states operating within the region" (Deloitte Touche Tohmatsu International 1996, 13).

All the small jurisdictions of the Gulf Cooperation Council and Saudi Arabia as well are monarchies. Their rulers have been able to sustain their control through the provision of various social benefits through the use of oil revenues. In general, policies to benefit the material status of the citizenry have been reflected in the expansion of government bureaucracies and pay scales for public employment rather than direct financial handouts.

Since the mid-1980s, oil has become a much less reliable source of predictable revenues that can be used by the regimes in question to maintain their power. Social contracts that buy the acquiescence of resident populations to centralized government control must be assured of the continued infusion of necessary funds. If global energy markets are to be the major source of such funds, then uncertainties in those markets add additional concerns, beyond the previously present specter of possible oil depletion.

The current situation vis-à-vis oil is dictating the need for the small monarchies of the Gulf to diversify their economies and perhaps forge international linkages that go well beyond those already in place. Such linkages unquestionably mean a more diverse intercourse with the global market system, and of course more contact between resident populations and foreign elements both cultural and economic.

As Paul J. Stevens has suggested, "Only Saudi Arabia has explicitly ruled out upstream involvement by foreign companies." The smaller countries "with various degrees of enthusiasm and urgency, are seeking to obtain foreign investment by international oil companies" (1997, 87). Beyond that, Bahrain and the United Arab Emirates have been developing offshore financial capabilities.

Despite what oil has done for Saudi Arabia and the smaller Gulf states, there is little doubt that their future economic security demands serious efforts at diversification. "To insure long-term economic security, countries whose economies are based upon depletable resources must adopt policies that will enable them to maintain their standards of living after the resource is exhausted" (Askari, Bazzari, and Tyler 1998, 225). If the actual exhaustion of oil reserves seems somewhat remote, a continuing reliance upon that resource to the exclusion of other options may be a doubtful policy. Economists are well aware of the pitfalls of relying upon primary products as tradable commodities in the global economy. The terms of trade have ceased to favor primary commodities, including, in recent years, oil.

Askari and colleagues have written a severe, perhaps even bitter prescription. "For the countries of the Gulf Cooperation Council (GCC), development of a viable private sector to replace the public sector's large contribution to national output from oil is essential." Those authors call for policies to enhance the business climate, coupled with the elimination of distorting economic policies. Specifically, they prescribe cuts in government spending and reductions in or the abandonment of indiscriminate subsidies. Beyond those suggestions, they call for the privatization of public enterprises, the reduction of public sector employment, and the deregulation of markets, "including the labor markets," and the introduction of a competitive real exchange rate (225).

F. Gregory Gause, III identified an interacting selection of security choices facing GCC countries. Among the issues facing the countries in question were such things as military security, fiscal problems, economic development, demographic growth, and political demands. Gause seems quite accurate in suggesting that choices made in one area may constrain the ability of governments to cope with other issues (1997, 63).

Gause points to the problems associated with growing, increasingly youthful populations, which are putting enormous pressure on welfare states that were developed in the 1970s and 1980s "when populations were smaller and revenues greater." Gulf states maintained government spending levels in the face of falling oil revenues during the 1980s "by drawing down their reserves and . . . by borrowing on the international market and relying on transfer payments from neighbors" (68).

As Gause went on to explain, such expedients are no longer available. Kuwait and Saudi Arabia have been suffering ongoing financial damage from the Gulf War and can no longer live off reserves. Oman can no longer rely on international capital markets to finance ongoing deficits, while Bahrain, which was relying on Saudi Arabia to assist with its budget deficits, is faced with a declining Saudi ability to assist. Qatar and the United Arab Emirates, though possessing larger financial reserves and smaller population–resource ratios, are feeling fiscal pressures as well (68, 69).

Certainly the governments of the countries under discussion are aware of the need to change. Still, Gause is of the opinion that the belt tightening efforts already in evidence are not adequate. "The governments will simply be unable to fund the generous and extensive social welfare policies . . . at current rates of population growth." Demographics are against them with respect to the absorption of growing numbers of university trained job seekers, the need to educate growing numbers of children, and the possible increases in health care needs in the face of expanding life expectancy (70).

Declining revenues from oil, together with rising populations, are pressuring the small nations of the Gulf to privatize their economies, reduce government spending, and generate stronger international linkages. Privatizing enterprises or production facilities in economies where both the size of the labor force and its remuneration have been inflated, will undoubtedly cause a certain amount of social and political unrest. Privatization almost invariably leads to belt tightening among profit-seeking enterprises. The private sector can hardly be expected to accept a social contract that includes overextended corporate bureaucracies and overinflated pay scales.

The only solution appears to be economic growth and diversification. The easiest method for growing the economies of the Gulf states is of course more investment from abroad. This may take the form of production for export, perhaps involving units of foreign multinational firms. It may involve growing international services that might include tourism and international business services.

Of course, such adjustments mean more foreign linkages and undoubtedly more contacts with foreign nationals, both resident and visiting. Such changes also may generate a certain amount of unpleasantness for a citizenry striving to maintain its cultural and religious roots. The rulers are faced with a dilemma. In their encouragement of foreign linkages they must accommodate the sensitivities of their citizens. Yet they must encourage those linkages if they hope to maintain acceptable living standards. Clearly the rulers of the nations in question recognize their dilemma better than most observers of the situation. Unfortunately, recognition on their part will hardly insure their success.

SOME SPECIFICS ON THE GULF ECONOMIES

In this section, each of the economies in question will be dealt with separately. Those included will be Bahrain, Kuwait, Oman, Qatar, and the United Arab Emirates. No attempt will be made to add to what has been said about Saudi Arabia earlier in this volume.

Bahrain is comprised of about thirty islands lying off the shores of Saudi Arabia, midway along the southern shore of the Persian Gulf. Its major cities include Manama and Muharraq. Jeffrey Nugent and Theodore Thomas described the skyline of Manama as having been recently changed "by the addition of highrise, luxury hotels, commercial buildings and parking structures, in the heavily congested commercial center" (1985, 5).

Those authors saw Bahrain as "attempting to discern a way to blend the rich traditions of the Arab and Islamic cultures indigenous to the gulf with the values of urban, industrial and Western societies." They saw the state as quite modern in appearance and described heavy automobile traffic, a modern road system, a busy international airport, a major port facility, and a dry-dock and ship repair yard, not to mention an aluminum smelter, a major oil refinery, hotels, and offshore banks (5). Indeed, Bahrain was seen as having "succeeded in diversifying its oil-dominated economy by developing regional banking and other services and a variety of light and heavy industries" (3).

According to Coopers & Lybrand, "Initiating an operation in an environment outside your own is fraught with risks" (1996, 3). They went on to explain that Bahrain, which they described as the commercial hub of the Gulf, has modified its framework so as to accommodate and facilitate both investments and business ventures.

Bahrain is an archipalagic state lying some 24 kilometers from the eastern coast of Saudi Arabia. Bahrain Island, the nation's largest land mass, "is connected by causeways to Muharraq, the second largest island, and to Sitra, where most of the industrial units are located" (1996, 4). Another causeway, perhaps 30 kilometers in length joins the island to the Saudi mainland, thus increasing intercourse between the two nations (1996, 4).

The nation's population is approaching 600 thousand and is increasing at a rate of roughly 2.5 percent per year. Roughly one-third of the population are foreign. Coopers & Lybrand explain that Bahraini women are eager to work and that educational standards have been more advanced than in neighboring nations. Eighty-five percent of the population subscribe to Islam, but other religions are permitted. "A long tradition of association with other cultures, a stable government and a strong sense of national identity have made Bahrain a pleasant place to live" (7). The nation has also maintained good relations with the remainder of the Arab world (10).

International transportation linkages are strong. The international airport boasts thirty-nine international airlines and averages 3.6 million passengers per year. As mentioned, Bahrain Island is connected to Saudi Arabia by causeway. The nation "is ideally located at the center of trade routes for VLCCs, which spend more time loading and unloading in the Gulf than in any other waters." The Organization of Arab Petroleum Exporting Countries as early as 1968 proposed Bahrain as the host for "the world's first purpose built yard to serve VLCCs." The nation has gained a significant share of world business in that regard because of fast turnaround times, geographical convenience, and high quality workmanship (13).

The nation has been the entrepot for the region and also its distribution center, although Saudi ports and those of other Gulf states are becoming competitive. The government has actively encouraged and promoted nonoil exports, but oil still dominates the trade account (13). Despite this, Bahrain has been described as "one of the most diverse economies of the Gulf region." Arab World explains that sixty years of oil production have given the nation (proportionately) the Gulf's largest collection of manufacturing industries and the biggest community of international bank branches (Arab World Online LLC 1997a, 1).

According to Coopers & Lybrand, aluminium is the nation's oldest industry after oil and gas. Following an expansion from the period of 1990 to 1992,

Aluminium Bahrain is now capable of producing 460,000 tons per year. The smelter supplies raw materials for a rolling mill, an extrusion factory, cable manufacturers, and aluminium powder production (1996, 19).

Bahrain's aluminium operations also include two automobile wheel factories. The aluminium sector has been led by Aluminum Bahrain, "a joint venture majoritively owned by the government and shared with Saudi Arabia's Public Investment Fund." Bahrain also boasts several companies dealing in smelter products, and has developed a major petrochemical complex at Sitra, as well as a sulfur derivatives plant (Arab World Online LLC 1997a, 3).

The tourism industry attracts two million visitors per year (3). Foreign visitors number both vacationers and business travelers. Hotels supply more than 2 thousand five-star rooms and a growing number in the three- and four-star range (Coopers & Lybrand 1996, 22). All hotels are fully licensed.

More recently, Bahrain has been described as "the Middle East's pre-eminent financial hub," and "a key player in world financial and banking services." The nation is described as "an international and regional interbank money market centered on its offshore banking sector." The offshore financial sector has assets in the U.S. $70 billion range and a daily foreign exchange turnover from all its financial institutions of some U.S. $4 billion (Arab Net 1996, 1).

It hosts international law firms, insurance companies, certified public accountants, and various consultants in a rather sophisticated service sector. The presence of such activities has "stimulated the evolution of other related financial establishments including the Bahrain Stock Market, the money exchange sector, the real estate and construction business and other commercial enterprises" (1). The nation boasts some ninety commercial banks, investment houses, and offshore banking units, as well as more than fifty representative offices, money, and foreign exchange brokers, and perhaps sixty local, foreign, and exempt insurance companies (1).

Kuwait is a small country situated between Saudi Arabia and Iraq on the Persian Gulf. It achieved its independence in 1961, and as of 1995, its population stood at 1.8 million. According to Arab World Online LLC, the nation is a welfare state with "one of the most comprehensive domestic social aid and extensive overseas financial aid programs in the world" (1997c, 2).

In 1992, Kuwait had proven oil reserves of 94 billion barrels. "Kuwait has . . . purchased refineries in the Netherlands, Denmark and Italy with a capacity of 200,000 bpd and over 4,800 service stations in Europe." Beyond oil the nation "has an estimated 1.5 billion cubic meters of natural gas reserves. . . . However . . . production of gas is limited by the absence of any known reserves independent of petroleum." In fact, as Arab World Online explains, much of Kuwait's gas is flared to facilitate oil production or reinjected to maximize petroleum output (3).

The main outputs from manufacturing are produced by the oil refineries. "The Petrochemical Industries Company supplies ammonia, urea, ammonium sulfate and sulfuric acid" (3). That company exports sodium hypochlorite, sulfuric acid and caustic soda (30). Union Carbide of the United States has a 45 percent share in a $2 billion plant at Shuaiba, which was scheduled to open in 1997 (3).

Y. S. F. Al-Sabah explained that it was Kuwait's geographical position in relation to the major trade routes that made it politically significant to the major powers (1980, 2). Among those interested were the British, the Germans, and the Russians. The British interest was based on Kuwait's location with respect to their trade routes to India and the Far East. The German interest was fueled by a rivalry with Britain. Interest in India and the Far East was also a factor in the Russian involvement.

Such interests predated the emergence of oil. The preoil economy in Kuwait was dependent upon fishing, pearl-diving, seafaring, boat-building, herding, and trade. Al-Sabah saw those occupations as the pillars of the Kuwaiti economy up to the outbreak of World War II (12).

"From the beginning of drilling in the 1930s right up until 1970 there was no control over the operating practices of the oil companies." Al-Sabah saw British Petroleum and Gulf Oil Corporation as accumulating large profits, which were used to finance oil refineries and petrochemical plants exterior to Kuwait. He saw such endeavors being accomplished through bank financing, with the control of crude oil sources as collateral. Similar financial arrangements supported the building of oil tankers and terminals. He suggested that as a result "No industry was built in Kuwait, and there was neither backward nor forward linkages to the oil industry in Kuwait" (27, 28–29). Better arrangements might have avoided bottlenecks in the Kuwaiti economy that Al-Sabah perceived in 1980.

According to Arab World Online LLC, Oman has been a historical trading center because of its central location vis-à-vis the Middle East and the Far East (1997d), however the country may not be as strong economically as various other Gulf States. In recent years, the nation's public infrastructure, including transportation linkages, housing, and educational establishments, has undergone significant expansion. The nation has been criticized for "the establishment of an oil based rentier welfare state," which has inflated government outlays (Gulf States Newsletter 1995).

The nation's most recent five-year economic plan (1996 to 2000) calls for "a special emphasis on the reduction of government spending, job creation and privatization." Oman's population, which stands at about two million, is expected to double by 2010. Parallel to the population increase, a reduction in oil revenues is predicted, a rather serious prognosis since those revenues account for 85 percent of export earnings, 80 percent of government revenues, and 40 percent of the nation's GDP (Arab World Online 1997d).

Clearly there is a need for the diversification of the nation's economy, a diversification that seems doubtful in the absence of increasing foreign linkages. "Agriculture and fisheries employ the bulk of the workforce but generate only 3% of GDP." Agricultural output has been rising but water shortages have been described as an increasing problem. Fish landings have remained static in quality and quantity in recent years (Gulf States Newsletter 1995).

In an attempt to encourage foreign investment, Oman has applied to join the World Trade Organization (WTO). The economic counselor to the office of the Sultan has emphasized the nation's desire to increase foreign investment: "Oman is not as affluent as its neighbors and that is why we are trying to be as lenient as possible towards foreign investment. We want and welcome both foreign capital and technology" (Arab World Online 1997d).

Despite this interest in foreign investment and technology, "Foreign investment is allowed only through joint stock companies or joint ventures." Investors from abroad are in general permitted to own a maximum of 49 percent of shares in a particular project. In the case of industrial projects, the Ministry of Commerce and Industry can permit foreign ownership of up to 65 percent (University of Missouri at St. Louis 1997). "In some cases, 100% foreign investment in a company is permitted with the approval of the Development Council for projects with capital of no less than $1.3 million" (Arab World Online LLC 1997d).

The nation's economy has been driven by oil and gas. Gas is currently being promoted, and the government hopes to make liquefied natural gas a cornerstone of the economy and a significant export industry. Agriculture accounts for roughly 2 percent of GDP, and although heavily subsidized, Oman has not been able to dispense with the need for imported foodstuffs. Major crops include dates, alfalfa, limes, tomatoes, eggplant, carrots, and bananas (1997d). The government does have an interest in self-sufficiency in food production.

Manufacturing accounts for only about 5 percent of GDP and is largely composed of light industry. The government has been encouraging industrial activity and has been investing in industrial zones. Rusalyl, near Muscat (the capitol) comprises 1.5 million square metres and houses sixty-eight plants. Other locations include Nizura, Sohar, and Rasyut (Gulf States Newsletter 1995).

Firms "are encouraged to move to these zones since they are provided with fixed-price sets rental, advance factories, cheap power and water supplies, training and housing facilities and participation in government-sponsored export drives" (1995). The government is hoping to expand its industrial base. "Future plans include a fertilizer plant, a petrochemicals complex, an aluminum smelter and a steel plant" (Arab World Online 1997). As yet, industrial diversification seems modest at best. Progress in that regard will undoubtedly require expanded international business linkages.

Qatar occupies a peninsula between Saudi Arabia and the United Arab Emirates. With a population of nearly 534 thousand, the nation has relied upon oil revenues for its prosperity. With the prospect of dwindling oil reserves the government has been turning towards liquefied natural gas as the future catalyst for the economy (Arab World Online LLC 1997e).

A change in emphasis in the direction of gas appears to be a sound policy choice. "Qatar boasts the third largest reserves of liquefied natural gas (LNG) in the world behind the former Soviet Union and Iran." International energy consultants (Gaffney, Cline, and Associates) were said to have reported Qatari proven gas reserves as 30 percent of world supplies at the same time as the nation was accounting for only 5 percent of world consumption. Spectacular increases have been predicted for gas exports "from the present level of 120,000 cubic feet to 2.6 trillion cubic feet by the year 2010" (1997e).

It seems clear that the switch in emphasis will leave energy in place as the most significant sector of the economy. Though most economists advise diversification as a part of any national development program, it would be difficult to argue against Qatar's chosen expansion route. "Assuming present annual average crude oil production of around 500,000 b/d, Qatar's oil reserves are expected to last another two decades or far shorter than other Persian Gulf countries" (United States Energy Information Administration 1997). The agency quoted here suggests that new technology could lead to additional reserves and new output.

At the same time, "State owned Qatar General Petroleum Corporation (QGPC) hopes to boost Qatar's sustainable crude oil production capacity to 700,000 b/d by 2000." However the government believes that the economic future of the nation lies in developing its gas potential. "Qatar has two liquefied natural gas (LNG) projects underway: Qatar LNG Company (Qatargas); and Ras Laffan LNG Company (Rasgas)" (1997). Beyond those, U.S.–based Enron is discussing a possible plant.

Beyond the energy sector, the government has promised heavy and light industry concentrating on in-country resources (Arab World Online LLC 1997e). Inexpensive energy has helped in the emergence of steel and iron operations, and reserves have encouraged chemical, fertilizer, and petrochemical production. The nation also produces cement.

The United Arab Emirates (UAE) hold a rather unique position among offshore financial centers, inasmuch as they provide significant linkages between the Arab world and the global economy. The nation "is an independent federation of seven emirates comprising (broadly from southwest to northeast) Abu Dhabi, Dubai, Sharjah, Ajman, Muh Al-Qiwain, Ras Al-Khaima, and Fujeira" (Deloitte Touche Tohmatsu International 1996, 1).

Prior to 1971, the area had been known as the Trucial States, and was bound by treaties with the United Kingdom (1). The emirates are well connected to each other as well as to neighboring countries by a newly laid network of roads. "Modern telephone, telex, and telecopier systems connect the United Arab Emirates with most of the world," and "major international couriers are well represented and provide service at competitive rates" (2). Clearly the emirates possess the transportation and communications linkages to support effective offshore financial services.

Despite a climate conducive to such services, the emirates are pursuing more general developmental goals. "The economy is influenced by fluctuations in the international oil market because oil, gas and related petrochemical industries continue as the most important economic sector." In order to reduce the petroleum dependency of the oil-producing emirates, both federal and individual emirate governments have launched programs to encourage foreign investment in fields believed to be of national benefit. Of special interest are agricultural and manufacturing projects deemed helpful in moving the nation toward self-sufficiency (Ernst & Young 1990, 3).

The governments of the individual emirates are active in trying to attract investments of expertise and capital. Aside from a sound transportation and communications infrastructure, the emirates boast "a virtual absence of taxation," and "a well-structured financial sector with no exchange control regulations." Free trade zones have been established and financial reporting requirements at both federal and local levels are minimal (3).

The ongoing, successful expansion of nonpetroleum sectors of the economy (5.45 percent in the period of 1994–1995) is directly attributable to government policy. Among the advantages in investing in the country are the availability of cheap energy, access to cheap regional labor markets, and the absence of duties on raw materials imports and finished product exports, as well as the proximity to major open markets in the region (Deloitte Touche Tohmatsu International 1993, 7).

Arab World Online LLC credits the United Arab Emirates as being one of the most dynamic economies in the Gulf. "With oil revenues and proceeds from free trade zones leading the way the UAE is making a concerted effort to meet its 20-year diversification plan" (1997f, 1).

The industrial sector includes textiles and clothing, footwear, electrical appliances, power station transformers, auto parts, and furniture, as well as stationery and paper products, air conditioning and refrigeration equipment, plastic containers, surgical gloves, and ophthalmic lenses (7).

Ernst & Young listed key sectors of the economy, beyond oil, gas, and related industries, as including "utilities, communications, construction, banking and financial services, manufacturing projects and tourism." Such activities tend to be positioned near the major urban centers of Abu Dhabi, Dubai, and Sharjah (1990, 4).

According to Deloitte Touche Tohmatsu International, the nation offers incentives to foreign investors that can supply needed technical expertise and are willing to work in collaboration with UAE nationals. Such investors are given various privileges and exemptions. Beyond those, no direct incentives, "such as capital grants, subsidized loans, preferential contract schemes or import quotas, or laws that protect domestic industry are available" (1996, 7).

Though general incentives to foreign investors are hardly extensive, the nation does offer a rather attractive tax climate, and beyond that, has developed free trade zones. "Foreign companies establishing businesses in the free-trade zones are offered special concessions, including an exemption from the requirement of having local ownership or a local sponsor" (Ernst & Young 1990, 9). Free trade zones feature duty-free imports, but normal duty rates are imposed if they are resold domestically. Exports are unrestricted and not subject to export duties (9).

Abu Dhabi, which is the federal capital, has larger oil revenues than the other emirates. Indeed, it produces about 70 percent of the nation's output of crude oil, "has significant natural gas reserves and has developed associated petro-chemical industries." It is the only emirate enjoying oil refining capacity, with refineries located at Ruwais and Umm Al Nar. Beyond the energy sector, the emirate has a substantial complement of medium- and small-scale manufacturing industries. Included are such products as cement, concrete blocks, bricks, paper and plastic bags, flour, and processed foods (4).

Dubai has been a trading center and has served as an entrepot within the Middle East and more recently "among markets of the Near and Far East, Europe and the United States." That emirate accounts for roughly 30 percent of the nation's crude oil output. Beyond that, it boasts aluminum smelting and produces copper and aluminum cables, lubricating oil, and cement. It has one of the world's largest dry docks that can accommodate the largest vessels afloat (5).

The government has promoted Dubai as a commercial, financial, trading, and tourist center. The Jebel Ali industrial port and Free Zone complex is one of the world's largest man-made ports and "provides excellent facilities for trading, manufacturing and service industries" (5). "The zone is the home of approximately 950 international operations." The harbor contains "sixty-seven berths, over fifteen kilometers of quay, and a container terminal with the most up-to-date handling equipment that is capable of handling any class of ship." In Dubai, Port Rashed has thirty-five berths and a modern container facility (Deloitte Touche Tohmatsu International 1996, 8).

"Dubai's ports are served by a large and growing number of international lines with worldwide links combined with feeder services to Iran and other regional markets." The emirate's state-of-the-art cargo village "helps insure the world's fastest sea–air transfers in as little as four hours." Such transport facilities are supported by unlimited, low-cost warehousing and storage facilities, as well as a modern highway network (Government of Dubai 1998, 2).

According to the government of Dubai, that emirate ranks as one of the of the world's leading trading centers. Support for that assessment is offered by the description of the emirate as "the gateway to a market of more than one billion people, covering the Gulf states, Middle East, CIS, East Africa and Asian sub-continent" (1). They point to well-established trading links throughout the Gulf Cooperation Council, Iran, and neighboring markets. Beyond such linkages, they claim to have a strong commercial tradition and a wide choice of potential trading partners.

They also point to a buoyant and prosperous domestic market and a rapidly developing manufacturing sector. The latter sector produces a wide range of high quality export goods, ranging from aluminium ingots to electronics. They see their port and airport facilities as having no regional rivals in the realms of size, flexibility, and efficiency. Related to such advantages is a strong shipping and transportation sector (1).

In support of Dubai as an attractive setting for regional headquarters, the Ministry points to pro-business government policies and one of the most liberal regulatory environments in the region. Specific advantages include no taxes on profits or incomes, no foreign exchange controls, and a stable, freely convertible currency. Other advantages include a sophisticated service sector, including major international hotels, banks, lawyers, accounting firms, advertising agencies, and consultants (1).

The Ministry points to quality office accommodations and an effective, competitively priced labor force. They claim to possess "the major regional conference and exhibition venue in the Middle East," as well as air linkages involving sixty-five airlines. They also point to an international lifestyle that is tolerant and virtually crime free (1).

MAJOR ACCOUNTING FIRMS AND THEIR SERVICES

According to Bavishi (1991), all the small nations under discussion host partners in major international accounting firms. Collectively partners resident in those jurisdictions outnumber their counterparts in Saudi Arabia. Bavishi listed eighteen partners in Bahrain of whom fourteen were affiliated with the Big Six. All the partners were based in Manama. Kuwait had eleven partners resident in Kuwait City, six of whom were affiliated with Big Six firms.

Muscat, the capitol of Oman, was hosting fourteen partners. Twelve of the partners in question were affiliated with Big Six firms. Qatar had only eight partners, four of whom boasted Big Six affiliations. All the accountants in question were located in Doha. The United Arab Emirates were well supplied with accountants. Bavishi listed forty-three partners, twenty-eight of whom were affiliated with the Big Six (1991).

In discussing the services offered by the major accounting firms in the nations under consideration, it might be counterproductive and repetitive to detail each service offered by each firm in each jurisdiction. Instead, an attempt will be made to feature the offerings of example firms in selected jurisdictions with an eye to illustrating their real and potential role throughout the region.

One of the Big Six that is very active in Bahrain is Coopers & Lybrand. Operating as Coopers & Lybrand/Jawad & Habib & Co., the firm offers a wide menu of services. Among areas covered are management consulting, information technology services, and human resources consulting. Beyond those areas, the firm is also active in the areas of financial services, business assurance, business recovery, insolvency, litigation support services, and company formation (Coopers & Lybrand International 1997).

Speaking of management consulting, the firm asserts that its personnel are well informed on local and gulf-wide issues and are thus ready to add value to their clients' organizations in the areas of their specific skills and experience. In view of Bahrain's interest in developing its tourism industry, the services offered by the firm in that area are potentially quite important. The firm stands ready to assist with business strategy appraisal and formulation. It conducts market surveys, feasibility studies, operation reviews, and economic, social, and environmental impact studies. Beyond such endeavors, it stands ready to assist with marketing strategy and planning, project finance, concept design and evaluation, and project management. It can also assist with management selection and contract negotiation (1997).

In the area of information technology, the firm can assess the effectiveness of actual or proposed information systems and can also establish plans for the future direction of information systems. Beyond those services, it can help in system delivery and can assist with software quality management. The firm can also assist with information system security by identifying and countering threats to confidentiality. With respect to business contingency planning, the firm provides disaster recovery capability aimed at business interruptions (1997).

Assistance with human resource management is also available through the firm. More specifically, it can assist with the setting of corporate objectives and with improving management performance, as well as with executive search, recruitment, and management. Beyond those services, the firm can help in identifying the appropriate management organization structure and appropriate personnel requirements (1997).

Financial services are a very significant component of the economy of Bahrain, and the firm is also active in this area. Specifically, it stands ready to assist with corporate strategy and organizational change as well as with human resources and training. It also stands ready to assist with financial management, management information, and risk control. It can help with treasury and cash management, and with corporate finance, financial audits, taxation, and regulation (1997).

The menu of business assurance services is intended to enhance business control, thus adding value to organizations. According to the firm, services provided include accounting, statutory audits, and audit-related services ranging from internal to environmental audits. Beyond such offerings, the firm deals with computer-assurance services, risk-management advice, forensic accounting, and corporate training. They are also willing to assist owner-managed businesses in similar areas (1997).

The firm is also active in the area of business recovery and insolvency. In explaining their posture, they state that they do not assume insolvency to be inevitable and try to supply innovative, commercial solutions to business problems. They see their role as supporting financial stakeholders in managing risks. The firm also supplies a range of litigation support services (1997).

Another major accounting firm operating in Bahrain is KPMG Fakhro. The services available through that firm are extensive. Its general practice department deals in various traditional accounting services. Included are audits, reviews, and compilations, as well as accounting and bookkeeping and business–share valuation. In addition, the firm deals with offer documents, investment memoranda, and prospectus, as well as procedure manuals. It offers accounting advice, control reviews, and risk assessment reviews. It can provide forensic accounting support and liquidation advice. It stands ready to perform feasibility studies. It offers Saudi tax advice, and deals in investment placement, and debt restructuring and scheduling advice (KPMG Fakhro 1997).

The firm's investigation and insolvency department conducts investigations and deals with arbitration, legal custodianship, and liquidation. Its shares department is prepared to administer public issues and to provide registrar and transfer agent services. The legal department handles company formations and flotation, including formalities and prospectus. It helps with registrations of trademarks and the translation of legal documents and liquidations. It assists in the drafting and review of contracts of legal documentation, as well as in the preparation of business law compilations (1997).

The firm also boasts extensive offerings through its management consulting department. These services are divided into three subgroups—financial management, human resources, and information technology. The first of these subgroups includes strategic business planning and strategic cost management. Beyond those services the firm stands ready to conduct feasibility studies, market appraisals, and efficiency and effectiveness reviews. It can also assist in executive search and selection, remuneration studies, and psychometric testing. Its offerings in the area of information technology include strategy and system selection and implementation. It also offers system diagnostics and reviews and systems disaster planning. Beyond those services, it can assist with requirements definitions (1997).

In a promotional brochure, Arthur Andersen enumerates the various services that are available to clients through its Kuwait office. "The Kuwait Auditing Office was founded in 1963 by Bader Al-Bazie." Bader Al-Bazie joined Arthur Andersen in 1990, and "Arthur Andersen personnel with significant global experience were transferred to Kuwait to provide a unique blend of local and international experience" (Arthur Andersen 1997d).

By 1997, the office employed over one-hundred professionals and boasted a client base in excess of four hundred. The firm offers a wide range of services to corporate clients, small businesses, and individuals. Among its conventional offerings are various forms of tax consulting and audits, reviews, and compilations. In the area of taxation, it assists in planning and filing. It also assists with the tax inspection process and in the obtention of Tax Clearance Certificates. In addition, it provides updates on current tax practices. On the international level, it deals with foreign tax credit studies and cross-border planning and provides international trade and customs consultations (1997d).

The firm has offerings in the area of assistance to business systems. These include information and systems planning and the selection and implementation of packaged software, as well as database and graphical user interface, design, and development. Beyond those concerns, the firm deals with executive information systems and groupware implementation. It also offers network management and systems support (1997d).

Arthur Andersen also provides assistance with computer risk management, corporate finance, and valuation services. In the area of computer risk management the firm offers logical access security, and computer-based analyses and investigations. It also deals with MIS productivity and with application systems both pre- and post- implementation. It also provides third-party reviews of computer service centers (1997d).

In the corporate finance area, the firm offers assistance with mergers, acquisitions, joint ventures, and divestments. It assists with private placements of debt and equity and with due diligence. It is also willing to help with capital structure and restructuring. With respect to valuation services, the firm offers business valuations, machinery and equipment valuations, and property tax–cost segregation studies (1997d).

Operational consulting comprises yet another segment of the firm's service menu. In that area, the firm offers activity-based costing and cost management. It can also assist with process management, reengineering, and quality management services. Best practices are also included in its offerings (1997d).

In the area of corporate recovery, the firm offers turnaround and prebankruptcy consulting. It also offers judicial bankruptcy accounting and financial restructuring. Litigation service offerings include information management and economic consulting, as well as expert testimony and consultation. In addition, the firm offers services to in-house counsel, demonstrative evidence, and claims preparation and consultation (1997d).

The firm stands willing to assist small businesses with their accounting needs, including the preparation of monthly financial statements, cash flow monitoring, and payroll processing. They are also involved in the privatization area, in which they offer preprivatization studies, privatization plans, commercialization consulting, and implementation services. Offerings in the area of healthcare consulting include such things as productivity reviews, reimbursement, strategic planning, and marketing and feasibility studies (1997d).

The firm can also provide contract services and assistance with outsourcing. In regard to family wealth planning, the firm stands ready to assist in succession planning, ownership and management structures, and compensation arrangements. Clearly the firm, through its varied service capabilities has the potential for causing wide-ranging impacts throughout the economy of Kuwait (1997d).

It seems clear that the international involvements that appear to be increasing in Qatar can benefit from facilitative business services of the sort provided by the major accounting firms in various locations around the world. The former Big Six firms were represented in Qatar by Arthur Andersen, Ernst & Young, and Price Waterhouse.

The Middle East practice of Ernst & Young dates from 1923 and boasts fifteen offices in eleven countries, with a combined professional staff in excess of eight hundred (Ernst & Young 1997a). Their commitment to the region appears to be self-evident. "Our decentralized organizational structure enables us to make available all the resources of an international professional services firm but apply these in a manner that is sensitive to the local business environment" (Ernst & Young 1997a).

If Ernst & Young were accurate in describing their capabilities, they have exposed the core of what such firms can do for Qatar or similar nations. Provided that the major accounting firms truly understand their host environments, they are well equipped to assist businesses in those locations with their international involvements. Of course, they should also be well positioned to assist businesses or organizations wishing to locate or transact operations in specific destinations. Thus, Ernst & Young and their rivals may have much to offer in Qatar.

The firm sees the auditing of financial statements as their main business in the Middle East (Ernst & Young 1997b). However they see themselves as having "one of the largest management consultancy practices in the world" (Ernst & Young 1997c). The success of that practice is attributed to the ability of their consultants "to provide new ideas, imaginative thinking and apply the most up-to-date techniques" (1997c).

Among management consultancy services offered are business planning and control, financial planning, and control and performance improvement (1997c). Beyond such services, the firm engages in business process reengineering, organizational change management, organization and management development, and human resource management. It deals with information and computer systems, mergers and acquisitions, privatization, and off-set services. If need be, the firm in Middle Eastern locations, including Qatar, can call upon its consulting staff in locations throughout the world.

The firm offers a wide variety of accounting and financial services. Included are advice regarding the selection and implementation of accounting systems and reviews of systems already in place, with an eye to insuring their relevance, timeliness, and accuracy, not to mention their proper control. They deal in fraud prevention, risk assessments, and detection services. They give advice on accounting for complicated or unusual transactions, and of course stand ready to assist in preparing financial and management accounts (1997d). The firm can also assist its clients on tax matters. This includes both advice and the actual preparation of tax returns (1997e, 1997f).

The firm has also involved itself in business community training. "One practical means we have developed of assisting our clients in particular, and the business community, in general, is by sponsoring a program of training courses in accounting, auditing, information technology and related areas." The significance of such programs beyond the client base of the firm seems obvious. Ernst & Young have fully equipped training centers in various offices in the Middle East (1997g).

The firm has developed a menu of more than twenty courses. Some are aimed at meeting international qualifications. Such courses enable clients to provide training for their employees. One such course prepares students "to sit for the US Certified Public Accountants qualification." Ernst & Young "have developed specific training programmes for a wide range of organizations" (1997g). Certainly such services should provide positive externalities for the economies where they are offered.

A FINAL OVERVIEW

The jurisdictions that have been discussed in this chapter are all relatively small and owe their current status in the global economy to their ability to respond to international demands for energy resources. Indeed, on the global level, energy has superseded trade routes and other geopolitical considerations in terms of how the wealthier nations of the world view those jurisdictions. Because energy resources are depletable and because those resources, like other primary products, have an unstable and perhaps weakening position as compared to various manufactured products and services in the world economy, it seems reasonable to suggest diversification as a prudent goal for the economies in question.

If successful, diversification seems to presume greater international business and economic linkages and thus a greater dependence upon the global economy. In digesting that reality, the jurisdictions in question must consider how much diversification seems indicated and what form it should take. Of course, the generation of diversification is hardly a buyers market activity. Rather, it depends on what interests foreign elements may have or develop in the economies in question, and on to what extent indigenous populations may be willing to accept the results of those interests.

In dealing with such considerations, it seems obvious that ongoing or expanding linkages to global energy markets will undoubtedly lead to deepening involvements with foreign elements. Those involvements may take the form of investments on the part of multinational firms, coupled with an expansion of resident foreign employees. It may also serve to generate more extensive international financial arrangements, including perhaps the hosting of externally focused financial intermediaries and other business-related service groups.

Of course, success in attracting manufacturing and other nonenergy related corporate divisions and facilities can be expected to accelerate the type of changes alluded to here. Kuwait and Qatar may be best advised to pursue their future economic interests through energy-related activities. Bahrain and the United Arab Emirates, while continuing their involvements with energy, have already emerged as substantial offshore financial centers and are pursuing the expansion of their manufacturing sectors as well. Oman is in the process of attempting to achieve economic advancement through diversification, while at the same time continuing to rely on an energy sector, which, though perhaps not as robust as those to be found in neighboring jurisdiction, still plays a significant part in the nation's economy.

All the jurisdictions that have been the focus of this chapter seem destined to pursue their economic futures in the global economy. In doing so, it appears as though they will have increasing involvements with global business and economic facilitators. What such service groups seem willing and able to offer has been exemplified in this chapter by details concerning the service menus of selected major international accounting firms. Though it cannot be said that such service organizations are all that will be needed in guiding the expanding foreign linkages developing in the jurisdictions that have been highlighted here, it seems clear that they will have a potential for very positive involvements.

Part Three

Legal and Institutional Parameters for Business and Accounting Practice

Chapter Eight

Business and Accounting Environments in Egypt

In this chapter, the operating climate faced by business interests and, more specifically, the major accounting firms is reviewed. The laws and procedures governing the business sector will be considered. By reaching a better understanding of the operating parameters facing the private sector, it is hoped that the nation's potential for material improvement can be better assessed. More specifically, it is hoped that the information presented here will aid in the assessment of the facilitative role that the major accounting firms can play in linking Egypt to the global economy, as well as in strengthening the nation's domestic economy.

Egypt continues its movement away from policies of central planning and nationalization and toward a more market-oriented economy. Under International Monetary Fund and World Bank auspices, privatization and restructuring of some sectors of the economy, agriculture and tourism in particular, has advanced. The Public Enterprise Office oversees planning and management of public-sector reforms and privatization. Egyptian industry is still largely controlled by the public sector. There has been a reduction in government's share of commercial business.

Stock exchanges operate in Cairo and in Alexandria. In excess of one-thousand Egyptian companies are listed on the Cairo exchange. Under the Capital Markets Law, Law 95 of 1992, all individuals and companies, foreign or domestic, may buy shares on these exchanges. There are no financial futures or commodities markets in Egypt. The country does not function as an international financial center, and there are no special provisions for offshore services (Price Waterhouse 1995, 34–36). Except for some basic goods, price controls are not in effect for private sector products.

There are no foreign exchange controls in effect as a result of agreements with the International Monetary Fund. Market forces now set free exchange rates. Also there are no barriers for repatriating capital, profits, royalties, or fees (Ernst & Young 1995–1997). A foreign exchange trading market is operated to support tourism and local business. The currency unit is the Egyptian pound, which is divided into one-hundred piasters. Regulated by the Central Bank of Egypt, the banking system has over one-hundred commercial banks and specialized financial institutions. Branches of foreign banks may operate in Egypt, and, as approved by the Ministry of Finance and the Central Bank, may issue bonds and guarantees for public corporations and government projects.

A number of Egyptian commercial banks can provide bank services that are consistent with Islamic Law. Since the charging of interest is forbidden under Shari'a', profit and loss sharing arrangements are used for business finances (1995–1997).

Businesses may form in Egypt as proprietorships, foreign company branches or representative offices, joint ventures, simple limited partnerships, general partnerships, partnerships limited by shares, limited liability companies, and joint stock companies. The limited liability company and the joint stock company provide a separate legal personality and liability limited to company investment. The Companies Department of the Ministry of Economy and Foreign Trade regulates Egyptian companies in accordance with the Companies Law 159 of 1981, which contains rules, procedures, accounting, and reporting requirements (Deloitte Touche Tohmatsu International 1994a, 25). This law may also require participation by Egyptian nationals. As an alternative, foreign investors may choose to operate under the provisions of Investment Law, Law 230 of 1989, administered by the Central Authority for Investment. The requirement for Egyptian national ownership can be avoided under this law (Ernst & Young 1995–1997).

Smaller retailers and merchants are the primary users of the proprietorship form. The sole proprietor is generally the operator of the business and is responsible for all liabilities of the business. Government approval is not required. Financial statement audits are not required. Proper accounting records must be kept to support tax returns and payments (1995–1997).

Representative offices of foreign companies are permitted to conduct market and product surveys but such entities may not conduct commercial activities. Local expenditures must be covered by funds from abroad, and filings with the government must be made to this effect (Price Waterhouse 1995, 51). The representative office is viewed as nonresident in nature and is not subjected to Egyptian income taxes. The individual who operates the representative office may not enter into binding contracts for the head office. Should the representative office enter into contracts or carry on commercial activities for the head office, it may be declared a permanent establishment that must meet the tax obligations and requirements for a foreign company under the Companies Law.

Apart from a representative office, liaison offices or technical and scientific service offices may also be established to coordinate services within Egypt. These offices must provide detailed annual reports, including expense reports with the Ministry of Finance (Ernst & Young 1995–1997).

Foreign company branches may operate in Egypt after obtaining the approval of the Companies Administration Department. Such approval is subject to renewal in five years. Before beginning business operations in Egypt, copies of the articles of incorporation and bylaws of the foreign company, as well as the company resolutions that authorized the Egyptian branch, must be officially translated into Arabic and notarized by the home country Egyptian consulate. Branch records, books, and audit requirements for the foreign company branch operations are the same as for joint stock companies (Price Waterhouse 1995, 51). The branch needs to be registered in the Commercial Register and needs to keep account books for branch operations, which are audited by local registered auditors.

Joint ventures in Egypt may be incorporated or unincorporated. Unincorporated joint ventures are permitted among any legal Egyptian business entities. For certain joint ventures with foreign investors, Law 230 of 1989 applies and the venture is considered an Investment Law project. A joint venture may be used to share income from operations in which case it may be viewed by the tax authorities as a partnership for income tax purposes. In other cases where the venture is structured not to share in net income but to share in production activities or to share output from operations, partnership returns are not appropriate. In this case, each joint venturer includes its portion of revenues and expenses from the venture operations in their separate tax returns. Incorporated joint ventures are viewed as ordinary corporations and are taxed as such (Ernst & Young 1995–1997).

General partnerships require unlimited liability for all partners, who each have equal rights and privileges unless stated otherwise in the partnership agreement. A general partnership is formed by preparation of a partnership agreement in accordance with a model written agreement. The agreement is notarized and registered with the Ministry of Finance and filed in the Commercial Register. Egyptian nationals must represent at least 51 percent of the ownership. This restriction is waived if the partnership is approved as an Investment Law project under Law 230 of 1989.

A simple limited partnership can be formed on the same basis as a general partnership, but may have one or more partners whose liability is limited to capital contributions, as long as there are one or more general partners with unlimited liability for partnership obligations. Such a partnership is registered in the same way as the general partnership. One general partner name must appear in the name of the partnership. To maintain limited liability status, a limited partner's name must not be used in the partnership name.

A partnership limited by shares may be formed in accordance with Law 159 of 1981, with provisions similar to those for joint stock companies. The Egyptian ownership requirement and some rules relating to the board of directors are waived in the case of the partnership limited by shares. At least one partner must assume unlimited liability for partnership obligations with the limited partners' liability limited to contributions of capital (Price Waterhouse 1995, 50).

Law 159 governs joint stock companies. At least three individuals must be members of the corporation. For most shareholder companies or corporations, Egyptian nationals must own at least 51 percent of the company's equity. This Egyptian ownership requirement is waived if shares remain unsold to Egyptian nationals one month after initial offering. A waiver of the Egyptian ownership requirement may also be obtained by petition. And, the requirement is waived for a company that is approved as an Investment Law project under Law 230 of 1989.

The investor in shares has liability limited to the amount of share value. Total authorized capital may exceed that issued at formation. One or more classes of stock may be issued. Ordinary and preference shares are two common types issued. Voting and dividend rights of the classes of stock are established in the incorporating documents. The shares must be of equal value and have a par value between 5 and 1,000 Egyptian pounds. Shares must be negotiable without restriction. Total capital of at least 500,000 Egyptian pounds is required for a public offering. Capital of 250,000 Egyptian pounds is required if shares are not issued publicly. Paid in capital may be in the form of cash or in-kind contributions. In-kind contributions are subject to a substantial valuation process. At a minimum, 25 percent of issued capital must be paid at corporate formation with the remaining capital paid within ten years (Price Waterhouse 1995, 49).

However the capital structure is formed, articles of incorporation must be in accordance with a model from the Minister of Economy and Foreign Trade. The articles and necessary support must be submitted to the Companies Department. Approvals must be obtained from the Committee for the Scrutiny of Company Formation Applications and from the Minister of Economy and Foreign Trade. Once approved, the incorporation document is published in the Official Gazette and appears in the Commercial Register.

Shareholders must appoint at least three directors, the majority of whom are required to be Egyptian nationals. For Investment Law project companies, this requirement is waived. The total number of directors must be an odd number. The directors are charged with the responsibility to manage the company and are responsible for following the company articles of incorporation and Egyptian laws.

An annual shareholder meeting must take place in Egypt within six months of the company's year-end. Ordinary shareholder meetings may conduct company business matters, approve financial reports and statements, and appoint the company auditor. An extraordinary meeting must be called to amend company articles of incorporation. Such amendment usually requires a two-thirds vote of shareholders. In any shareholder meeting, voting may be in person or by proxy, vested in another shareholder by power of attorney.

Shareholders in a company that has lost half or more of its capital may place the company in dissolution by appointing a liquidator, or a board of liquidation, who is required to act in the company's best interest in meeting company debts and obligations. The liquidation authority will prepare an inventory of all assets and liabilities which, upon approval by the board of directors, must be recorded in the Commercial Register (Price Waterhouse 1995, 49).

The procedures to form a limited liability company in Egypt are essentially the same as those for joint stock companies. The limited liability company, however, is in effect a private company. Capital of at least 50,000 Egyptian pounds must be paid in at formation. Capital shares may not be offered to the public and are not negotiable. Share value is required to be at least 100 Egyptian pounds. Shareholders may number at least 2 and no more than 50. Existing shareholders have a first right of refusal for any company shares being sold by other shareholders. As with a joint stock company, a legal reserve must be added to at the rate of five percent of annual net income until a total of 50 percent of total capital is reserved.

Corporate mergers or reorganizations of companies require advanced approval by shareholders of each associating company. Approval of the Capital Markets Authority must be obtained. A resolution containing specifics must be published in the Official Gazette. Two or more companies may be consolidated into a newly formed company or may be combined into an existing company.

Joint stock company employees have rights to share in corporate profits. The share is set at no less than ten percent of distributable profits and no greater than the total wages of the workers. Employees of branches of foreign companies also have these profit sharing rights.

Egyptian companies must keep proper records for all business transactions. A general journal and an inventory ledger are required to be kept in Arabic. Documents which support the accounting records such as contracts and original invoices, must also be kept in Arabic. Before the general ledger is used, it must be notarized. Most business accounts are kept in Egyptian pounds. Oil companies and companies in free trade zones may keep their records in U.S. dollars (Price Waterhouse 1995, 59).

Financial statements include the balance sheet, income statement, and the statement of changes in financial position. The statements must be prepared in Arabic and include comparative figures for the preceding year. The financial statements of oil and gas industry companies must be prepared on a concession basis. Financial statements must be filed with both the Tax Department and the Companies Administration Department (62).

Law 159 contains recommended income statement format and content. Any departure from these recommendations must be disclosed. The recommended format includes the operating section with computation of cost of goods sold, the trading section including gross profit, the profit and loss section with the computation of net profit, and the distribution section with required allocations of net profit as per company statute (62).

Company authorized capital is set during incorporation. Authorized capital may be greater than contributed at the time of formation. Any changes to the capital account that would lower total capital must have the prior approval of the Companies Administration Department. Capital is shown in three categories—authorized, issued or subscribed, and paid-up. At the time of incorporation, paid-up capital must constitute at least 25 percent of that issued, with the remainder to be paid within ten years by a predetermined agreement (62).

Marketable securities viewed as current assets are carried, using the lower of cost or market value. Long-term marketable securities are valued at historical cost unless a long-term impairment of the carrying amount has occurred. Inventories are accounted for on the lower of cost or market basis with actual, average, or first-in–first-out methods being used. Long-term real property is valued at cost. Depreciation is charged over estimated useful lives of buildings, equipment, and machinery using the straight-line, declining-balance, or unit-of-production methods.

Affiliations of companies may be carried out using the purchase or the pooling of interest methods, whichever is appropriate. Financial statements for groups of companies may be prepared using either the consolidation or equity methods (63).

Contingent losses are charged against income in the period in which an asset has been impaired or a liability incurred. Material but unrecorded contingencies should be disclosed. Letters of guarantee and letters of credit are recorded by means of contraaccounts. Reserves are not permitted for general business risk contingencies against which insurance has not been purchased. Reserves of profits, such as reservation of retained earnings, are permitted by statutory regulations. Deferred income tax accounting is not practiced in Egypt. There are few differences between financial and tax accounting (64).

Footnote disclosures must be made as part of the financial statements. Disclosures include organizational relationships, accounting policies in use, material related-party transactions, major company commitments, material subsequent events, material contingencies, and analyses of major accounts (64). Subsidiaries are required to disclose their parent company relationship (65).

An annual financial statement audit is required under Law 159 of 1981. This law requires that financial statements consist of the balance sheet, the profit and loss statement, and the statement of changes in financial position or the statement of cash flows (60). Each joint stock company is required to appoint an auditor who is licensed to practice in Egypt by the Ministry of Finance (Deloitte Touche Tohmatsu International 1994a, 30).

Requirements to become a licensed auditor in Egypt are more strenuous than are seen in many countries. Only Egyptian nationals may be licensed auditors (30). A university degree in accounting and ten years of experience are required before licensure. Under certain circumstances the experience requirement can be waived: if the applicant is a member of the Egyptian Society of Accountants and Auditors, or such a society approved by the Egyptian Society of Accountants and Auditors (Price Waterhouse 1995, 60).

Under Law 159 of 1981, the Ministry of Finance governs standards relating to auditors. Auditors must be independent as to the companies audited. Such activities proscribed for the auditor are being a founder in the company formation, being on the company board of directors, or being a company employee; nor may the auditor have a family relationship with company management (60).

Law 159 and Decree 92 of 1982 of the Ministry of Investment Affairs contains audit standards and guidance (60). The auditing guidelines set by the International Federation of Accountants (IFA) are appropriate in Egypt since the Egyptian Society of Accountants and Auditors holds IFA membership (Deloitte Touche Tohmatsu International 1994a, 30). When an entity being audited has foreign affiliations, generally accepted audit standards from those other countries, such as the United States, may also be followed (Price Waterhouse 1995, 60).

The audit report required in Egypt is somewhat expanded over reports from other countries. The report must state that the audited financial statements are prepared in compliance with rules and regulations. The statements reflect the company statement of financial position and results of operations. The decree goes beyond items required in many other countries. The audit report must state that all data or company explanations that the auditor considers necessary have been obtained. A statement is required from the auditor that the company has inventory and accounting records appropriate for their business; that the financial statements correspond with the accounting records; and that all board of directors resolutions that have accounting content have been appropriately included. The statement must also indicate whether in the course of the audit illegal acts by the company were noted (60).

Egyptian law is permissive as to accounting principles. Any generally accepted accounting principle may be used that is sound and results in the accurate portrayal of the financial position and results of operations in financial statements. Though Egypt has not in the past had an organization that makes pronouncements, the Society of Accountants and Auditors currently has a project in which it is reviewing various generally accepted accounting standards toward the end of establishing a standards setter (64). Accounting pronouncements by the American Institute of Certified Public Accountants, the Financial Accounting Standards Board, and the International Accounting Standards Committee are all currently acceptable for preparing financial statements in Egypt (61).

Differences are few between accounting for income for financial reporting purposes and tax reporting requirements. Income from the audited financial statements of corporations must be adjusted for any differences to arrive at income for tax returns (64). Annual income tax returns are due to be filed within a month after the annual general meeting of shareholders approves the financial statements.

Chapter Nine

Business and Accounting Environments in Saudi Arabia

This chapter assesses the operating climate and legal environment facing business in general and the major accounting firms in Saudi Arabia. Various laws and procedures governing business practice will be reviewed. The purpose is to arrive at an understanding of the operating parameters of the private sector in the nation's economy. That understanding, it is hoped, should help in assessing the facilitative role that the major accounting firms can play in forming international business and economic linkages for the Saudi economy.

The Ministry of Commerce regulates all business enterprises in the Kingdom of Saudi Arabia through its Regulations for Companies. Businesses must also observe Ministry of Finance regulations for taxes and other matters, Ministry of the Interior rules pertaining to social customs and immigration, and labor regulations covering personnel in Saudi Arabia. As a matter of law, businesses must join the chamber of commerce and industry located in the major cities if their business involves importing, exporting, or bidding on government contracts (Ernst & Young 1991, 5).

The Kingdom's central bank is the Saudi Arabian Monetary Agency. The Saudi riyal (SR) is the unit of currency in Saudi Arabia. It is divided into 100 halalahs. The exchange rate is fixed against the U.S. dollar. Other country rates fluctuate. The currency may be freely converted through banks or money exchanges (4). There are no exchange controls or monetary restrictions for the importation or repatriation of funds, including profits and salaries of foreign workers (13).

Only Saudi bank branches may operate in the Kingdom. There is no official stock exchange, but the banks have established a network that makes a market in Saudi company shares. Through use of bank branches and computerization, shares of Saudi public companies are widely available. However, in general, only Saudi or Gulf Cooperation Council country nationals may own or deal in such shares (9). Bonds and related instruments can be issued by Saudi businesses through foreign-bank head offices in cooperation with a Saudi bank (7).

Since the expansion of Islamic banking systems within the Islamic world, many Saudi businesses conduct their businesses according to the Shari'a'. Charging interest is prohibited. Islamic banks and businesses arrange financing with profit-and-loss sharing rather than interest paying contracts (8).

Saudi Arabia business entities may take on a number of different organizational and legal structures. Requirements, rights, and obligations for most businesses are contained in the Regulations for Companies enacted by Royal Decree in 1965 and amended in 1982 and 1992 (21).

Sole proprietorships may be operated by Saudi nationals but are not permitted for foreigners. Joint ventures are not recognized as separate entities but as associations of authorized business entities for a specific purpose. Several forms of partnership are recognized: general partnerships, limited partnerships, and professional partnerships. Business organizations may also be incorporated as limited liability companies or as joint stock companies (Price Waterhouse 1991, 57–58).

A Saudi national may form a sole proprietorship by registering the business in the Commercial Register in the Ministry of Commerce. Owners of proprietorships have unlimited liability. This business form is used generally in the mercantile areas. A registered company may not be a sole proprietorship. Therefore if one person achieves complete ownership of a company, the company must be dissolved (Ernst & Young 1991, 21).

Partnerships may be established as general partnerships, limited partnerships, limited liability partnerships, and professional partnerships. In a general partnership, all partners assume unlimited liability for partnership obligations up to the extent of their personal assets. This form is a common organizational arrangement among Saudi nationals. There are no minimum capital requirements. The partnership agreement must be filed with the Ministry of Commerce. Unless arranged differently in the partnership agreement, the general partnership is dissolved upon the death of a partner, the legal incapacity of a partner, or the bankruptcy or insolvency of a partner. Ownership interests may not be transferred without unanimous partner agreement (24).

Two forms of limited partnerships may be formed in Saudi Arabia by filing a partnership agreement with the Ministry of Commerce. The first form must have at least one general partner who assumes unlimited liability for partnership debts. In the second form, which requires a minimum of four partners, liability for all partners is limited to their capital contributions. For either form of limited partnership, minimum capital is SR 1 million, with paid-in capital at least 50 percent at formation. Partnership capital must be evenly divided among negotiable shares that are not divisible.

A professional partnership may be used to form a joint practice of a locally licensed professional partnership with a foreign partnership. A model partnership agreement was issued in 1991. Regulations require Ministry of Commerce approval. Such approval is contingent upon a number of factors. The foreign organization must have been in existence at least ten years and must have a distinguished international reputation. Expertise and training for Saudis must come from the foreign firm. The foreign firm must have a resident representative. Saudi partners are required to own at least 25 percent of capital in the joint partnership (23–24).

Joint ventures of business entities may be carried on in Saudi Arabia. A joint venture is not viewed as a legally separate entity. Title to contributed capital remains with the organization that contributed it. Establishing a joint venture does not require special incorporations, permissions, registrations, or licenses. It can be established by any means, including de facto, based on the circumstances of the operations. If a joint venture agreement is made, it should include the objectives of the joint venture, venturer rights and obligations, and distribution of profits and losses.

The joint venture in Saudi Arabia can also take on the form of a joint adventure. In a joint adventure, the business arrangements between the venturers are unknown to third parties. In this case, where the third parties are not aware that they are dealing with a joint adventure, recourse may be taken only against the venturer dealt with. Should a third party be aware of the joint venture nature of the entity, the joint adventure will be treated as a general partnership for its affairs with such a third party (25).

Consortiums are similar to the joint venture but are generally formed to complete large projects. The business agreements are between existing legal entities with no separate legal status taken on by the consortium (25).

The bylaws of some partnerships may allow variable capital, that is, a partnership's bylaws may allow capital to be increased by additional payments from existing partners or by taking in new partners. Such business organizations can also reduce capital of existing partners (Price Waterhouse 1991, 67).

A cooperative company may be formed that is for the purpose of reducing costs or maintaining the quality of products to consumers or partners of the company. The form may be of a joint stock company or limited liability company. Shareholders have equal rights. Capital is in registered shares of equal value. Share value must be set at least SR 10 but may not be more than SR 50 (67).

Foreign companies may establish representative offices with the approval of the Ministry of Commerce. Only Saudi nationals or 100 percent Saudi-owned entities may act as commercial agents. These agents must be in residence within Saudi Arabia and be registered with the Ministry of Commerce. Foreign companies may not sell their products directly in Saudi Arabia. Products must be sold through Saudi Arabian commercial agents who then market locally (Ernst & Young 1991, 26).

If a foreign company has business with the Saudi government, liaison offices may be established to coordinate Saudi operations with the home office. A license must be received from the Ministry of Commerce. The liaison office may not carry on commercial business. The liaison office is required to file a detailed activities report and annual audited reports with the Ministry of Commerce, which will demonstrate that the office was paid for by the foreign corporation's home office.

The provisions of the Foreign Capital Investment Code apply to a permanent establishment and operation of branches in Saudi Arabia. Such branch approval is generally only given for high-technology defense projects (26). There must be overriding reasons for such branch operations to be 100 percent foreign controlled. When approved, foreign corporate branches generally must have a separate stated amount of capital. Branch books of account must be kept in Arabic and maintained in Saudi Arabia (Price Waterhouse 1991, 86). Information which must be provided to establish a branch includes: audited financial statements of the foreign company from the past three to five years; the bylaws of the foreign entity; board of directors approval to authorize a branch in Saudi Arabia; and a copy of the grant of power of attorney to the legal representative who will act as the company's agent in the Kingdom (Ernst & Young 1991, 26).

The Companies Regulations provide for limited liability companies to be formed. Many of the aspects of a partnership as well as many of the aspects of a joint stock company apply to these entities. Owners of the limited liability company are referred to as "partners" in the regulations. Ownership shares carry liability limited to contributions. The number of shareholders may be from two to fifty. Insurance, savings, or banking business may not be undertaken by a limited liability company.

Original promoters file an application for registration with the Department of Companies within the Ministry of Commerce. A summary of the approved charter should be published in the Official Gazette. Owners' capital is issued in indivisible, nonnegotiable shares of equal value. Sale of shares to the public is not permitted. Initial capital must total at least SR 500,000 for service and contracting companies. For entities formed for a manufacturing project, 25 percent of the total project cost is required to be paid in by owners.

Limited liability companies should be operated directly by the owners or designated actual managers. When shareholders total more than twenty, a control board of no less than three shareholders must be provided for in the charter. Once per year, a general shareholder meeting should be held. Other meetings may be called by the board of managers, the auditor, or shareholders who hold 50 percent or more of the total capital.

Each limited liability company must create a reserve from profits and add to the reserve each year no less than 10 percent of net profits until the reserve totals at least 50 percent of total capital. An auditor must be appointed in a similar fashion as for joint stock companies, discussed in the following paragraphs (Price Waterhouse 1991, 60–61).

The Saudi joint stock company may be formed by at least five founders who are signatories to the charter, who participate in the company organization, or who are contributors-in-kind. Founders may limit share purchases to only themselves.

Should they choose to sell shares to others, an announcement in the form of a prospectus in the official Gazette must invite public participation. The prospectus should include, among other requirements, information about the corporation's objectives and home office; classes of stock to be issued with all particulars; privileges of founders or others; plans for profit distribution; and the date of the Royal Decree or Ministerial Resolution which incorporated the company. The prospectus must be made available to any prospective shareholder. Additional information beyond the required information may be included in the prospectus document, such as that required by stock exchanges and the like.

Companies formed to be concessional, to run a public utility, to receive subsidies from the government, to provide banking services, or to be a partner with the government require a Royal Decree. Such a decree is issued based on Council of Ministers approval (Price Waterhouse 1991, 62).

The capital of the joint stock company is represented by negotiable shares of equal value, which must not be less than SR 50. For public companies, paid-up capital must total at least SR 10 million. A private company must have at least SR 2 million in capital. Shares may be registered or bearer. Subscriptions are made through Ministry of Commerce-designated banks (Ernst & Young 1991, 22). Shareowners are liable for full payment of the agreed subscription value of shares. Legal liability of the shareholder is the total par value of shares owned or subscribed. Share ownership may be transferred by an entry in the company's shareholders' register.

A joint stock company, after equity capital is fully paid, may issue negotiable, registered debentures to Saudi nationals only (Price Waterhouse 1991, 63–64). Nonvoting preferred shares up to a total amount of 50 percent of capital may be issued (Ernst & Young 1991, 22).

Each joint stock company is required to have a board of directors of no less than three members, with term of office restricted to three years. A director must own at least two hundred company shares, which are set aside to guarantee the director's liability (22). Remuneration for directors is set forth in the company charter. If directors received a percentage of company profits, such percentage may not be greater than 10 percent of net profit after a dividend of at least 5 percent of total share capital is provided for.

Directors must not enter into a transaction with the company in such a way as to have a personal interest, except with prior approval of the stockholders in a general meeting. If the transaction was made via public bid, the director must disclose any personal interests to the board of directors.

At least twenty shares must be owned or represented by proxy for an individual stockholder to be admitted to the annual meeting or extraordinary meetings of shareholders. A quorum of 50 percent of outstanding stock is required for a general stockholder meeting. If the quorum is not reached, another meeting is called requiring no quorum, except that a delayed extraordinary meeting must have 25 percent of shares outstanding as a minimum quorum. Any matters of the company can be dealt with and voted upon in a general meeting. Extraordinary meetings may change the company bylaws, except that stockholders cannot be deprived of their rights, financial liabilities cannot be increased, the company objectives cannot be changed, the head office cannot be moved to another country, or the company's nationality cannot be changed (Price Waterhouse 1991, 64).

Auditors are appointed at the annual general meeting. The auditors must be licensed to practice in Saudi Arabia. Auditor duties are not completely specified, though the auditor has a right to inspect books and records, ask for explanations and details as necessary, and verify all assets and liabilities. A general meeting is required at least once per year to examine the audited financial statements. This meeting should be held within six months after year-end (Ernst & Young 1991, 23). The auditor reports to the general meeting. Such reports must include a statement about management's attitude on cooperating with auditor requests for particulars and explanations.

Should the joint stock company experience losses that equal 75 percent of capital, an extraordinary general meeting must be called by directors to determine that the company should dissolve or continue to operate (23).

A foreign company may do business as a government contractor, may set up a branch operation, or may open a representative office. Investments by foreigners in Saudi Arabia are governed under the jurisdiction of the Foreign Capital Investment Code. Though foreign investment may take most legal forms available, the limited liability company and the joint stock company, which do not require unlimited liability, are the usual forms selected. Other forms require a degree of unlimited liability.

Contracting with the Saudi Arabian government does not require compliance with the Foreign Capital Investment Code. Nor must government contractors or subcontractors comply with full Ministry of Commerce reporting requirements. Contractors must usually have a Saudi service agent. Such contractors need to obtain a separate Temporary Commercial Registration from the Ministry of Commerce for each government contract. Such registrations permit only work on government contracts, not private dealings. Contractors are expected to assign work to local Saudi contractors for not less than 30 percent of the government contract. Local sources should be used for supplies, transportation, shipping, insurance, banking, and leasing arrangements. Contractors must register with the Department of Zakat and Income Tax and are subject to taxes.

Professionals who are licensed to practice in home countries are permitted to operate in Saudi Arabia in conjunction with a local Saudi partner. Such foreign professionals are permitted to practice after obtaining an appropriate license to practice from the Ministry of Commerce (59).

The Companies Regulations and the Income Tax Regulations specifically require that accounting books and records be maintained in Saudi Arabia. They must be written in Arabic, or if written in English, must be translated into Arabic.

Specific accounting records required are the daily journal, which centralizes all original entries for posting to the general ledger; the general ledger; and an "inventory book," which is essentially a trial balance that contains all assets, liabilities, and results for the year. An income statement in Arabic is also suggested.

Requirements for accounting records were delineated by the Ministry of Commerce and reinforced by Royal Decree in July 1998 (51). Pages of the accounting records must be prenumbered and presented to the local Chamber of Commerce and Industry. The chamber is required to sign and stamp annually the first and last pages of each record. Entries in accounting records must be in chronological order. No corrections or interlineations are permitted in accounting records. Modifications must be made by separate entry.

Businesses must also keep minute books and stockholder registers. Records and supporting documentation must be kept for at least ten years. Computerized accounting systems have been adapted to these requirements. Such computer systems must be in Saudi Arabia. Auditors must authenticate a printout no less than once per quarter. Input and output procedures must be documented.

Accounting records must provide an audit trail from the trial balances for financial purposes to the applicable tax reports and declarations (Price Waterhouse 1991, 85). Virtually all business entities in Saudi Arabia are required to file annual tax returns that report income from audited financial statements as adjusted for tax purposes (Ernst & Young 1991, 30). These compulsory reports are made to the Department of Zakat and Income Tax, from which each business entity is also required to obtain tax and Zakat clearance certificates each year (37).

Foreign business unit records for operations in Saudi Arabia must be kept separately for Saudi Arabian operations. Such records must be kept in the Kingdom until a clearance certificate from the tax authorities is received.

Financial statements of all companies with limited liability must be audited by a certified public accountant registered to practice in the Kingdom. The audited financial statements must be filed within six months after year-end with the Ministry of Commerce and the Ministry of Industry and Electricity. Audited financial statements must also be filed with the annual final tax returns (30).

Royal Decree 4/43 of 1 August 1974 established the formal recognition of the accounting profession in Saudi Arabia. Customarily, only Saudi nationals are granted accounting titles. International accounting firms generally associate with a Saudi accounting firm and practice under the Saudi name.

Guidance and regulation of accounting and auditing in Saudi Arabia are found in a number of sources: the Regulations for Companies, the Foreign Capital Investment Code, the Income Tax Regulations, the Saudi Arabian Auditing Standards, and the Saudi Arabian Standards of General Presentation and Disclosure (51).

The Ministry of Commerce issues public accountant certificates and oversees disciplinary actions. Ministerial Decision 595, 16 March 1975, governs the awarding of public accounting certificates. To receive certification, an accountant must hold an approved degree in accounting and have appropriate experience in auditing or accounting. Enumerated qualifications and duties of the company auditor include independence, due care, and the requirements for proper audit documentation.

The financial accounting concepts and objectives approved as a basis for accounting standards by the Ministry of Commerce Decision 692, 11 November 1986, are similar to those issued by the American Institute of Certified Public Accountants. However, these have not been monitored or enforced. Business entities follow U.S., U.K., or international standards in general, but with many important differences (Price Waterhouse 1991, 89). New accounting standards are under development by a technical committee of the Saudi Accounting Association in close cooperation with the Ministry of Commerce (86).

Saudi Arabia has not created or appointed an organization or government body to be recognized as promulgators of accounting standards and practices. Nor has legislation been enacted that would set such standards. The effect is that financial statements are prepared using divergent methods and practices. Comparability has not been achieved.

As noted, many public accountants follow International Accounting Standards issued by the International Accounting Standards Committee. However, major exceptions to the international standards are necessary in Saudi Arabia. Companies seldom have consolidated financial statements. Deferred taxation is not used. Procedures for accounting for taxation are inconsistent. Companies do not disclose the details of related-party arrangements. Start-up costs of development-stage businesses are capitalized and charged to expense over an arbitrary period, frequently five years. Depreciation expense methods follow the income tax authorities requirements even for financial reporting purposes. Par value is used for stock dividends.

The basic financial statements are the balance sheet, statement of income and retained earnings, and the statement of changes in financial position, or cash flow. Though prior year statements are not required, in practice many companies issue comparative statements. Statements may be based on a fiscal or calendar year. Saudi income statements generally contain figures for net sales; other operating income; cost of goods sold; selling, general, and administrative expenses; interest and other income; and other deductions, including interest and taxes. Disclosure is required by the Ministry of Commerce guidelines for results of continuing operations, results of discontinued operations, and extraordinary items.

Reporting differs in a number of respects from that generally found in financial statements of the United States, the United Kingdom, or the International Accounting Standards. Transactions for treasury stock, stock dividends, or stock splits do not generally occur in Saudi Arabia. The LIFO method is not an acceptable inventory method for income tax reporting and so is not used for financial reporting, since income tax methods are generally followed for both income tax and financial reporting. Long-term assets are carried at cost.

Depreciation and depletion methods follow the tax requirements. Though the purchase method is used for reporting the affiliations of companies, and the goodwill arising is generally amortized over its useful life, consolidated financial statements are rarely prepared. Ministry of Commerce guidelines do not indicate when consolidated financial reports must be prepared. The cost method is used for investments in the voting stock of other companies.

Some limited liability companies do not charge income taxes through the income statement, but rather to shareholder accounts. The legal reserve of retained earnings required by law for some companies is shown separately in the balance sheet. It is not available for distribution to owners but may be used for net annual losses.

Disclosures in footnotes to financial statements vary substantially among companies. Information that is generally disclosed either on the face of the statements or in the notes include descriptions of the nature of the entity's business, legal form and its registered commercial number. Accounting policies are disclosed as to the revenue recognition, depreciation, amortization, and inventory valuation methods. The major components of property, plant and equipment, and of the inventory are described.

The Ministry of Commerce guidelines on disclosures in financial statements require the following: nature of operations; description of significant accounting policies; accounting changes and how such changes are accounted for; potential losses or gains; financial commitments; and any subsequent events (Price Waterhouse 1991, 92–93). Should the financials not be certified by a Saudi registered accountant, tax authorities indicate that the deemed profit basis will be used to assess taxes (84).

Chapter Ten

Business and Accounting Environments in Turkey

This chapter reviews the institutional and legal environments confronting the accounting firms and, of course, other business endeavors in Turkey. An attempt is made to provide an understanding of the various laws and institutions that influence or control business procedures and practices. Such an understanding seems essential if the potential of the accounting firms for facilitating international business and economic linkages with Turkey is to be gaged.

The Turkish Code of Commerce governs the formation of business organizations. Sole proprietorships, ordinary partnerships, limited partnerships, sleeping partnerships, limited by shares, branches of foreign companies, subsidiary companies, liaison offices, limited liability companies, and corporations are all permitted in Turkey within the provisions of the law. Businesses run as sole proprietorships are permitted for Turkish nationals and in some cases foreign residents. Foreign residents may not form proprietorships.

Partnerships formed in Turkey may be ordinary, limited, or general partnerships. All are governed by the Turkish Obligations Act and the Turkish Commercial Code. In ordinary partnerships, all partners have full liability for partnership obligations. A corporation may become partner in an ordinary partnership, but when a partnership has some form of limited liability, partnerships must be natural persons (Deloitte Touche Tohmatsu International 1994b, 35).

The ordinary partnership is viewed from a legal standpoint as a group of investors and does not have a separate legal entity. The ordinary partnership may not have a trade name and is not included in the Register of Commerce or the Register of Title Deeds. Partners share rights and obligations equally and assets are jointly owned. Partners are jointly and severally liable for the partnership obligations. The partnership agreement may be either oral or written.

Statutory provisions do not include a legal framework of management or operational requirements for the ordinary partnership (Ernst & Young 1995–1997).

Limited or general partnerships are regarded as commercial companies with legal entity separate and apart from its partners. Partnership agreements must be written. In limited partnerships, one or more active general partners must be liable without limits for partnership obligations. Limited partners are liable only for their contributions. General partnerships differ in that the company becomes the first party liable for obligations, followed by the partners (1995–1997).

In Turkey, joint ventures are permitted between legal entities or real persons to jointly undertake a specific project in a specified time, in accordance with a written agreement, and to share resulting profits. One of the joint venturers must be a company that is subject to corporation tax. The joint venture is itself subject to corporation tax, value added tax, and withholding tax. However, the joint venture is not a legal entity that has the right of ownership (1995–1997).

Companies may have liaison offices and branches in Turkey. Commercial business may not be undertaken by a liaison office, however. Such offices are permitted for the purposes of gathering information and representing foreign companies. Permission, usually granted for two years, must be obtained from the Foreign Investment Directorate in the Office of the Undersecretariate of Treasury and Foreign Trade.

The liaison office is not permitted to have revenues on its own account and therefore must be funded by the company home office. The office must keep books and legal records necessary to meet the requirements of public authorities in Turkey. The Turkish consulate in the company's home country must indicate approval of the parent company's statements in regards to the authorization and commitments to the liaison office, including power of attorney designation and the activities statements. Required documents include designating and granting a power of attorney to a company official to set up the office, an application letter to set the office up that details the reason for the office, an estimate of liaison office expenditures, and the number of liaison office employees.

The home country chamber of commerce must indicate that the investor is well established in the home country. Also needed are the parent company's previous annual reports and an investor-prepared commitment letter for expense payment from funds from non-Turkish sources.

Approved liaison offices are not subjected to corporate or personal income tax, as long as income is not generated in Turkey and expenditures are not made from Turkish sources of funds (Deloitte Touche Tohmatsu International 1994b, 35–36).

To form a branch of a foreign company in Turkey, an application with support documents must be submitted to the Foreign Investment Directorate. The home country chamber of commerce needs to vouch that the investor corporation is established and active. Parent company articles of incorporation, annual reports, and board of directors' approval to invest in Turkey must be provided. A branch feasibility study must include the amount of foreign currency that will be sent to Turkey as branch capital and details for all planned imports of machinery and equipment. A power of attorney to establish the branch in Turkey must be granted with copies of the representative's passport. As in the case of the liaison office, most of these documents need to be certified by the Turkish consulate in the home country (34). Tax liability is levied only on Turkish income for a branch. Subsidiary companies formed in Turkey are subject to full tax liability (28).

The formation of corporations or limited liability companies is permitted in Turkey. Limited liability companies differ from corporations in that share certificates are not issued. Instead, a shareholder register is kept as the legal ownership record. A minimum of two and a maximum of fifty shareholders are permitted. Minimum capital required is Turkish lira (TL) 10,000, which are divided into shares of TL 500 or multiples thereof. Net profit is distributed in proportion to ownership share total. Court approval is not required for establishing the limited liability company. If the limited liability company has more than twenty shareholders, one or more must be appointed as company auditor with authority and duties similar to the auditors of corporations. Liability of shareholders, as in corporations, is limited to capital contributions or subscriptions (34).

The Turkish Code of Commerce authorizes the formation of companies by Turkish nationals or by foreigners. The only distinction made is that foreign investors must obtain a permit from the Foreign Investment Directorate prior to filing for business formation with the Ministry of Industry and Commerce (29).

Turkish corporations may be formed by the investing founders contributing the entire corporate capital, or a public subscription of capital may be used. Founders prepare articles of incorporation and the prospectus for subscriptions to the new corporate stock. At least five shareholders must register these materials with the Ministry of Industry and Commerce for issuance of a permit to incorporate. Permits are subject to the Commercial Court's approval.

When shares or other corporate securities are held by the public, the corporation must also register with the stock exchange. Companies with more than one-hundred shareholders are subject to Capital Market Board regulations, which include directives on financial reporting, authorized share capital, and public disclosures including prospectus provisions. Minimum capital of TL 500,000 must be subscribed, of which a minimum of 25 percent must be paid by the corporate formation date. Founding shares may be issued that entitle founders to additional dividends (28–29). Legal capital reserves are to be set aside from income for protection of creditors.

Shareholder meetings may be ordinary general meetings or extraordinary general meetings. General shareholder meetings are called by the directors, or the auditors if directors fail to call a required meeting. An ordinary general meeting should be held within four months after the accounting period ends. Should the meeting be postponed beyond that date, approval is required from the Ministry of Industry and Commerce. An extraordinary shareholder meeting can be called by any shareholder or shareholders representing one tenth of the total outstanding shares. The meeting request must be in writing and must state the purpose of the meeting.

For most purposes, a simple majority vote for shares represented at the meeting is required to elect officers and to pass resolutions at a general meeting. To increase the number of shareholders' subscriptions, or to change the nationality of the company, takes a meeting quorum of all shares outstanding and a voting majority. Issuance of debentures, liquidation, decreasing company capital, or approval of offer of acquisition by public enterprises takes a quorum of two-thirds of all outstanding shares and a majority of those voting on the particular issue (32).

In the ordinary general meeting, directors and statutory auditors are appointed. Director remuneration is set. The profit and loss account, balance sheet, and directors' reports are approved. Dividend distributions are approved by the shareholders upon directors' recommendation. Articles of incorporation may be modified by shareholders at a general meeting.

Statutory auditors are required to be appointed who are not related to any of the board members. Statutory auditors may be shareholders. Their report is treated as a formality (32). Historically, audits have not been viewed as more than a formality by many in the Turkish business community (Price Waterhouse 1993, 98). Companies may hire independent auditors who are certified public accountants or the equivalent. In some cases, companies are required to have approved auditors and file appropriate reports.

All commercial enterprises in Turkey must maintain full sets of accounting records in the Turkish language with dual language books permitted. The records must reflect the recording of every transaction separately. The records must be kept in Turkish lira. Memorandum records are required for all foreign currency balances.

Annual financial statements must be based on these accounting records and must be denominated in Turkish lira. There are a number of requirements imposed by the Tax Procedure Law 213. Accounting books must include cash books, a general ledger that includes bank accounts, a journal, a stock or inventory ledger, a fixed assets register, accounts receivable and payable ledgers, the stamp tax book, and, for manufacturers, a cost ledger. The books must be stamped at the beginning and end of each year by a notary public. Computerized records may be used, with all hard copy output stamped by the notary public. Detailed printouts must be kept to substantiate summary records. Capital market companies and financial entities have official separate charts of accounts. The chart of accounts for other entities is not specified. The Commercial Law provides that hard copy accounting records must be kept in Turkey and retained for a minimum of ten years. Records kept on computer, microfilm, or the like are not acceptable (97–98).

Reports by approved independent auditors are required only for banks and other financial institutions and for publicly held companies. When there are over one-hundred shareholders in joint-stock companies and for entities that issue public securities, registration with the Capital Market Board is necessary. The Capital

Market Board requires that audited information on financial position be filed at regular intervals. (Deloitte Touche Tohmatsu International 1994b, 32). Companies that have shares or other securities on the stock exchange financial statements that have been audited by approved auditors must be published for shareholders and filed with the Capital Markets Board (Price Waterhouse 1993, 99).

The Turkish Central Bank requires banks to file reports approved by auditors on statutory financial statements. The reports are required in prescribed form and must include comments on the bank's financial position, ratio analysis, and internal control system information. Some banks voluntarily publish financial statements complete with a balance sheet, income statement, and notes in conventional international form, but the exact content and form is by agreement of the bank with its auditors (99).

In 1989, Law 3568, the Independent Accountancy, Independent Accountant Financial Advisor, and Sworn Financial Advisor Law was passed, becoming effective in 1990. This was the first Turkish law regulating the accounting profession, granting exclusive rights and responsibilities. The law provides that company-independent auditors have joint responsibility with company authorities for the records and accounts. It provides for required training and examinations for those who may practice the profession independently. Transactions and documents, which are required by law to be either controlled or certified officially, may receive such treatment from the authorized independent auditors with the same effect as government authorities.

The statute defines scope of work, procedures for practice, and forms of reports. Future changes to these will be made by issuing communiqués (100). The Central Bank approves the professional accounting firms that may perform bank audits. Such firms must be organized as public companies with a minimum of TL 100 million capital. The board of directors, a managing director, and an assistant managing director must have professional qualifications or hold a bachelor's degree, and have a minimum of ten years experience in law, economics, accounting, management, or banking. Auditors need five years experience in addition to a bachelor's degree in any of the above fields. The professional staff must all be resident in Turkey and must be at least ten in number. In 1988, the Capital Markets Law included a provision that those audit firms approved by the Central Bank to audit banks would have automatic approval for audit of capital markets companies.

Approved audit firms in conjunction with the Capital Markets Board in 1988 formed the Independent Audit Association, with the purpose of providing a discussion forum for the firms and the Board. The Association appears to be the first step to forming a professional accounting institution in the manner that has been so successful in other countries. Currently, the Association does not have the functions of controlling the profession by setting training, examination, and professional ethics; nor does it have the statutory functions of setting national accounting and auditing standards (100–101).

Turkish accounting principles are not set by statute. Financial statements for commercial entities are required by statute to agree with the books of account. General practice has been to omit adjustments that are not permitted under the income tax laws. This results in financial statements prepared under the income tax methods. Subsidiaries of international companies have recently tended to follow International Accounting Standards. The practice is not widespread, since keeping the books in accordance with International Accounting Standards is thought to reduce the flexibility for declaring dividends (102).

For companies listed on capital markets, the Capital Markets Board has set comprehensive accounting regulations. The Board recognized the requirements to keep books of accounting according to the tax law. Adjustments to the tax law accounting are necessary in order to prepare financial statements in accordance with the rules of the Capital Markets Board. Accounting principles required by the Board are close to International Accounting Standards. The standards on consolidation and equity accounting have, however, been excluded. Consolidation is not mandatory. The Board has used the principles of consistency, prudence, accruals, going concern, materiality, and fair presentation. Where board regulations do not cover reportable transactions, either industry practices or the International Accounting Standards should be used.

The Turkish Commercial Code requires boards of directors to submit financial information to shareholders at the annual general meeting. A balance sheet and income statement are necessary, along with a report on the company's commercial, financial, and economic situation. The board also submits its proposal to distribute profits and make set-asides into reserves. Financial statements are not required to be published, except for capital market companies, banks, and insurance companies.

Form and format for income statements are not set out with the result that information disclosed is kept to a minimum. The income statement typically begins with gross operating profit. General and administrative expenses may or may not be deducted when arriving at the gross operating profit figure. There are headings of general expenses, financial expenses, other income, and other expenses. Explanations beyond these headings are usually not provided. There is frequently no provision for income tax on the income statement. Distributions of profit to directors or employees are not listed and are accounted for only after the shareholders provide for them at the annual meeting.

The first item on the credit side of the Turkish balance sheet is, as a rule, shareholder equity. The section is subdivided into nominal capital, legal reserves, revaluation reserves, investment revaluation reserves, and reserves for possible losses. There may also be reserves for bad debts, employee termination benefits, accruals, and depreciation. Profits for the year, either before or after charges to legal reserves, are frequently shown as a separate item in the equity section. Losses frequently appear on the asset side of the balance sheet and are not, in fact, offset against profits. Treasury stock does not occur, since companies are not permitted to repurchase their own shares. Revaluation reserves or retained earnings may be used to issue stock dividends upon approval of the shareholders (104).

There are two reserves required by the statute. Annual appropriations of 5 percent of profits after taxes must be made until the reserve total reaches 20 percent of the paid-up share capital. A second reserve is required of appropriation from current profits of ten percent of any distributions made to shareholders that exceed 5 percent of the paid-up share capital. This reserve account can continue to grow without an upper limit. The reserve can be used to offset losses incurred.

Accounting is generally on the basis of tax accounting rules. These vary substantially from generally accepted accrual accounting bases. The tax rules do not permit provisions, reserves, and accruals. Movable fixed assets are originally recorded at cost but are revalued annually by a government issued multiplier, which has reference to the wholesale price index from year to year. The related "surplus" is credited to a nondistributable capital reserve. It is not normally taxed. The useful lives for these movable fixed assets are not used as the period for allocation of costs. Rather, tax rules dictate lives for annual depreciation charges (126, 105).

Bending the accounting rules in ways that increase income is usually tolerated. Thus, losses are sometimes covered by capitalizing interest, exchange losses, or other items that under GAAP would be expensed in the current period. This, of course, results in financial statement income reported at falsely high amounts. Lower of cost or market rules are not used for valuing inventories. Obsolete stock is rarely written off. Neither are recognized in the income tax procedures.

Land improvements are recorded originally at cost with subsequent revaluations made as permitted by tax laws. Depreciation is taken on the straight line basis of up to 25 percent per year. Buildings are recorded at original cost and may be revalued each year but depreciation is restricted to two percent of the original cost per year. For factories, the rate is 4 percent per year.

When another business is purchased, valuation is recorded at initial cost with no provisions for equity, pooling of interests, or purchase accounting. Marketable securities are carried at cost. Requirements for consolidation do not exist but are permitted. Some large businesses do prepare consolidated financial statements, but these do not follow international accounting practices. Companies owned 25 to 50 percent are consolidated as subsidiaries. Intragroup transactions and unrealized intercompany profits are not eliminated for consolidations. Minority interests are not eliminated. In general, there is no consistency of accounting principles used among the companies in the consolidated group (106).

Since financial accounting follows tax accounting rules, there is no basis for interperiod income tax allocation with its provisions for deferred income tax. Corporate income taxes are not recorded in the financial statements until approved at the annual meeting by the shareholders.

Some accruals for exchange gains and losses are mandatory for tax purposes, but in general, no provisions are made for accruals. Transactions are recorded only on the basis of invoice date and are usually recognized in the period when the invoice was issued, regardless of when the services were rendered. However, tax authorities are not likely to challenge when recognition of income accruals increases taxable income.

Interest is only recognized on the stated values for long-term loans. There is no recognition of implicit interest rates prevalent in international accounting practices (107).

A breakthrough for financial reports for companies listed with the Capital Markets Board became effective in 1989. These regulations require books to be kept on a tax basis, but allowed them to be adjusted by the use of tax disallowable expense accounts to conform with the regulations set forth by the Capital Markets Board for financial reporting.

The regulations spell out the form and content of the financial statements, which include the balance sheet, income statement, and statement of changes in financial position. Required content of financial statement notes include appropriate information on accounting principles, contingent liabilities, subsequent events, and other appropriate explanations of accounts.

Financial reports of capital market companies must be published in the Official Commercial Gazette and in no less than two daily newspapers. The Capital Markets Board requirements include very specific forms for each financial statement. Marketable securities must be valued at cost except where market is more than 10 percent below cost, in which case a provision to market value is required.

Inventories are carried at original cost, except where net realizable value is more than 10 percent below cost. Inventory methods must use consistent valuation principles between categories of inventory. Interest, financial expenses, and administrative overhead may not be included. Trade investments are generally accounted for at cost unless market values declines are deemed to be permanent. Losses on foreign exchange changes on long-term debt taken out for the purchase of property, plant, and equipment may be capitalized and allocated along with depreciation of the assets involved. Goodwill arising from a purchase acquisition of another business is expensed over five years. Consolidations are handled in the same way as described for noncapital market companies. Deferred income tax accounting is not presently covered by the Capital Markets Board financial reporting regulations, but International Accounting Standards for deferred income taxes should be applied. Disclosure in foot notes must be made for a wide variety of items (108).

Chapter Eleven

Accounting Environments in Selected Small Gulf States

In a continuing review of the legal and institutional climate facing business and accounting practices in the Middle East, this chapter presents a selective discussion of Gulf states. Bahrain and the United Arab Emirates have been chosen for special attention, since those jurisdictions have become major offshore financial centers and transportation hubs. As such, they have the potential for being major players in the growing linkages of the Arab world to the global economy. Beyond those jurisdictions, the business environment of Qatar will also be discussed.

BAHRAIN

Businesses in Bahrain are required to register with the Ministry of Commerce. Business entities organized as sole proprietorships are allowed only for Bahrain nationals. Foreign company branches or representative offices may be operated after approval and registration with the Ministry of Commerce. Such units set up as regional distribution centers for services or goods do not require sponsorship by a Bahrain national in the same general area of business. A Bahrain national must sponsor all other branches or representative offices. The parent company must be a viable entity and must take responsibility for all branch obligations. The unit must be registered in the Commercial Register and follow other procedures similar to other businesses (Price Waterhouse 1997a, 64, 65).

Partnerships may be any of three kinds: general, limited, or limited by shares. Partners must assume joint liability for partnership debts up to their total wealth. Limits are not set for minimum or maximum capital requirements. All partners must share profits and losses, with methods for allocating profits or losses stated in the partnership agreement. Partnership ownership shares may not be transferred to nonpartners unless provided for in the partnership agreement. Withdrawing partners will be liable only for obligations prior to withdrawing. Any new partners are held liable for all partnership obligations both before their entry and after (59). Foreign ownership rights in a general partnership may not exceed 49 percent.

The general partnership name must contain at least one partner's name with "and Partners" followed by "Bahrain Partnership Co." The partnership must be entered in the Commercial Register and the partnership agreement in summary published in the *Official Gazette* and in a local publication. The following information is required in the partnership agreement: partnership name and address; main office and branches; partners' names and nationality; total capital and percentage share for each partner; persons responsible for management and authorized to sign for the partnership; profit sharing arrangements among partners; and dates of partnership fiscal year (58).

Unless provided otherwise in the partnership agreement, partners must arrive at decisions by unanimous vote. Amendments to the partnership agreement require unanimous partner approval. Any partner may examine partnership books and records. Unless barred in the partnership agreement, any partner may participate in partnership management. Partners are not permitted to be in a business similar to the partnership's business unless other partners consent.

Any partner may participate in managing the business except where prohibited by the partnership agreement. Management of the partnership may be undertaken by a nonpartner. If a partner who is appointed to manage the partnership by the partnership agreement is removed by court order upon the request of a majority of the partners, the partnership is considered dissolved. A manager who is a partner but was not named so in the partnership agreement may be dismissed by a partnership majority without dissolving the partnership.

The general partnership can be dissolved by unanimous agreement of the partners. The death or bankruptcy of a partner will not cause the partnership to be dissolved if the remaining partners choose to carry on the business. Creditors may sue for payment from the partnership or personal assets of the partners. Any partner may examine the accounting records of the partnership and related records. The statutes of Bahrain contain no requirements for the keeping of accounting records and books by general partnerships, nor is there a legal requirement to appoint an auditor (60).

Many of the provisions of the law for general partnerships also apply to limited partnerships. The limited partnership, in addition to one or more general partners with unlimited liability, may have partners with liability for partnership obligations limited to contributions to the business entity. The trade name of the limited partnership may not contain the name of a limited partner. The limited partnership must have Bahraini national general partners who hold more than 50 percent of the partnership capital. Limited partners may not take part in the management. Should a limited partner do so, unlimited liability will be imposed. The limited partnership may be dissolved upon any partner's application to and approval by the court (61).

A partnership limited by shares is a mixture of general partnership and corporation provisions. One or more general partners must assume responsibility for all partnership obligations to the extent of their capital shares. The name of the partnership should contain one or more general partners' names. It may also contain an artificial name or a reflection of the objectives of the entity. Formation requirements are similar to those set out for corporations. The Ministry of Commerce has prescribed the format for the partnership limited by shares agreement. Official authorization for the partnership is not required.

At least four promoters are required to form the partnership, which must have at least one general partner and ten limited partners. Capital contributions must total more than BD 10,000. The capital must be equally divided in par value negotiable shares. Bahrain nationals only may be partners, unless foreign expertise or capital is needed, in which case no more than 49 percent of capital may be owned by foreign partners. The requirements to build a general reserve from earnings are the same as for corporations.

The partnership agreement should specify the names and responsibilities of the general partners who will manage and administer the partnership. Legal provisions are the same as for the general partnership for dismissal, rights, and obligations of the managers. Management salaries and other emoluments should be as stated in the partnership bylaws. If the management remuneration is stated in terms of percentage of net profit, the statute sets a limit of 10 percent of net income (63).

Provisions in the law for an annual general meeting of partners, both general and limited, is similar to that for corporations. The general partners must approve changes to the partnership agreement. A board of control of no less than three partners must be elected by vote of the limited partners to oversee partnership affairs, examine accounting records and reports, and call general meetings, should irregularities be found. The board also reports to the annual partnership general meeting (63).

The law does not set forth specifics on partnerships limited by share requirements for accounting books and related records. However, a statutory auditor must be appointed to report on whether proper account books have been kept. The general expectation is that records and books similar to those for corporations will be kept. A register of mortgages and loans other than debentures is required (64).

Bahrain corporations may be exempt joint stock companies, closed joint stock companies, or public joint stock companies. The exempt joint stock and the closed joint stock companies may be wholly owned by foreign shareholders. The public joint stock company may not have more than 49 percent foreign ownership (46).

An exempt company must have its main offices in Bahrain but must have only offshore operations. To engage in financial arenas, the exempt company must have Bahrain Monetary Agency approval. Such exempt organizations may not hold property or land in Bahrain. A maximum corporate operational life of twenty-five years may be extended with Ministry of Commerce approval.

The closed joint stock company form of incorporation is authorized for an entity that will not offer public shares. This corporate form does not require an Amiri Decree if there are at least five promoters guaranteeing that the incorporation will comply with the Commercial Companies Law. All shares must be fully paid and deposited in a bank authorized by the Ministry of Commerce. Company particulars must be placed in the Commercial Register and publicly in the *Official Gazette* and one other publication. Formation and registration procedures are the same as for an exempt company. Foreign interests may wholly own such closed joint stock companies if its business is that of an industrial company. Service companies setting up regional distribution centers for goods and services in Bahrain may also be 100 percent foreign owned (47–48). Capital in a closed joint stock company must be at least BD 200,000.

Public joint stock companies may only be established with the permission of the Ministry of Commerce. A promoter or promoters, some of whom may be foreigners, are required to agree to a memorandum of association and to apply for a company license. The particulars of the memorandum and the articles of association must comply with the contents and formats of the Ministry of Commerce. For public joint stock companies, foreign shareholders may not exceed 49 percent of ownership.

The main offices of corporations incorporated in Bahrain must be in Bahrain. Legal incorporation begins with the date of the decree. The registration of the new company is required to appear in the Official Gazette and another publication. The phrase "Bahrain Joint Stock Company" is required after the name of all incorporated companies. The Bahraini currency is used to denominate corporate capital, which must be in equal shares that are negotiable. Individual share value may be from BD 1 to BD 100. If shares are sold above par, the excess after expenses is set into a capital reserve, although procedures are not set forth in the legislation for operation of this reserve. Shares may not be issued at a discount. Share transfers are accomplished in accordance with the memorandum and the articles of association approved by the Ministry of Commerce. Shares may be issued for full cash payment or not less than 20 percent of share value during the subscription period, with the remainder paid within four years of the final incorporation date. Shares may be issued for property the value of which has been approved by two-thirds of shareholders paying in cash and an expert appointed by the High Court. (51). A corporation must hold in general reserve 10 percent of annual profits until such amount is 25 percent of the total par value of share capital (77).

For a public joint stock company, capital must total at least BD 500,000. In the formation of public joint stock companies founding shareholders must subscribe to at least 7 percent of total capital, but not more than 20 percent before a public prospectus is issued for public subscriptions. An exception can be made with the approval of the Council of Ministers to allow founding shareholders to subscribe to up to 40 percent of the corporate capital. At least sixty promoters are necessary to win approval of this exception (48–49).

After promoters receive approval from the Ministry of Commerce, the prospectus is published in the Official Gazette and at least one other local publication five days before subscriptions are to begin. The subscription period may be from fifteen days to three months and may be extended with the approval of the Ministry of Commerce for another three months. For the incorporation to proceed, all shares must be fully subscribed. The Ministry of Commerce may allow the promoters to reduce total capital or to subscribe for all remaining shares. All subscription applicants must be resident in Bahrain. A list of subscribers is required to be provided to the Directorate of Commerce and Company Affairs. An initial meeting of shareholders is convened within forty-five days from the end of the period for subscriptions. A quorum must represent at least one-half of all subscribed corporate capital. At this initial meeting, auditors and board of directors are elected. A report from promoters is received and the shareholders declare the incorporation to be complete. The newly elected board is responsible for providing to the Directorate of Commerce and Company Affairs the minutes and resolutions of the meeting, documentary proof that establishment procedures have been proper, and a listing of subscribers together with subscription totals (50).

There are no provisions for issuance of preferred, convertible, voting, or nonvoting stock. Companies may issue publicly registered debenture bonds after approval at an ordinary general shareholder meeting. Such debentures can only be issued to Bahrain nationals. Public issuance of debentures by subscription may only be through a national bank after a proper prospectus has been issued. Closed companies are prohibited from issuing negotiable bonds. Debentures may not be issued until shareholder capital is fully paid in, nor can the value of the debentures exceed the total paid in capital.

After incorporation, an increase in company shareholder capital requires the approval of shareholders in an extraordinary general meeting. Current shareholders have first right to subscribe. For a public offering, an audited prospectus is required and procedures are similar to original issuance at the formation of the corporation. Capital may also be decreased at an extraordinary general shareholder meeting, at which a report of auditors is read explaining the reasons for such a decrease (51).

A corporate board of directors elected by shareholders is responsible for corporate management. Members of the board should be three to twelve in number appointed for renewable three-year terms by secret ballot at the general meeting. A majority must be Bahrain nationals, except with permission of the Council of Ministers. Each director must own shares with par value of at least BD 2,500 and assign these shares to secure third party claims. No public servants may be board members unless the government is involved in the corporation formation. Directors may receive total remuneration up to 10 percent of corporate net profit, less proper reserves and expenses. Directors must be free from direct or indirect interests in contracts or transactions entered into by the company, unless exceptions are authorized by shareholders. They may not participate in other similar entities. Cash loans or loan guarantees may not be made by the corporation for a director. Any person may not be a director of more than three Bahrain companies and managing director of only one. Directors are expected to meet at least four times per year and have a quorum of at least half of the directors in order to conduct business. Boards of directors may not mortgage company assets, make loans that exceed three years in duration, sell the place of corporate business, or make guarantee bonds (52).

In an annual general meeting of shareholders at which all shareholders may attend and participate can be considered any matter except those matters reserved for an extraordinary meeting. The bylaws may restrict attendance and participation to shareholders who own a minimum number of shares. Extraordinary shareholder general meetings must be called to transact and approve the following: modify corporate articles of incorporation or bylaws, dissolve or merge the corporation, change share capital, or dispose of the entire business for which the company had been established. Approval by two-thirds of votes at a meeting of holders of 75 percent of the company's shares is required. Should a quorum not be available at a first meeting, the quorum for a second meeting called within thirty days will need only holders of 50 percent of the total shares. Should a quorum in this second meeting not be available, a third meeting's quorum will be those present. Decisions at any of these meetings will need only a majority of those present, assuming such business that is transacted is approved by the Ministry of Commerce. The following are not permitted, unless approved unanimously by shareholders or agreed to by an individual shareholder concerned: an increase in financial liability of a shareholder, a decrease in the percentage of net profit specified in the bylaws to be distributed to shareholders, limiting the right of a shareholder to bring legal action for damages against the board of directors, and changing the qualifications required in order for a shareholder to attend and vote in a general shareholder meeting (53). Once formed, a corporation continues to have a legal identity until liquidated by liquidators appointed by shareholders or by the court. Such liquidators must take an inventory of assets and liabilities to prepare a balance sheet for dissolution (54).

There are no statutory requirements that businesses in Bahrain keep books and records. In practice, businesses use accounting systems of their own choice and in the language of their own choice. English and Arabic are the usual languages. Corporations, limited liability companies, and partnerships limited by shares are required to keep shareholder registers. Corporations must maintain registers for board of directors' meeting minutes and for debentures and loans held by the corporation (74).

Annual audits are mandated for corporations, limited liability companies and partnerships limited by shares. Entities in the financial services sector must file annual audited financial statements with the Bahrain Monetary Agency. Auditor duties contained in the Commercial Companies Law require the auditor to attend the annual general shareholder meeting where the auditor should read the audit report (74).

In accordance with the 1996 Legislative Decree, which now regulates the auditing profession, the Ministry of Commerce must license auditors before practice in Bahrain. The decree established a code of ethics, academic preparation, and other requirements necessary to be licensed. Auditing procedures or standards have not been codified. Therefore, auditors may follow the standards of their own choice taking into consideration local customs and usage. The form of audit report for corporations, limited liability companies, and partnerships limited by shares is specified in the Commercial Code. The Bahrain Monetary Agency specifies bank audit reports content (75).

Boards of directors of Bahrain corporations and limited liability companies are required to report annually on the company's affairs. The statutory requirements contained in the Commercial Companies Law require the board of directors chairman to publish this report, which must include the balance sheet, profit and loss statement, the auditor's report, and a summary of the directors' report in local newspapers at least fifteen days prior to the stockholders' annual general meeting. Beginning in 1993, they were required to file the financial statements with the Ministry of Commerce (76).

The statutes do not require particulars as to financial statement form and content, except that companies are required to follow generally accepted accounting principles. Within Bahrain, no government or professional group has been charged with the formulation of accounting principles. The Ministry of Commerce, the Bahrain Monetary Agency, and other government agencies are encouraging all companies to use International Accounting Standards (74).

All accountants and auditors working in Bahrain may join the Bahrain Society of Accountants, the country's professional accounting organization. Only Bahrain nationals are eligible to be elected to the Society's Board of Directors. It remains to be seen how effective the organization will be in moving toward improvements in accounting and auditing (75).

Since 1992, the Bahrain Monetary Agency has required banks and other financial companies to adopt International Accounting Standards. The financial sector is more strictly regulated by the Bahrain Monetary Agency, which formulates regulations for banks more than other business sectors (77).

In general, accounting and auditing in Bahrain companies depends upon the level of accounting sophistication of company managers and auditors. International Accounting Standards are followed by most large entities.

Bahrain is host to a regional finance center with offshore banking units and investment banks. Such offshore units may not offer services to Bahrain residents.

The Bahrain Monetary Agency requires that all such offshore operations provide annual audited financial statements within ninety days after fiscal year-end (64).

QATAR

In the Islamic state of Qatar, the local currency unit is the Qatar riyal, which is divisible into 100 dirhams. The riyal is linked to the U.S. dollar in a fixed rate of exchange of U.S. $1 to QR 3.6411. The currency is fully convertible. No restrictions are made on repatriation of funds whether capital or earnings.

All registered businesses in Qatar are subject to oversight by the Ministry of Finance, Economy and Commerce. This ministry controls the prices of certain goods seen as essential, such as foodstuffs. Government and partially state-owned monopolies dominate many economic sectors. Greater privatization and competition is planned. In 1995, an Amir decree authorized the establishment of the Doha Securities Market, which lists only Qatari companies. Foreign ownership and investment is strictly controlled. Foreign companies may not be commercial importers. Foreign firms must sell to a Qatari agent, who in turn distributes products within Qatar. Patents may be registered for ten years and extended for five years only. Trademarks can be registered indefinitely for ten-year periods, but if not used for five years, can be voided by the court.

Business enterprises in Qatar may be formed as sole proprietorships, joint ventures, partnerships, limited liability companies, or corporations. The sole proprietorship form of business is permitted only for Qatar nationals or for nationals from other GCC countries. In fact, Law 20 of 1963 prohibits foreign nationals from entering into trade or industry in Qatar unless a Qatari partner owns at least 51 percent of the business capital. An exception is possible for foreign company branches. With the permission of an Amiri Decree, a foreign company may operate a wholly owned branch in Qatar. Foreigners may also operate through a local sponsor in such areas as advisory and professionals services. There are business activities that are reserved exclusively for Qatar nationals.

In Qatar, joint ventures are considered to be extensions of the existing venturing entities that are not separate legal entities. The share of each entity in the joint venture is viewed as a legal extension of each venture participant's existing organization. There are no separate registration or publication requirements. The business entities entering into a joint venture should prepare bylaws in which they state objectives, rights, and liabilities of each participant entity, and a plan for allocating profits or losses. The recourse of their parties is only to the venturing entity with which the third party dealt. If, however, the third party is lead to believe that the joint venture is a separate entity, the joint venture will be treated as a general partnership in regard to recourse for said third party. Though there are no stated rules for management of or the keeping of accounting books and records, the joint venturing participants must abide by the Qatar taxation laws (Price Waterhouse 1996a, 57).

There are three kinds of partnerships recognized. In a general partnership, two or more partners associate together through a partnership agreement. This agreement should include names, nationalities, and addresses of each partner; the objectives and duration of the partnership; the head office address; capital with percentage share from each partner; names of the partnership management or signatory authorities; and the plan for distributing profits and losses among partners. Every partner must share in profits and losses. The partnership should have bylaws agreed to by the partners. Once formed, the partnership agreement may be changed only upon a unanimous vote of the partners. Normally, the partners need a majority vote for other decisions.

Foreign partnership interests must be limited to no more than 49 percent unless an exception is granted by an Amiri Degree. Amounts for minimum or maximum required capital have not been set. Partners' interests may not be transferred to anyone other than another partner, except as provided for in the original partnership agreement. Partners have unlimited liability for partnership obligations.

Partners may examine the accounting books and records kept for the partnership. They also have the right to participate in management of the partnership unless the partnership agreement states otherwise. A nonpartner or a partner may manage the partnership. Managers have the right to take any management action unless the partnership agreement provides otherwise. The manager is not permitted to carry on a similar business or to contract for personal gain with the partnership except with the agreement of all partners. A partner manager who was specified as manager in the partnership agreement can be removed from management by court order only after a majority of partners have requested the action. Should such actions be taken, the partnership is considered dissolved. A manager who does not hold membership in the partnership can be dismissed by a majority vote of the partners.

A partner, asserting that another partner has not fulfilled partnership obligations, may sue for the dissolution of the partnership or the dismissal of a partner from the partnership. The partnership can be dissolved in a number of other ways including completion of the business of the partnership, unanimous decision of partners to dissolve, and the occurrence of large losses or bankruptcy (Price Waterhouse 1996a, 53).

The law does not specify content or types of books of account or records of the partnership. Nor does it require appointment of an auditor. Partnerships must adhere to the provisions of the tax law.

Limited partnerships have a minimum of one fully liable partner and limited liability partners. Fully liable partners share responsibility for partnership obligations to the extent of their personal wealth. Limited partners are liable only for their partnership investment. A limited partnership is formed in the same way as a general partnership. A limited partner's name must not appear in the partnership name; nor can the limited partner take part in partnership management. Other provisions of the general partnership also apply to the limited partnership.

The third type, partnership limited by shares, must have at least one general partner with unlimited liability and at least ten limited liability partners. This form combines features of the limited partnership with features from the limited liability company and the corporate form. The partnership limited by shares must be registered in the Commercial Register and its partnership details must be published in a local newspaper. The name of the partnership must include "partnership limited by shares." The format and charter of the partnership limited by shares must be that prescribed by the Ministry of Finance, Economy and Commerce. The charter and bylaws must be registered with the Ministry before activation of the partnership. Capital of this type of partnership must total at least QR 200,000. Shares are to be issued that have a par value and are equal in value. The enabling legislation does not include provisions for preferred stock, convertible stock, nonvoting shares, or the issuance of debentures.

Public sale of stock is permitted under the same provisions as a corporation which issues stock to the public. But, the provisions of transfer are the same as those for a general partnership. The rights and obligations of partners and managers follow the general partnership rules as specifically amended. Limited partnership management must be carried out by one or more unlimited liability partners. The names of such manager or general partners and their rights and obligations should be specified in the partnership agreement. The corporate laws for corporate directors apply to these manager–partners as to their authority and as to rights of dismissal. The rules applicable to liquidation of the general partnership apply to liquidation of limited partnerships.

A partner general meeting is required in which both general and limited partners rights are governed by the corporate law. Such a meeting may not take actions to amend the partnership agreement or arrangements relating to the trading activities of the partnership. The partnership is required to elect a board of control of at least three limited partners. Only unlimited partners may vote in the election of the board of control. This board is empowered to examine the accounting books and records of the partnership, to prepare a report for the general meeting of partners, and to call a general partner meeting when irregularities are thought to exist. There are no legislated requirements as to the form and content of accounting records and reports. The partnership must comply with rules set out in Qatar tax legislation. For partnerships limited by shares that have over QR 500,000 in capital, a statutory auditor is required. Duties and responsibilities of the auditor are the same as for statutory auditors of corporations (Price Waterhouse 1996a, 56).

Under the Commercial Companies Law of 1981, a limited liability company must have at least two shareholders who have unlimited liability for company debts. Total shareholders may not exceed thirty in number. Qatar or GCC nationals must own at least 51 percent of the limited liability company shares. An exception is possible through the grant of an Amiri Decree. The phrase "with limited liability" must be included after the company's name. This type of company may not operate in the field of banking, investment, or insurance brokerage. Company capital must total at least QR 200,000. Shares must be equal in value with a par value of at least QR 1,000.

The company must be registered in the Commercial Register maintained at the Ministry of Finance, Economy and Commerce. The formation must be published in a local newspaper. All shares must be distributed and paid in full by the original subscribers before business may commence. Shares may only be sold at par. Therefore no capital stock premium can occur.

The articles of incorporation and bylaws should include the company name; the head office address; the amount of capital and how subscribed; any restrictions on share transfer; the name, address, and nationality of each share subscriber; the name of company management; and the plan of distribution of profits and losses. Loans can not be raised by sale to the public. There are no provisions for preferred, convertible, or nonvoting shares. Shares are not freely transferable. Shares may be assigned to another existing shareholder. Should a transfer to a nonshareholder third party be planned, existing shareholders must be notified and given a one-month period to purchase the shares on the same terms as the third party.

A board of directors elected from or chosen by the shareholders operates the company. Should the total number of shareholders be less than ten, the nondirector shareholders will constitute a board of control. This board may make proposals for profit distributions. It may examine all books and records of account, request the directors to report on company management, and request that financial statements be prepared and submitted to the shareholder general meeting.

An annual shareholder general meeting should be held, at which the reports of the auditor and the board of control are heard. Company financial statements should be presented at this meeting, as should the directors' proposals for profit distribution. A majority of 50 percent of outstanding shares is normally required for approval of actions, with 75 percent being necessary for changes to the articles of incorporation or bylaws and for liquidation of the company. There are no statutory requirements on dividends but a reserve that is unavailable for dividends must be maintained of 10 percent of annual net profit, until the total funds reserve equals 50 percent of share capital.

Limited liability companies must keep a register of all shareholders. The Commercial Companies Law indicates that bylaws must contain provisions for company accounts but form or contents are not specified. Companies must comply with taxation requirements. Should capital of the company be above QR 500,000, an auditor is required. The statute lists no restrictions upon or duties expected of the auditor (Price Waterhouse 1996a, 50).

Corporations may be formed under the Law of 1981. Corporations can be formed outside the Law of 1981 by the Qatar government or a government authority. Such formations may be accomplished alone or in partnership with one or more founders. In these cases, the corporation is subject to the agreements between the contracting parties at time of incorporation and to the provisions in its articles of incorporation.

An Amiri Decree is normally used to form a public corporation. But, formation of a closed corporation may be without an Amiri Decree if shares are not publicly sold; there are less than six shareholders; contributed capital is at least QR 200,000; and an official published document in the *Official Gazette* indicates that the corporation bylaws and articles of incorporation conform to the law. Such a corporation has the attributes of a limited liability company.

The formation of a public corporation requires the submission to the Minister of Finance, Economy and Commerce of an application to be registered as a commercial corporation and for the issuance of a decree. Articles of incorporation and bylaws must be submitted that follow the format set out by the Ministry. These should include the corporation name and head office address, which must be in Qatar; purposes and duration of the corporation; shareholder names, nationalities, and addresses; and share capital amounts and numbers of shares. When the Decree of Incorporation is granted and published in the *Official Gazette*, the public corporation may proceed to the sale of shares to the public. Prior to issuing a prospectus, the founding shareholders must pay in capital equal to the value of at least 10 percent of the shares but not more than 20 percent. They must also receive permission from the Minster of Finance, Economy and Commerce to proceed with issuance of the prospectus and public sale of shares.

The incorporation will proceed only if all shares have been fully subscribed. Only residents of Qatar may subscribe. All shareholders must be Qatari nationals except that subscribing shareholders may be GCC nationals. In exceptional cases, permission may also be received from the Ministry of Finance, Economy and Commerce for foreign ownership in cases where foreign investment or foreign expertise is needed. No maximum number of shareholders has been set. The minimum number is five.

In the case where total shares are not fully subscribed, the total capital may be reduced by the founding shareholders with the permission of the Ministry. In such an eventuality, subscribers may choose to withdraw. Final incorporation takes place when a detailed listing of share subscribers is submitted to the Comtroller of Companies, and an initial meeting of shareholders is convened to elect auditors and the board of directors (Price Waterhouse 1996a, 42).

The capital of a Qatar corporation is required to be denominated in Qatar currency divided into negotiable shares of equal value. Capital must be in an amount sufficient for the purposes of the corporation with a minimum capital paid-up of at least QR 500,000 for a public corporation or QR 200,000 for a closed corporation. Par value must be at least QR 100, but no more than QR 1,000. Shares may not be issued at a discount but may be issued at a premium. No provisions exist in the law for preferred, convertible, or nonvoting shares. There are no provisions for loans or debentures. Corporate shares are transferable by registration taking place at time of sale between the buyer, the seller, and a company official. Only a Qatari national may purchase shares if held currently by a Qatari.

Authorized capital may be increased after the original total amount has been paid in. Existing shareholders have a preemptive right to purchase any additional shares issued in proportion to their holdings. Authorized capital may be reduced after the corporation experiences losses, but approval of two-thirds of members present at an extraordinary general shareholder meeting is required.

The board of directors elected by shareholders administers the corporation. Their number is required to be at least five and no more than eleven. Each must own at least 1 percent of the outstanding shares, or shares valued at QR 10,000 at a minimum, which are assigned to secure rights of third parties. Should the government participate in the corporation, it has the right to appoint and remove its own directors, who are not required to hold shares. An individual may be a director of no more than three corporations unless such director owns at least 10 percent of the shares of each. Any person may only be the managing director or chairman of one Qatar corporation. Directors may not have an interest in transactions or contracts of the corporation without the permission of the shareholders. Directors may not be involved with administrative functions of a similar corporation. The corporation may not guarantee or grant a loan to a director. Corporate bylaws should enumerate director remuneration.

All shareholders of ten or more shares are always permitted by law to attend the annual meeting. Shareholders with less than ten shares may attend unless a minimum holding was set in the corporate bylaws. Any matter may be discussed and voted upon at a general meeting except those specified as requiring an extraordinary meeting: modification of the original articles of incorporation or bylaws; dissolution or amalgamation of the corporation; share capital increases or decreases; or sale or disposal of the corporation. Larger quorums and passage percentages are required at extraordinary meetings.

Within four months of the close of the year-end, an annual shareholder meeting must be held to consider the financial statements and reports of directors and auditors. A statutory reserve that is not normally available for distribution to shareholders must be set aside of at least 10 percent of annual corporate net income, until the reserve totals 50 percent of share capital. This reserve may be used to pay dividends of no more than 5 percent in a year when corporate profits would not support such a payment.

Corporations may be liquidated under a number of conditions: the object of incorporation has been obtained; the corporation is bankrupt; the time period fixed for corporate duration has expired; or legal requirements or a court order dictates. The directors must call an extraordinary general meeting for possible liquidation if corporate losses total at least half of the original capital. Liquidators may be appointed by a civil court or by the corporation. Such liquidators must prepare a balance sheet upon dissolution that indicates the remaining share of each shareholder. The final accounting must be audited.

Corporations are required to keep registers of shareholders and of meeting minutes of the board of directors. Corporate accounting records and books must be kept, but specific guidance is not provided for financial reports. Books of account may be prepared in any language. English and Arabic are the most commonly used.

Income tax laws require all businesses to keep a general ledger, an inventory book, subsidiary records required, and all supporting documents. In practice, only business entities that have partial or complete foreign ownership are taxed, and therefore only they are legally required to keep books of account. Foreign investors are responsible to file properly and to pay the correct amount of corporate income tax on business in Qatar. Qatar does not levy personal taxes, value added taxes, or sales taxes.

Qatar corporations are required by the Commercial Companies Law to appoint an auditor who is listed on the Register of Auditors kept by the Ministry of Finance, Economy and Commerce. The tax authorities also enforce this requirement. Each firm that must file income tax returns must include a full set of audited financial statements for their activities in Qatar. Thus, all businesses in which foreign investors participate are required to have an annual audit and to prepare full sets of financial statements (Price Waterhouse 1996a, 47).

Beyond the rudiments, there are no accounting principles or practice requirements stated in Qatar legislation. There are no government or professional bodies that have the responsibility to formulate accounting and auditing practices. The form and content of financial statements is not addressed. Legally, corporations, limited liability companies, and partnerships limited by shares must produce a balance sheet and income statement. A directors' report is also required.

Tax returns must be accompanied by the full complement of audited financial statements common in developed countries. This includes the statement of sources and applications of funds. Most businesses that must file with the tax authorities follow International Accounting Standards. However, because most reporting is in conjunction and in compliance with tax rules, book and tax differences arise if at all, very rarely.

Law 7 of 1974 contains provisions designed to ensure that the auditor maintains objectivity and independence. The company auditor is required by law to report whether proper books of account have been kept and whether the financial statements fairly present the position of the company. In practice, auditors follow International Accounting Standards.

A standard audit report has not been formulated. By law, the audit report for corporation financial statements must cover the following matters. The auditor must indicate that sufficient information was obtained for satisfactory performance of the audit; the statements contain all the requirements of the law and of the company's bylaws; the statements fairly and truly present the company standing; regular account records have been kept by the company; inventory taking was in accordance with established principles; information in the directors' report is in accordance with records of the company; to the extent of information availability, no violations of the Commercial Companies Law or the bylaws of the company occurred, which may have a material effect on the financial position of the company; and if violations were noted, indication of whether they are continuing. Audit reports for a partnership limited by shares and a limited liability company cover the same points. The auditor's report for all three types of entities is presented to the annual general owners' meeting. Declarations filed with the income tax report are fully audited and detailed. The reports and all accompanying documentation is required to be signed by both the auditor and the taxpayer (Price Waterhouse 1996a, 69).

THE UNITED ARAB EMIRATES

Businesses operating in the United Arab Emirates must adhere to federal rules and the local rules of each emirate. Local regulations are subject to more frequent changes than the federal and of course apply only within each emirate. The UAE currency is the dirham (DH), which is divided into one-hundred fils. The dirham is fully convertible and is pegged to the U.S. dollar (Price Waterhouse 1996b, 8). The U.S. dollar is equal to DH 3.671. This peg was established in 1980 (19). The repatriation of foreign investments and earnings has not been restricted (32). The UAE maintains no protective duties (27). Only a few items have price controls, and these are generally medicines or petroleum products (41).

The banking system is well developed but there is no official stock exchange. An Abu Dhabi commercial bank carries on an unofficial over-the-counter market for a small number of public joint stock companies in the country, twenty-three in number in 1996 (44). Only UAE nationals may trade in this market (41).

Regulations applicable to all emirates are contained in The Federal Commercial Companies Law, Federal Law 8 of 1984 as amended by Federal Law 13 of 1988. This legislation allows businesses to be organized as sole proprietorships, joint ventures, partnerships with mixed liability, simple limited partnerships, general partnerships, partnerships with limited liability, private shareholding companies, or public shareholding companies. With the exception of the joint venture, each of these forms is viewed as a separate legal entity.

Businesses of all forms operating within the United Arab Emirates must file and be added to the register of companies for the emirate in which it is established. Each business entity must also be registered in the Ministry of Economy and Commerce Commercial Register and with the municipal chamber of commerce. Each business must obtain from the economic department of the appropriate emirate a license that specifies authorized activities for the organization.

Licensing arrangements differ from emirate to emirate. There are generally separate licenses for each major type of business to be undertaken—for example, a trade license for trading activities, a professional license to practice a profession, or an industrial license for manufacturing. A license must be obtained in each emirate in which the business seeks to operate a business (Deloitte Touche Tohmatsu International 1996, 18). In general, licenses are granted only to industrial projects owned by UAE nationals or owned at least 51 percent by gulf nationals. Companies established in the free zone area are excepted and may be 100 percent foreign owned (7–8).

The sole proprietorship form of business enterprise is not subject to the Federal Commercial Companies Law. This form is open only to UAE and GCC nationals. Foreign ownership of sole proprietorships is not permitted (Price Waterhouse 1996b, 70).

The primary corporate form of enterprise in the UAE is the public shareholding company, which is authorized to issue capital in negotiable shares of equal value. Liability of owners is limited to the par value of shares owned. A public company capital must total at least DH 10 million. The entire company capital must be subscribed to, with at least 25 percent of nominal share value paid in at formation and the remainder normally payable within five years from incorporation date. Treasury shares are permitted. A legal reserve must be created equal to 10 percent of net profit, until one-half of total share capital is reached. Such a reserve may not be used for distributions to shareholders.

Companies formed in the United Arab Emirates must have at least one owner who is a UAE national. Corporate ownership must be at least 51 percent owned by UAE nationals. Corporate founders must be at least ten in number with a majority being UAE nationals. Company memorandum and articles of association are prepared consistent with a model issued by the Ministry of Economy and Commerce. These must detail the name of the company; its main office location, which must be in the UAE; company duration; reasons for company formation; founders names, addresses, occupations, and nationalities; total capital and total shares including type of shares and value; rights and privileges of each share; and estimated incorporation expenses. The fiscal year of the company must be set in the articles of association (Deloitte Touche Tohmatsu International 1996, 37). Corporate applications must be filed with the ministry and must include an economic feasibility study, together with the memorandum and articles of association (33). Should the time to establish the company be long, the articles of association may indicate that a fixed interest rate will be paid to shareholders during the period of corporate establishment (37).

Within sixty days, the Ministry will issue its decision in the official gazette. A rejection of the incorporation is assumed if approval is not published within that time frame. Upon approval of the incorporation application and prior to inviting public subscription, founders must subscribe to no less than 20 percent but no more than 45 percent of the authorized capital. The public subscription period must be for at least ten days and no more than ninety days. All shares must be subscribed before the company is considered established (33–34).

A shareholder statutory meeting must be called within thirty days after the subscription period closes to approve founders' plans and to elect the company board of directors and company auditors. A majority of the board and its chairperson must be UAE nationals. The law does not indicate that they must be resident in the UAE. A final formation report is then submitted to the Ministry containing a list of subscribers and the number of shares each subscribed to. The minutes of the statutory meeting indicating approval of shareholders for the memorandum and articles of association are included with the final formation report. Within thirty days, the ministry must issue a decree of incorporation, which is published in the *Official Gazette*, along with the memorandum and articles of association (34).

The corporate board of directors must have at least three but not more than twelve members with terms of office that do not exceed three years, subject to renewal. Directors may be liable to the company for duties performed in a negligent manner. A director may not be a board member of more than five public companies in the United Arab Emirates; nor can a person be chairperson or vice chairperson of more than two United Arab Emirates company boards. An individual may only be managing director of one United Arab Emirates company. Before 1 January of every year, the names of officers and the names and nationalities of board members must be provided to the Ministry, endorsed by the chairperson of the board (37).

Director remuneration should be set out in the articles of incorporation or bylaws. The monetary arrangements may not exceed 10 percent of net profit after a dividend of 5 percent of paid-in capital is set aside. Shareholders by law may dismiss board members by action at a general meeting. New directors must be elected as replacements. These actions must be reported to the Ministry of Economy and Commerce. Company employees are not empowered to have representation on the board of directors; nor may they form work councils (35–36).

Within the four months that follow the close of the company year, an ordinary general meeting of shareholders is required. Such a meeting will be convened upon the request of the company auditors. The place of meeting is not established by law, but the expectation has been that meetings would be held in the United Arab Emirates. A meeting may also be convened upon application of the holders of 30 percent or more of company capital. Further, should holders of 40 percent or more of capital request for proper cause, an extraordinary meeting must be convened. The number of company shares owned determines voting rights at shareholder meetings. Voting may be accomplished by proxy. The memorandum and articles of association may only be altered, upon the vote of at least 75 percent of shares, at an extraordinary shareholder meeting to change company capital, to extend company life or to liquidate the company.

Disclosures or financial statement requirements are not set out in law. By common practice, the reporting that is similar to that of the United Kingdom or the United States is acceptable. Companies are also encouraged but not required to use International Accounting Standards. Consolidated financial statements are normally prepared for UAE parent companies but are not required by law or regulation.

Auditors must be appointed each year at the annual general shareholder meeting. They must be independent of the company and have a license to practice in the United Arab Emirates. Such company auditors must be listed in the register of auditors and accountants under the Federal Law 9 of 1975 (38). The auditors have responsibility for their audit report and for financial statement accuracy. They may be held liable for any negligence on their part.

The auditor attends the general shareholder meeting and reads the audit report to the meeting. The auditor's report must include the auditor's opinion on the following. Was access to information necessary for the audit duties sufficient? Are the balance sheet and profit and loss account factual, in accordance with requirements of law and the company articles, and do they present a true and fair view of the company's financial position? Were proper accounting books kept? Was the inventory taking in accordance with established practices? Is the board of directors' report consistent with company books? Were there in the year audit violations of the company articles of association? (38)

Only after company share capital has been fully paid and company financial statements for at least one year have been published can the United Arab Emirates company issue debentures to the public. Approval of a general meeting of shareholders is required. Prior to public subscriptions for debentures, detailed information must be published in at least two local Arabic daily newspapers. The Ministry must be provided, within one month after debenture subscription, detailed subscription information, such as names and nationalities of subscribers with their subscription amounts (39).

If a public company has lost half of its capital, an extraordinary meeting of shareholders must be called to consider dissolution. Upon the failure of the board to call the meeting or in the event that stockholders do not choose to dissolve the company, a lawsuit seeking company dissolution may be filed by any interested party (39).

Differing from the public company, three or more founders may establish a private company. Minimum capital required is DH 2 million. The same procedures and rules described for the public company apply, with the exception that shares may not be issued to the public. A private company may be converted to a public company by proper procedures and approvals (40).

Two partners as a minimum may form a partnership with limited liability, otherwise known as a limited liability company. There may be as many as fifty partners. A UAE national must own a minimum of 51 percent of the entity capital. Partners shares are not negotiable. Loans may not be raised by public subscriptions. All partners have liability limited to their capital contributions. The company name must include "limited liability." Any purpose within the law may be carried on, except for banking, insurance, and placement of funds for others (40).

The limited liability partnership must be organized with capital of at least DH 150,000 (DH 300,000 in Dubai), divided into shares of equal value of at least DH 1,000. UAE nationals must own capital shares representing 51 percent of total capital. A partners register must be kept at the main partnership office, which contains the name, residence, and occupation of each partner. Total value and number of shares owned by each partner must be listed. A record of share transactions must also be kept in the partnership register (41). Once established, the limited liability partnership must set aside a legal reserve of 10 percent of annual net profit until the reserve equals one-half of total capital.

Partnership management becomes the responsibility of one or more managers selected by the partners. Public liability attaches to these managing partners in a manner akin to that for directors of a corporation. Auditors are selected at a general meeting of the partners. Each year the managing partners are responsible for preparation of the annual balance sheet, and the profit and loss statement, as well as a report of entity activities over the past year.

An annual meeting of partners must be held to review the manager's report, the financial statements, and the auditor's report. The partners must declare dividends. A register of minutes and resolutions of each meeting must be kept (42).

A general partnership with unlimited liability may be formed by two or more persons who are UAE nationals. This form is not open to foreign investors or partners. All partners are fully liable for partnership obligations. In a memorandum of association, the partnership name, address, and purposes must be spelled out. The names of all partners, their domiciles, their dates of birth, and their nationality are included. The capital contributions of each must be listed. The partnership's fiscal year, the date of formation, and, if applicable, the expiration of the partnership must be included. The arrangements for partnership management must be declared including persons permitted to act on behalf of the partnership. Distribution of profits and losses must be indicated (43).

Partners may not engage in a competing business unless permitted by the remaining partners. If the partnership is granted a general trade license, minimum capital must be at least DH 300,000, and the partnership must file audited financial statements with the Ministry of Economy and Commerce each year. There are no requirements to publish the annual financial statements (43).

A simple limited partnership may have one or more general partners who accept unlimited liability, and silent partners whose liability is limited to their capital contributions. Partners must all be UAE nationals. Corporations are not permitted to be partners. The partnership agreement should include similar provisions to the general partnership. The partnership name must not include that of a silent partner. The general partners must accomplish all dealings with external parties. Any internal management role of the silent partners must be spelled out in the partnership agreement. The Ministry of Economy and Commerce does not require the filing of financial statements.

A partnership with mixed liability must be formed by two or more general partners, who are responsible for management, and two or more silent partners. General partners have unlimited liability, while silent partner liability is limited to capital contributions. Capital contributions of limited partners must be at least DH 500,000. Only UAE nationals may be partners. Partner name, nationality, and residence must be included in the memorandum of association. The memorandum must be signed by all general partners, and by silent partners if founders. For general partners, the entity is similar to that of a general partnership. However, rules for formation are similar to those for a public shareholding company (44).

In the UAE, joint ventures may be arranged between two or more parties, corporations, or individuals for the purpose of sharing profits in a venture carried out by one party on behalf of all. The agreement should set forth the rights and obligations of each party in the joint venture, including how profits and losses will be apportioned. The company law requires that the joint venture be carried out in the private name of one of the joint venture parties, who must be a UAE national. The joint venture agreement does not have to be registered in the Commercial Register.

Foreign companies may form a branch in the UAE with the permission of the Ministry of Economy and Commerce or the Dubai Economic Department, if the branch is in Dubai. Prescribed and authenticated forms must be submitted that include a certification by competent home country authorities that the foreign company is well established and registered in the home country. A resolution by the foreign company's board of directors must set out planned branch activities together with the UAE national who will be the company's agent responsible for the branch activities. The foreign company must submit copies of the articles of association attested to by competent home country officials. A report must be submitted that indicates the company's history of operations abroad in the area of operations proposed for the branch. The company's audited balance sheets for the two prior years are also required.

Branch operations may not include industrial activity, transport operations, or commercial activities, because the UAE national must participate in these kind of businesses. Branches established must prepare separate and audited financial statements for branch activities. Branches must be registered in the same way as all other business entities in the UAE (45).

All the businesses recognized under the Federal Commercial Companies Law must maintain accounting records that are appropriate for the scale and nature of the business. Such records of account with supporting documents must be kept for at least five years. The records must show the financial position of the business, and by law, must include a journal and a general ledger.

Audited financial statements must be prepared and filed annually by public and private joint stock companies, free zone establishments, limited liability companies, and branches of foreign companies. A UAE registered auditor must carry out the audit. The auditor has the power to examine all relevant information when auditing the financial statements. The auditor is to determine that the statements prepared by the board of directors actually presents fairly the financial position of the business. The auditor must also indicate whether all of the provisions of federal laws and the company's articles of association have been carried out during the year. The audited financial statements are required to be filed with the Ministry of Economy and Commerce in the case of public and private joint stock companies, limited liability companies, and branches of foreign companies. Free zone establishments must file the audited financial statements with the appropriate free zone authority (Price Waterhouse 1996b, 82–83).

In regard to public accountants in the UAE, the Ministry of Economy and Commerce keeps separate registers that list practicing auditors, trainee auditors, and nonpracticing auditors. Those seeking to be registered must apply to the ministry and provide necessary documentary evidence of their qualifications. If accepted, the auditor is given a certificate of registration and placed on the appropriate roll. UAE and foreign auditors can be registered, but the conditions for the foreign auditor are stricter.

After receiving the certificate of registration, the auditor can apply for a license to open a practice. Prior to passage of new federal legislation in 1995, auditing firms were exempt from the requirement to have UAE partners in majority ownership. Since passage of the 1995 law, all accounting and auditing practices must have at least 51 percent of their owners who are UAE nationals.

The UAE has not constituted a body to set and enforce audit standards. Auditors in the UAE must be independent of clients and must keep confidential all client matters and information. If an auditor is found negligent, damages may be collected for clients. Auditors may also be prosecuted in a criminal case. Auditors usually apply the International Standards on Auditing (83).

Nor has a body been constituted to formulate and oversee generally accepted accounting principles in the UAE. The larger accounting firms generally follow International Accounting Standards. The Companies Law requires only the preparation of the balance sheet and profit and loss accounts without setting out further details. The law does not include the concept of consolidated financial statements with the result that statements prepared for statutory purposes must be on an individual company basis (86).

Banks are more heavily supervised. UAE Central Bank Circular No. 445 sets out the format and disclosures that must be made in bank financial statements. Directors of each public or private joint stock company and of each limited liability company are required to file an annual company activity report with the Ministry, but no precise requirements have been issued. The general practice has been for public joint stock companies to file quite detailed reports, while the private companies and the limited liability companies tend to file basic and brief reports (85).

Unlike most jurisdictions, taxes and tax reporting are not a major problem and thus do not create problems for financial reporting methods. Each emirate has legislation on taxes that include corporate income tax provisions, but in practice these provisions are not enforced. Only oil and gas production companies and branches of foreign banks pay taxes on earnings. Personal income taxes are not levied. There are no sales taxes or value-added taxes. The exception is for alcohol and cigarettes tax. A municipal hotel tax is collected based on services. There is a municipal tax on rents in most emirates of 5 percent for private dwellings and 10 percent for commercial properties (87).

Part Four

Implications for Regional Growth and Change

Chapter Twelve

A Summary of Institutional Specifics

Earlier in this book, the institutional environments impacting business and accounting operations in various Middle Eastern jurisdictions were discussed (Chapters 8–11). Of course, such environmental factors have major impacts upon the present operations and future potential of the economies in question. Efficient domestic laws and procedures are capable of significant contributions to effective business climates, suitable for economic expansion and business growth. Conversely, inhospitable laws and procedures can easily develop into impediments to progress. Certainly domestic institutional circumstances are especially important where they impact international business and economic operations.

In this chapter, an overview of the institutional environments of various jurisdictions discussed earlier will be provided. The purpose is to assess the efficiency of existing institutional environments in facilitating business and economic operations. It is hoped that such an appraisal can establish a basis for comprehending the real and potential impacts that the major international accounting firms are capable of in the Middle Eastern nations under discussion. The jurisdictions concerned will be divided into two groups for examination. First, the institutional environments of Egypt, Saudi Arabia, and Turkey will be considered. Following that, a similar treatment will be afforded various smaller Gulf nations. The chapter will conclude with a brief overview.

THE LARGER NATIONS

The jurisdictions under review in this section were discussed in some detail earlier in this book (Chapters 8–10). Specifically they include Egypt, Saudi Arabia, and Turkey. Though they are arguably the most prominent of the nations under discussion, their economies are rather dissimilar, and though they share Islam as their predominant religion, they are culturally quite different. The review presented here will step back from the detail contained in earlier chapters in an effort to capture the overall climatic business influences at work.

As noted earlier, "Businesses may form in Egypt as proprietorships, foreign company branches or representative offices, joint ventures, simple limited partnerships, general partnerships, partnerships limited by shares, limited liability companies, and joint stock companies." The country does control foreign access to some extent. For example, representative offices of foreign companies are permitted in order to conduct market and product surveys but cannot conduct commercial activities.

Further control of foreign business activity can be seen in relation to partnerships, which must have more than 51 percent ownership by Egyptian nationals. However, that ownership requirement can be waived in the case of the partnership limited by shares. As with partnerships, most corporations must have at least 51 percent of stock owned by Egyptian nationals, although various grounds exist for waiving this requirement.

Egyptian companies are required to keep proper records for all business transactions. Financial statements include the balance sheet, the income statement, and statement of changes in financial position. Such statements must be prepared in Arabic and must include comparative figures for the preceding year. In the case of the oil and gas industry, such statements must be prepared on a concession basis.

"Footnote disclosures must be made as part of the financial statements. Disclosures include organizational relationships, accounting policies in use, material related-party transactions, major company commitments, material subsequent events, material contingencies, and analyses of major accounts" (chapter 8). Subsidiaries must disclose their parent company relationship.

Joint stock companies must appoint an auditor, licensed to practice in Egypt. Licensing requirements for auditors are said to be more strenuous in Egypt than in many countries. Licensing requires a university degree in accounting and ten years experience, in addition to Egyptian citizenship. The experience requirement may be waived for members of the Egyptian Society of Accountants and Auditors or societies approved by that organization.

The auditing guidelines established by the International Federation of Accountants are acceptable in Egypt. Organizations with foreign affiliations can follow the generally accepted audit standards of other nations, such as the United States. However, audit reports required in Egypt are somewhat more extensive than those from other countries. They must be explicit in saying that the audited financial statements were prepared in compliance with rules and regulations.

"The statements reflect the company statement of financial position and results of operations" (chapter 8). The audit report must state that all data or company explanations that the auditor considers necessary have been obtained. The auditor must state that the firm has inventory and accounting records appropriate for their business, that their financial statements correspond to their accounting records, and that all resolutions of the board of directors that have accounting content have been included. The auditor's statement must also indicate that any illegal acts on the part of the company have been noted.

With respect to accounting principles, Egyptian law is permissive. "Any generally accepted accounting principle may be used that is sound and results in accurate portrayal of financial position and results of operations in financial statements" (chapter 8).

In the case of Saudi Arabia, the following information includes a summary of points made in Chapter 9. Government involvements in the regulation and control of enterprise were delineated earlier. Beyond government involvements, all businesses concerned with exports or imports or in bidding on government contracts must join the chamber of commerce located in major cities.

Business enterprises can take on various organizational and legal structures, among which are sole proprietorships, partnerships, and corporations. The sole proprietorship format is not available to foreigners and is generally to be found in the mercantile area. Various forms of partnership exist. The professional partnership mode can be used to form a joint practice comprising a locally licensed professional partnership and a foreign partnership. In such operations, the foreign firm is expected to provide expertise and training for interested Saudis. Professionals licensed in their home countries can practice in Saudi Arabia in conjunction with a Saudi partner. The foreign professionals must secure the appropriate local licenses.

The discussion in the preceding paragraphs speaks to the manner in which foreign accountants, including representatives of the major accounting firms, can come to practice in Saudi Arabia. Presumably they are expected to operate in partnership with local accounting interests. It appears as though such arrangements have great potential for strengthening international business linkages between Saudi Arabia and the global economy.

Foreign companies are permitted to establish representative offices with appropriate government approval. However, only Saudi citizens and entities that are 100 percent Saudi owned are permitted to act as commercial agents. Such agents must be registered and must be a resident in the country. Foreign firms are not permitted to sell their products directly but rather must deal with local agents. Such firms that have business with the government may establish liaison offices to coordinate Saudi operations with their home offices. Those offices are not permitted to carry on commercial business and must file detailed activities reports, not to mention annual audited reports. The reports in question must demonstrate that the offices were paid for by the home offices of the foreign corporations.

Approvals for the permanent establishment and operation of branches are generally only given for high technology defense projects. Such branches must have overriding reasons if they are to be 100 percent foreign controlled. The establishment of such branch operations requires audited financial statements of the foreign company for the past three to five years, the bylaws of the foreign organization, approval of the board of directors for the establishment of a branch, and a copy of the grant of the power of attorney to the legal representative to act as the firm's agent.

Foreign companies can operate as a government contractor, set up a branch operation, or open a representative office. Foreign investment can take most legal forms available, but the limited liability company and the joint stock company, which do not require unlimited liability, are the forms most frequently selected.

Firms contracting with the government require a Saudi service agent. They must have separate registrations for each government contract. Such registrations limit the work involved to government contracts and the contractors must assign no less than 30 percent of the work to Saudi contractors. In addition, firms are expected to use local sources for supplies, transportation, shipping, insurance, banking, and leasing arrangements. Contractors must register with the Department of Zakat and Income Tax and are subject to taxes.

Regulations governing both companies and taxes require that accounting books and records be kept in the country. Among required records are the daily journal, centralizing all original entries for posting to the general ledger; the ledger itself; and an inventory book containing all assets, liabilities and results for the year.

Businesses are also required to keep minute books and stockholders registers. Records and documentation must be held for ten years. Computerized accounting systems have been developed to cover those requirements. In such cases, the systems must be kept in the country, and auditors must authenticate a printout at least once per quarter. All input and output procedures must be documented.

Accounting records are expected to provide an audit trail from trial balances to tax reports and declarations. "Virtually all business entities . . . are required to file annual tax returns that report income from audited financial statements as adjusted for tax purposes" (Ernst & Young 1993, 30). These reports form the basis from which businesses must obtain annual tax and Zakat clearance certificates. Foreign business unit records for operations in the nation must be kept there until a tax clearance certificate is obtained.

All limited liability companies must have their financial statements audited by a certified public accountant registered to practice in Saudi Arabia. Financial statements should describe the nature of operations, provide a description of significant accounting policies, state accounting changes and how they are accounted for, describe potential losses and gains and financial commitments, and any subsequent events.

Corporate auditors are appointed at annual meetings and must be licensed to practice in the country. The reports of auditors must include a statement about management's attitude toward responding to the requests of auditors. For certification, an accountant must have an approved degree and appropriate auditing or accounting experience.

Financial accounting concepts and objectives approved as a basis for accounting standards in Saudi Arabia are similar to what have been issued by the American Institute of Certified Public Accountants. They have neither been monitored nor enforced. Businesses follow U.S. or U.K. or international standards, however with many important differences.

No organization has been put forward as the promulgator of accounting standards or practices, and beyond that, no standard setting legislation has been enacted. Thus, financial statements are prepared by divergent methods and practices, and comparability has not been achieved. However, many accountants do follow the International Accounting Standards issued by the International Accounting Standards Committee. Nonetheless, major exceptions to international standards are necessary.

The basic financial statements include the balance sheet, statement of income and retained earnings, and a statement of changes in financial position or cash flow. Reporting differs in various ways from what is generally found in financial statements made according to the U.S., U.K., or International Accounting Standards.

The nation's currency exchange rate is fixed in relation to the U.S. dollar. Saudi currency may be freely converted. There are no exchange controls or monetary restrictions with respect to the importation or repatriation of funds.

In regard to Turkey, highlights from Chapter 10 are summarized. A variety of business formats can be employed. These include single proprietorships, various partnership forms, branches of foreign companies, subsidiary companies, liaison offices, and limited liability companies and corporations. Turkish nationals and, in some cases, foreign residents can operate sole proprietorships.

Limited or general partnerships are seen as commercial companies with their legal identity separate from their partners. Foreign companies are permitted to have liaison offices and branches in the country. However, liaison offices are not permitted to conduct commercial business, but rather are intended for the purposes of gathering information and/or representing foreign companies. Liaison offices cannot have revenue, and thus must be funded by the company home office. Since no income is generated, liaison offices are not subject to taxation by Turkey. Liaison offices must be approved by a Turkish Consulate in their home country, and in addition, the firm must be endorsed by their home country chamber of commerce as being well established in that country.

Foreign companies wishing to form branches in Turkey must also get the approval of their home country chamber of commerce to the effect that they are established and active. Various support documents cited earlier in Chapter 10 must be certified by the Turkish Consulate in the home country. Such companies are taxed on the Turkish income of the branch. Subsidiary companies set up in Turkey are subject to full tax liability. Companies may be formed by Turkish nationals or by foreigners, though foreign investors require permits. Companies may hire independent auditors who are certified public accountants or the equivalent.

All commercial enterprises in the country are required to keep full sets of accounting records from which annual financial statements are to be determined. Accounting books are expected to include cash books, a general ledger to include bank accounts, a journal, a stock or inventory ledger, a fixed asset ledger, accounts receivable and payable ledgers, the stamp tax book, and in the case of manufacturers a cost ledger. A hard copy of accounting records must be kept in the country for a minimum of ten years.

As noted earlier, "Reports by approved independent auditors are required only for banks and other financial institutions and for publicly held companies." The Central Bank requires banks to file reports approved by auditors on statutory financial statements. Such reports must comment on the bank's financial position, ratio analysis, and internal control systems information. Some banks voluntarily produce financial statements in conventional international form. Of course, the existence of such information increases the stature of the bank in the eyes of the global business community.

The form and content of financial statements, including balance sheets, income statements, and statements of changes in financial position are spelled out in government regulations. The required content of financial statement notes includes appropriate information on accounting principles, contingent liabilities, subsequent events, and other appropriate explanations of accounts.

Since 1990, the law gives company independent auditors joint responsibility with the companies themselves for records and accounts. The law requires training and examinations for those wishing to become independent auditors. The law permits authorized independent auditors to certify transactions and documents. It defines the scope of work procedures and practices and the forms of reports. The Central Bank approves the professional accounting firms that may perform bank audits.

In 1988, the Independent Audit Association was formed. That organization appears to be the first step toward a professional accounting institution. To date it does not have the function of controlling the profession through training, examinations, and auditing standards.

SELECTED SMALL GULF STATES

This section presents an overview of the business and legal environments facing selected jurisdictions discussed in Chapter 11 of this volume.

Various forms of business enterprise are permitted in Bahrain. Among them are sole proprietorships, which may only be operated by citizens of Bahrain. Foreign company branches and representative offices are also permitted with proper registration and approval. If such operations are established as regional distribution centers for goods and services, they do not require sponsorship by a citizen of Bahrain in a similar pursuit. All other branches or representative offices require sponsors. The parent company is expected to be a viable entity and must take responsibility for all branch obligations.

Partnerships may be of three types: general, limited, or limited by shares. Foreign ownership rights in general partnerships are limited to 49 percent. Partners may not participate in a similar business without the consent of other partners. Many legal provisions aimed at general partnerships also apply to limited partnerships. The latter form must have more than 50 percent of its partnership capital in the hands of local citizens. Partnerships limited by shares are a cross between general partnerships and corporations. Though the Ministry of Commerce has prescribed its format, official authorization for it is not required.

Only local citizens may be partners unless foreign expertise or capital are needed, whereupon no more than 49 percent of the capital may be owned by foreign partners. Specific requirements for accounting books and related records for partnerships limited by shares have not been set down by law. However, a statutory auditor must be appointed to report on whether proper account books have been kept. It is presumed that books and records resembling those for corporations will be kept.

In Bahrain, corporations may take the form of exempt joint stock companies, closed joint stock companies, or public joint stock companies. The first two varieties may be wholly owned by foreign shareholders, while the third form may not exceed a foreign ownership of 49 percent. An exempt company must have its main offices in Bahrain, but is expected to limit its operations to offshore. It may not own property or land in Bahrain and must have the Bahrain Monetary Agency approval to engage in the financial arena. Such corporations have maximum corporate operational lives of twenty-five years unless extended by the Ministry of Commerce.

Closed joint stock companies are not expected to offer public shares. Formation and registration procedures are the same as for an exempt company. If their business is that of industrial companies, closed joint stock companies may be wholly owned by foreigners. One-hundred percent foreign ownership is also permissible for service companies establishing regional distribution centers for goods and services in Bahrain.

Public joint stock companies require the permission of the Ministry of Commerce to establish themselves. Foreign shareholders may not exceed 49 percent of ownership. The corporate main offices of firms incorporated in Bahrain must be located there. All subscription applicants must be domiciled in Bahrain.

As noted earlier, "There are no statutory requirements that businesses in Bahrain keep books and records. In practice, businesses use accounting systems of their own choice and in the language of their own choice." Corporations, limited liability companies, and partnerships limited by shares must have annual audits. Beyond those types of operations, firms in the financial services sector must file annual audited financial statements with the Bahrain Monetary Agency.

Since 1996, the Ministry of Commerce must license auditors before they can practice in Bahrain. In that year, a legislative decree established a code of ethics, academic preparation, and other licensing requirements. However, auditing procedures and standards have not been codified. Thus, auditors may choose their standards, in keeping with local customs and usage. The Commercial Code specifies the form of audit for corporations, limited liability companies, and partnerships limited by shares. The content of bank audit reports is specified by the Bahrain Monetary Agency.

The boards of Bahrain corporations and limited liability companies must report annually on company affairs. Specifically, they must include company financial position, a balance sheet, and a profit and loss statement. Though companies must follow generally accepted accounting principles, the law does not specify particulars with respect to the form and content of financial statements. Though no government or professional group has been charged with formulating accounting principles, various government agencies are encouraging all companies to use International Accounting Standards. "Since 1992, the Bahrain Monetary Agency has required banks and other financial companies to adopt International Accounting Standards."

As suggested earlier, "In general, accounting and auditing in Bahrain companies depends upon the level of accounting sophistication of company managers and auditors." Most large entities follow International Accounting Standards. The country is host to a regional offshore financial center, with offshore banking units and investment banks. Such entities may not offer their services to local residents. Nonetheless they must provide annual audited financial statements to the Bahrain Monetary Agency.

In the United Arab Emirates, businesses can be organized as sole proprietorships, joint ventures, various types of partnership, and public or private shareholding companies. Each business must obtain a license specifying authorized activities from the emirate in which it operates. Licensing arrangements differ between emirates, and businesses are required to have licenses from each emirate in which they wish to operate. Generally speaking, licenses can only be obtained for industrial projects owned by a UAE national or owned at least 51 percent by Gulf nationals. Of course, companies established in the free trade zone are excepted and may be wholly owned by foreigners.

Sole proprietorships are open only to UAE or Gulf Cooperation Council nationals. The public shareholding company is the primary corporate form of business in the country. All companies formed in the UAE must have at least one owner who is a citizen. Corporate ownership must be at least 51 percent domestic. Private shareholding companies are subject to the same rules as their public counterparts, except that shares may not be issued to the public.

In the case of limited companies, a citizen must own a minimum of 51 percent of the entity capital. These organizations that are actually partnerships can carry on any purpose under the law, exclusive of banking, insurance, and the placement of funds for others. Auditors are selected at a general meeting of the partners. Annual balance sheets, profit and loss statements, and reports on activities over the past year must be prepared.

"A general partnership with unlimited liability may be formed by two or more persons who are UAE nationals." If this partnership obtains a general trade license, it is required to file audited financial statements with the Ministry of Economy and Commerce each year. A simple limited partnership may have one or more partners who accept unlimited liability and silent partners with limited liability. All partners must be citizens, and corporations may not be partners. The provisions of the partnership agreement should be similar to those of a general partnership. Mixed liability partnerships are also permitted, with rules for formation similar to those for a public shareholding company.

Foreign companies may form branches in the UAE. Those that do must submit prescribed and authenticated forms that include certification by home country authorities that the firm is well established and registered. A report indicating the company's history of foreign operations in the area of operations proposed must be submitted. Audited balance sheets for the two prior years are also required. Branch operations must exclude industrial activity, transport operations, and commercial activities. Branches must prepare audited financial statements for branch activities.

Audited financial statements must be filed annually "by public and private joint stock companies, free zone establishments, limited liability companies, and branches of foreign companies." Audits must be conducted by registered auditors. Audited financial statements must be filed with the Ministry of Economy and Commerce by public and private joint stock companies, limited liability companies, and branches of foreign companies. Free zone establishments must file audited financial statements with free zone authorities.

Disclosures or financial statements are not detailed in law, but reporting similar to that of the United Kingdom or the United States is acceptable. Companies are encouraged to use International Accounting Standards. "Consolidated financial statements are normally prepared for UAE parent companies but are not required by law or regulation." There is no constituted body to set and enforce audit standards, but auditors usually apply the International Standards on Auditing. The larger accounting firms generally follow International Accounting Standards.

As mentioned earlier, all registered businesses in Qatar are subject to oversight by the Ministry of Finance, Economy and Commerce. Government and partially state-owned monopolies dominate many economic sectors. Foreign ownership and investment is strictly controlled and foreign companies may not be commercial importers. Foreign interests must sell to an agent, who then distributes the products. Patents are issued for ten years and are renewable for five.

Business ventures in Qatar can take the form of sole proprietorships, joint ventures, three forms of partnership, limited companies, and corporations. Only citizens or the nationals of Gulf Cooperation Council member states are permitted to form sole proprietorships. Foreign nationals are prohibited from entering trade or industry in Qatar unless a Qatari partner owns at least 51 percent of business capital. There are activities reserved exclusively for local citizens. However, by decree a foreign-owned company may operate a wholly owned branch. It is important to note that foreigners may also operate through a local sponsor in areas such as advisory and professional services. This of course holds great significance for the actual or potential imputes of major international accounting firms.

Joint ventures are considered as extensions of existing entities. There are no stated rules for management or for the keeping of accounting books and records, but participants are expected to adhere to the Qatar laws governing taxation.

Three forms of partnership exist. In general, partnerships interests must be limited to no more than 49 percent unless an exception is granted. As might be expected, partners have unlimited liability for partnership obligations. Laws do not specify the content or types of books of account or records, nor do they require the appointment of an auditor. However, such partnerships are expected to adhere to the provisions of the tax law.

In limited partnerships, at least one partner must be fully liable, while others need not be. Limited partnerships are formed in a similar fashion to general partnerships. In partnerships limited by shares, there must be at least one general partner with unlimited liability and at least ten limited partners. This last form of partnership combines certain features of the limited partnership with features from the limited liability company and corporate form. There are no legislated prescriptions regarding the form or content of accounting records and reports, but for partnerships limited by shares with capital in excess of QR 500,000, an auditor must be appointed.

A limited liability company must have at least two shareholders with unlimited liability, and local citizens or Gulf Cooperation Council nationals must own at least 51 percent of the limited liability shares, although exceptions may be granted by decree. Such firms are prohibited in banking, investment, or insurance brokerage. The same capital threshold as with partnerships limited by shares triggers the need for an auditor, but the duties of such a person are not stated explicitly by the law.

As mentioned earlier, "The formation of a public corporation requires the submission to the Minister of Finance, Economy and Commerce of an application to be registered as a commercial corporation and for the issuance of a decree." Only residents of Qatar may subscribe. All shareholders must be local citizens except for subscribing shareholders who may be Gulf Cooperation Council nationals. In cases where foreign investment or foreign expertise is needed, foreign ownership may be permitted by the Ministry.

Though corporate accounting records and books are required, specific guidance concerning financial reports is not supplied. Corporations are required to appoint an auditor. Each firm filing an income tax return is required to include a full set of audited financial statements covering their activities in Qatar. "Thus, all businesses in which foreign investors participate are required to have an annual audit and to prepare full sets of financial statements" (Price Waterhouse 1996a, 47).

Local laws do not specify accounting principles or practice requirements, nor are there any government or professional bodies with responsibilities toward formulating accounting and auditing practice. Nonetheless, corporations, limited liability companies, and partnerships limited by shares are expected to produce balance sheets, income statements, and directors' reports.

SOME CONCLUDING OBSERVATIONS

"With the emergence of the global economy, international linkages and operations have become crucial elements in the development potential and material strength of the jurisdictions under consideration" (McKee and Garner, 1996, 137). Though that statement was directed specifically at a selection of economies in the Pacific Basin, it appears to apply equally well in the current context. All the nations that have been reviewed in this chapter are certainly dependent on successful economic and business linkages for the nurture and development of their domestic economies.

The success of such linkages can be encouraged or impeded in specific jurisdictions by rules and regulations imposed upon the business community. From the point of view of successful international linkages, it appears to the current investigators that the jurisdictions under discussion may benefit from a business climate somewhat more welcoming to foreign business interests.

It appears as though growth and ongoing prosperity could be better achieved in those nations through careful attention to economic diversification. Certainly few would argue against more diversification in the nations that are strongly dependent on petroleum and related exports. One road to greater diversification is through an infusion of foreign investment capital and, to some extent, multinational business interests. That road would become somewhat smoother if some of the institutional constraints governing foreign ownership limits, exclusionary rules directed at corporate operations, and hurdles imposed upon foreign professional personnel were eased to some extent.

This is hardly a recommendation for seriously compromising local customs, traditions, or religious practices. Foreign business interests that seem unwilling or unable to accommodate such concerns are hardly desirable. Institutional and legal constraints may prove more productive if aimed at such practitioners, as opposed to the erection of more general barriers that may seriously impede material growth potential.

"Although domestic laws and procedures are important to the generation of a strong business climate, how those laws and procedures impact international linkages and business operations is also important." McKee and Garner went on to suggest that the compatibility of domestic laws and procedures with the operation of international business interests will encourage or retard such operations (1996, 137). Certainly those concerns apply in the present context.

Some of the constraints concerning foreign business participation in the various jurisdictions under discussion may well impact the existence and/or operating procedures of the major international accounting firms in those jurisdictions. The operating mode of those firms in the Middle East has often been the formation of partnerships with local firms.

Irrespective of how those firms have emerged as players in the nations concerned, it is clear that they have a potential for positive impacts. In cases where local accounting standards have not been established and institutionalized, they provide a window on international standards and procedures. They may also provide a training ground for local residents interested in accounting. Beyond such things, through their consulting operations, they have much to offer both domestic and international business interests. Indeed, they may be of major assistance as facilitators of international business linkages. Once again it seems clear that their acceptance may contribute positively to the economies concerned.

Chapter Thirteen

Implications for Growth and Change

This chapter reviews the economic situation facing the nations that have been examined in this book, with an eye to assessing their potential for economic improvement. The first section deals with the prospects facing the larger nations of the region—Egypt, Saudi Arabia, and Turkey. Following that, the smaller nations of the Gulf Cooperation Council are reviewed. Beyond appraisals of the economies as they exist, the intent is to focus on pertinent directions for public policy. The facilitative roles of major accounting firms as purveyors of business services are also reviewed.

PROSPECTS FOR LARGER NATIONS

As mentioned earlier, Egypt is the largest nation in the Arab world. Though it did suffer a reduced credibility in that community based on its coming to terms with Israel, it is still an important contributor to the voicing of Arab concerns to the world at large. Certainly the United States, not to mention various other Western nations, have ongoing interests in maintaining ties to Egypt. Such ties can certainly be strengthened by any growth in business and economic dealings.

Egypt is not alone among Middle Eastern nations in having much to gain from linkages with the world economy, as well as with the non-Islamic world. It relies on the world economy as its source for various manufactured goods and, of course, must find ways for paying for those goods with exports. This is a dilemma that Egypt shares with many emerging nations. Beyond the demands of that dilemma, Egypt must conduct its international business affairs within parameters that are supportive of its cultural and religious traditions. As suggested earlier, "Visible breaches in value systems and religious principles may . . . generate suspicion among the nation's Arab neighbors" (Chapter 4). Such breaches may also generate repercussions among the nation's domestic population.

During the time of the Nasser regime, the economy of Egypt was heavily socialized. The nation entered the 1990s with 7.3 percent of the population or 25.3 percent of the work force employed by the government in some capacity (Ayubi 1997, 298). Ayubi described a bureaucracy expanding more rapidly than population, employment, and production (299). These circumstances suggest that efforts at changing the direction of the economy will be confronted by a very strong ideological obstacle.

Ayubi is quite critical of the actual pace of policy shifts and accuses the state of pursuing privatization for its own purposes (340). Other writers have been critical of the nation's bureaucratic apparatus and have called for cutting back the civil service from its current complement of 3.5 million people. Those authors also suggest a revision of salary scales to bring them into line with realistic living standards, as well as to minimize corruption. They are also in favor of gearing promotions and remuneration to performance (Handoussa and Kheir-El-Din 1998, 59). Despite such suggestions, International Monetary Fund researchers are satisfied with the progress of privatization (El-Erian and Fennel 1997, 11).

Agriculture has been seen by some as Egypt's main source of growth (Handoussa and Kheir-El-Din 1998, 63). That sector was described by the U.S. Department of Agriculture as one of the most "liberal and progressive" components of the Egyptian economy. Despite such recognition, less than 4 percent of the nation's land is arable (Arab World Online LLC 1997b).

Handoussa and Kheir-El-Din identify the manufacturing sector as having been at the center of Egyptian growth strategy since the 1950s. Thus, it has been receiving the "lion's share" of public investment by a government that is emphasizing import substitution and diversification (1998, 65). As mentioned earlier in Chapter 4, the government has picked the development of technology as one of its primary tools for the overall development of the nation (Technology Development Program 1998). During the period from 1975 to 1992, growth rates in manufacturing were averaging nearly 9 percent. Despite such success, manufacturing's share of GDP has held steady at 17 percent, due to the expansionary performance of petroleum, utilities, and services (Handoussa and Kheir-El-Din 1998, 65).

According to Arab World Online, oil and gas accounted for nearly 10 percent of GDP in 1993 and 1994. During that time, oil products accounted for more than 52 percent of exports. Though certainly significant, oil and gas are hardly as important in Egypt as they are in various other Middle Eastern nations. At the nation's current output of 860,000 barrels per day, oil reserves are expected to last only fourteen years. If that prediction is accurate the government would be well advised to restrict its reliance on oil in its development plans. Indeed there is evidence that the government is turning more to its natural gas reserves (1997b).

A government-sponsored Technology Development Program may have positive impacts upon the manufacturing sector. That program has among its objectives the elimination of major problems and obstacles in the way of technological development and the endorsement of that type of change as the correct path to follow. The program looks to coordination and cooperation between the private sector and related government entities. Toward that objective the program introduces pilot projects, encourages coordination and cooperation and private sector investment in the technology industry (Technology Development Program 1998).

Like many economists, Handoussa and Kheir-El-Din feel that manufacturing expansion can be stimulated by exports. They see the manufacturing sector with a well-diversified production base, that has substantial existing capacity in upstream processing, over a broad horizontal range. In addition they point to an abundance of experienced labor, willing to work at competitive wages. They also point out that "a wide range of labor-intensive industries is based on sales to a large and protected domestic market—and now shows signs of being profitable in export marketing, even if on a small scale." They suggest a change of emphasis, from inward to outward, in search of more rapid expansion, one that is able to utilize existing capacities and to accelerate toward higher value added products, and that encourages increasing specialization on the part of the producers of both goods and auxiliary services (1998, 65).

In addition, they see the need for accelerating the pace of incoming foreign direct investment, coupled with strong links between domestic firms and multinational corporations, in hopes of creating employment opportunities and encouraging the adoption of modern technology and managerial practices. They hope such reforms will facilitate the nation's serving as the locus of international industrial activities for European and Middle East markets. They suggest the development of high-tech industries able to use the existing pool of engineers, technicians, and other professionals. As industries to be targeted, they suggest microelectronics, telecommunications, and computers. Beyond that, they call for the development of the numerous traditional microenterprises as ways to integrate with the modern industrial complex (65, 66).

Earlier in this book, the major impediments to the nation's industrial development were identified as shortages in finance and foreign exchange, competition between industry and agriculture over scarce resources, poor production standards and productivity, excessive control, and a destructive bureaucracy. It was suggested that infrastructure and other facilities must be built up in technical education and training, transportation and communications, ports, construction, energy supply, and storage and distributional facilities.

Industry can become a major sector in the nation's development plans. Toward that end, attention should be given to improving export performance, especially with respect to the nation's Arab neighbors. In seeking economies of scale and comparative advantage, structural reform appears to be needed, as opposed to merely marginal growth. Better regional trade relations should offer greater opportunities for more efficient industrial firms, who in turn will be better able to avail themselves of economies of scale and efficient resource use.

A reasonable understanding of Egypt's economic potential requires an understanding of its role in the Arab world and how its culture and traditions relate to economic and business linkages to the world at large. The business linkages in question can presumably be facilitated or encouraged by the offerings of the major international accounting firms. This seems especially true in the present environment, as the nation moves toward an economy more attune to market forces. The menu of services available through selected accounting firms has been outlined earlier in Chapter 4.

Saudi Arabia is of considerable significance in the modern world because it is host to major Islamic religious sites and also because of its role as a major supplier of petroleum products to the world at large. Dating from the mid-1970s, the government elected to utilize expanding oil revenues for developmental purposes, especially industrialization. This resulted in investments in processing plants employing hydrocarbon resources, as well as to the construction of airports, hospitals, roads, and ports. By the mid-1980s, such expenditures reached a total of U.S. $500 billion (Library of Congress 1997c).

As previously mentioned in Chapter 5, funds spent on development are in large part aimed at promoting private sector investment. In addition to infrastructure projects, this entailed aiding private firms in the supplying of electric power. It also entailed improving water supply capabilities and bringing telecommunications up to international standards (1997c).

Major investment initiatives in the nation have been capital intensive, thus providing limited opportunities for manual or unskilled labor. Labor demands have been for highly skilled and qualified managerial and supervisory personnel. Often those demands have been filled by expatriates, notably Egyptians. The best opportunities for less-skilled workers were to be found in the service sector.

Oil revenues have been used to import state-of-the-art modern technology that has done little by way of creating employment opportunities for the nation's citizens. If anything, the nature of what has been imported has generated pressure to expand capital imports, including spare parts and computerized equipment. Thus, as might be expected, the processes of labor absorption and accompanying improvements in human material welfare have been slowed.

Sustained growth and prosperity for Saudi Arabia will require more economic diversification than oil can provide. As oil resources are depleted over time, the economy will be faced with the need to accumulate offsetting productive resources in other endeavors. Present oil revenues can be of assistance in the pursuit of that end. As Ayubi has suggested, most private sector firms are small in size and concentrated in the supplying of consumer products. The firms in question are not very efficient and are employing rather primitive managerial and accounting practices. Beyond that, he suggests that private sector companies are heavily dependent on subsidized borrowing from state financial bodies (1997, 377).

In Saudi Arabia, religion has the potential for making a substantial impact upon the economy. The Muslim holy sites, aside from their religious significance, have already generated an economic impact. Islam has the potential to constitute a strong and sustainable subsector of the Saudi economy. Every Muslim is expected to make the once-in-a-lifetime pilgrimage known as the Hajj if possible. That pilgrimage occurs annually. Though its activities last little more than a week, they generate a significant infusion of foreign exchange, as well as full- and part-time employment opportunities. The economic importance of the Hajj may not be readily apparent, compared to its religious significance.

Unquestionably, the Hajj has a significant impact, but it falls short of maximizing the material benefits available to the nation from the hosting of religious observances or the visitation of major Islamic sites. The sites are significant in their own right and are unquestionably capable of attracting Islamic visitors on a continuing basis. Through the encouragement of religious visitors, substantial positive economic effects could be generated. Indeed, economic benefits to be generated through religious tourism may well be more reliable and long lasting than are the gains from the energy sector. Supporting a religious foundation for the economy may actually provide a stable base upon which various secondary and tertiary activities can be built.

Religion aside, the government has shown a willingness to adopt an escalating international involvement. One indication of this dates from 1981 with the formation of the Gulf Cooperation Council, an arrangement through which the Saudis became political partners with smaller Arab jurisdictions of the Persian Gulf. Their involvement soon became economic as well as political. They may have been assuming security responsibilities in the region that had previously been the preserve of the British.

For their part, certain small principalities were providing a window on the world for the Saudis. As an example, Bahrain and the United Arab Emirates have emerged as offshore financial centers that may be in a position to facilitate Saudi international dealings to some extent. The freedom of economic movement that has emerged between the members of the Council, including Saudi Arabia, represents a major movement on the part of the latter nation away from its previous insularity.

In 1995, Saudi Arabia introduced the Sixth National Development Plan. It called for the further development of technical skills amongst the Saudi population and an increasing emphasis on the private sector (U.S.–Saudi Arabian Business Council 1997b, 4). There appeared to be little mention of foreign linkages. Among various goals aimed at growth, the plan set an annual production sector expansion quota.

As stated earlier in Chapter 5, "The two main roles of the Saudi government in its effort to diversify the industrial base are to provide the infrastructure and incentives to encourage industrial development and to generate industrial projects to take advantage of the Kingdom's oil resources" (U.S.–Saudi Arabian Business Council 1997c, 4). These may be significant goals, but nevertheless the nation would be well advised to forge more substantial international industrial and service ties beyond those attributable to oil.

During the last quarter of the present century, major groupings of international business services have emerged. Their clients have included multinational firms as well as various governmental agencies in settings around the world. The major international accounting firms have been very active among those service groupings. Those firms may have a significant potential for improving international linkages to the Saudi economy. However, they are operating in that nation through offices in Jeddah and Riyadh exclusively. Their impacts should be expected to be strongest in the centers housing them.

Price Waterhouse offers through its local associates a wide range of services to both domestic and international clients (1991, 138). As was detailed earlier in Chapter 5, the firm can assist with audits and accountancy, Saudi taxation, international assignment tax services, training seminars and courses, and management consulting (139). The firm sees petroleum companies as capable of benefiting from its network in various ways. It can provide up-to-date knowledge of oil and gas taxation in the operating jurisdictions, as well as in the home countries of its clients (1997b, 1).

The firm professes to have considerable contact with government petroleum regulators, as well as with private firms. It stands ready to assist clients in various capacities, including accounting, litigation, information technology, the establishment of systems, and the acquisition and management of operating facilities (1). As previously mentioned in Chapter 5, "Price Waterhouse also helps its petroleum clients reengineer their systems and procedures to reduce costs with best-in-industry and best-across-all-industry benchmarking analysis" (Price Waterhouse 1997b, 4).

Assuming that other major accounting firms can offer similar service menus, it would appear as though the Saudi economy may have much to gain from their operations. Such firms should be capable of facilitating both domestic and foreign corporate operations. Their own operations have the potential for creating demonstration effects in the local economy and should be capable of facilitating economic linkages at all levels.

Though Turkey is not an Arab nation, it has the potential to become a major player in the regional economy of the Middle East. Beyond that region, "Any understanding of how Turkey relates to the world economy, not to mention the nation's potential for ongoing diversification and growth, requires knowledge of how the nation perceives its relationship with Europe and how religious and cultural factors influence that relationship" (Chapter 6).

Indeed, it has been suggested that the changing relationship between the state and religion is likely to be one of the most important debates in Turkey during the 1990s (Ayata 1993, 63). Ayata pointed to big business interests in Istanbul as the most significant deterrent to religious fundamentalism (66). Nonetheless, it appears as though Islamic concerns, together with a strong argument for economic and political ties to the Islamic nations of the Middle East, are factors deserving consideration in any policy initiatives aimed at economic development and expanding international linkages.

Certainly relations between Turkey and the Arab world are greatly influenced by Islamic ideology. However, Yesilada has suggested that it was economic difficulties experienced by Turkey and an infusion of financial capital from oil-rich Arab nations that led to improved relations with the Arab world. Nonetheless, during the 1980s Turkish nationalism combined with Islam in pursuit of what Yesilada has termed "the only viable channel for creating a strong Turkey." The prevalent ideology embraced a union of religion and the state in search of a society supported by Islamic foundations (Yesilada 1993, 177), and beyond that a coalition embracing government and the military ruled by the Shari'a'.

In a structural transformation dating from 1980, the Turkish economy began moving away from direct regulation and government control and toward a more liberal posture embracing market forces. Through its new posture, the government was pursuing its ultimate goal of integration with the world economy. Global integration has been accelerated through the strengthening of exports, foreign exchange rate policies, and tax rebate practices. In the process of these adjustments, the private sector has gained an increasing share of the industrial base (MFA 1997a).

Structural adjustments included the liberalization of capital movements aimed at increasing the competitive power of the economy. As mentioned earlier in Chapter 6, "The Turkish banking system has been made compatible with . . . universal banking" (MFA 1997a). An interbank money market aimed at unifying the money market and establishing a national cash flow between financial institutions dates from 1986. Reforms aimed at increasing the efficiency of the financial system through interbank competition were introduced.

Changes included the freeing of interest and foreign exchange rates. New firms were permitted to join the banking system and foreign banks were welcomed. Parallel to that, Turkish banks began international operations. As early as the mid-1980s, special finance houses operating within Islamic banking principles emerged. The government introduced various legal and institutional arrangements designed to encourage the development of capital markets. Banks expanded their service menus to embrace the negotiation of security issues and trading in securities. Beyond such dealings, they underwrote fund management, established mutual funds, and entered the arena of financial consultation (1997a).

By the fall of 1995, as many as twenty-two foreign banks were in existence in Turkey. They formed a significant element in the Turkish banking system through the new concepts and practices that they were able to introduce. Indeed, they have been said to have changed attitudes toward competition and dynamism in the banking system (1997a). Perhaps their operations are suggestive of the impacts that facilitative business services may have upon the economy. Certainly such involvements can be assumed to be improving the foreign linkages enjoyed by the nation's economy.

As economic development has proceeded, agriculture has declined in importance relative to growing manufacturing and service activities. Nonetheless, Turkey has considerable strength in the agricultural sphere and is self-sufficient in food. In spite of the relative decline in the importance of agriculture, "Turkey is still the largest producer and exporter of agricultural products in the Near East and North African region" (*Agriculture* 1997). The domestic market for agricultural products has been strong as a result of a rising population and higher incomes (*Agriculture* 1997). Agriculture can be expected to play an ongoing role parallel to manufacturing and service activities. Ready markets for Turkish food products in the Middle East should guarantee an ongoing role for the agricultural sector.

Manufacturing activities are gaining in importance in the Turkish economy due to abundant natural resources, the geographical proximity to export markets, an improving infrastructure, the existence of a large domestic market, and liberal economic policies (MFA 1997a). Clothing and textiles have been the most prominent manufacturing activities. The nation was seen as an ongoing net importer in most process industries. It was also said to be becoming an importer of engineering products with the exception of metal products. Indeed, Turel saw the pace of such imports accelerating (Turel 1993, 76).

Nonetheless, manufacturing activities have a significant place in the nation's economy. The exports of that sector represented nearly 86 percent of the export total in 1994. A sustainable export performance has been seen to be dependent upon competitiveness in international markets. In addition to prices, factors thought to impact competitiveness included the closing of technological gaps with developed countries, the improvement of product quality, the development of trademarks acceptable in international markets, the production of environmentally friendly products, and the diversification of both products and markets (MFA 1997e).

It is significant with regard to export potential that the nation holds an association agreement with the European Union and has signed a trade zone agreement with the European Free Trade Association. As quoted earlier in Chapter 6, "On March 6, 1995, the Turkish–European Community Partnership Council approved Turkey's accession to the Customs Union with the European Union (EU)." Technical aspects of the union allow for the free flow of goods, harmonization of trade policies and legislation, arrangements concerning agricultural products, and simplification of customs formalities (Arthur Andersen 1997c, 121). Such arrangements may be expected to change the nation's economic relations to other players in the global economy.

According to Deloitte Touche Tohmatsu International, the nation is attractive to foreign investors. "The government maintains a liberal policy toward all forms of foreign investment" and "the political and social climate is stable." In addition, energy costs are relatively low, and the nation holds a rather large domestic market. Labor costs are also low and workers are plentiful (1994b, 1–2).

Arthur Andersen reports the introduction of free trade zones as early as 1985. The zones were intended to raise investment in export-oriented production, as well as to accelerate the acquisition of foreign capital and technology. In addition, the zones were seen as "providing inputs to the economy in an economical and orderly manner," as well as raising the utilization of foreign trade opportunities and foreign financial instruments (1997c, 125).

As Turkish dealings in the global economy expand it seems clear that facilitative opportunities for the major international accounting firms will also increase. Deloitte & Touche, the Deloitte Touche Tohmatsu International member firm in the nation, provides a full range of audit, accounting, management consulting, and tax services through offices in Istanbul and Ankara. The firm serves domestic and international clients, large and small (1994b, 59).

Price Waterhouse Turkey is internationally oriented, and most of its clients have international connections either through extensive trading operations or because they have foreign parent companies (Price Waterhouse 1993, 169). The firm's service menu covers three areas—auditing, taxation, and management consulting. As suggested earlier in Chapter 6, the firm's operations suggest the types of facilitative services that accounting firms may offer in the jurisdictions hosting them.

It seems clear that the major accounting firms are well aware of the potential impacts of the services they offer. An official of Arthur Andersen, quoted earlier in Chapter 6, saw his firm to be focused on assisting its clients to improve their performance through the application of knowledge, experience, and expertise acquired through worldwide business dealings over a long period of time. The firm assesses problems and puts together teams of experts to deal with them (Arthur Andersen 1997b). In Turkey, Arthur Andersen offers a wide range of advisory services, aimed at strategic market sectors.

As mentioned earlier in Chapter 6, "Many nations have faced serious difficulties due to the encroachment of a global economic system that seems to threaten their customs and values." Turkey appears to be stronger, larger, and in possession of more resources than many such nations. Nonetheless it appears to be facing a complicated mix of issues in finding its way. Few would suggest that the major accounting firms or other multinational business service suppliers can easily solve Turkey's dilemmas. Nonetheless, the major accounting firms can certainly provide some assistance and support. Certainly they contribute to the confidence level of their international clients who may wish to conduct business in Turkey. They may very well be helping to put together sound international linkages. It must be remembered, however, that the firms will only be able to assist by remaining within the parameters of Turkish customs and traditions.

THE SMALLER NATIONS OF THE
GULF COOPERATION COUNCIL

In addition to Saudi Arabia, the Gulf Cooperation Council comprises Bahrain, Qatar, Kuwait, Oman, and the United Arab Emirates. Dating from 1981, the organization was originally intended as a security umbrella, but it has also taken on economic significance. The original agreement called for eventual economic integration to facilitate the free movement of goods, as well as labor and capital. In addition, the agreement was aimed at the coordination of economic and financial policies (El Mallakh 1981, 152).

In 1983, the agreement was expanded to abolish customs duties on agricultural livestock and manufactured products from within its member state. In addition, ships of member nations were given free access to all ports, and both passengers and cargo were exempted from taxes and fees. The products of member states were to be free of taxes and fees when transiting the territories of members. The "citizens of one GCC state specializing in medicine, law, engineering, accounting and local consulting firms" could operate in other member states without obtaining permits or paying taxes. Citizens of individual states were permitted to establish businesses in others, on condition that at least 25 percent of the shares are subscribed by citizens of the states where the company is established (153–154).

The organization was intended to encourage cooperation on matters such as economics, finance, defence, education, health, trade, travel, transport, customs, and legal issues. The major intent of the agreement was the establishment of a united economic system. A new tariff system for extra regional imports was established and "decisions have been made to give more freedom to the private sectors of the member states" (Deloitte Touche Tohmatsu International 1996, 13).

Dating from the mid-1980s, oil has become a less reliable revenue source for the regimes of the region. This of course represents problems for those regimes, since social contracts with resident populations must be assured of the continued availability of funding. As suggested earlier in Chapter 7, where global energy markets are the major funding source, then uncertainties in those markets are causing problems beyond the previously existing fear of possible oil depletion.

Problems related to oil are driving the need for the nations in question to diversify their economies as well as to seek international linkages that go well beyond what have been in place. The new linkages signal a more extensive intercourse with global markets, as well as more contact between resident populations and foreign elements. Askari, Bazzari, and Tyler have called for policies to improve the business climate as well as to eliminate distorting economic policies. Among their recommendations are cuts in government spending and the reduction or actual abandonment of indiscriminate subsidies. They also call for the privatization of public enterprises, the reduction of public sector employment, the deregulation of markets, and the introduction of a competitive real exchange rate (1998, 225).

Gause has pointed to problems related to expanding populations that put severe pressure on the welfare states that were developed in the 1970s and 1980s. He suggested that the states in question maintained government spending levels, in spite of the falling oil revenues during the 1980s, by utilizing their reserves and by borrowing internationally and relying on transfer payments from their neighbors (1997, 68).

As suggested earlier in Chapter 7, "Declining revenues from oil, together with rising populations, are pressuring the small nations of the Gulf to privatize their economies, reduce government spending, and generate stronger international linkages." It seems clear that privatization in economies, where both wages and employment have been inflated, will bring about a certain amount of social and political unrest. Privatized enterprises almost invariably indulge in cost cutting and can hardly be expected to subscribe to a social contract that commits them to overextended corporate bureaucracies and exaggerated pay scales.

The solution would appear to rest with economic growth and diversification. In seeking growth in the small states in question, an obvious line of advance lies with increased investment from abroad. This may be directed toward production for export, involving production facilities owned by foreign multinational corporations. It may also take the form of expanding international service subsectors that may include tourism and international business facilitators.

Adjustments such as those suggested will mean increased foreign linkages and more contact with foreign nationals, whether resident or visiting. These adjustments may be the source of a certain amount of discomfort for a citizenry striving to maintain its cultural and religious roots. The rulers appear to be facing a dilemma. If they elect to encourage expanded foreign linkages, they must accommodate the sensitivities of their citizens. The option of rejecting such linkages may not be viable if they hope to maintain acceptable living standards for their citizens.

The nations in question all are relatively small, have varying degrees of involvement with the petroleum industry, and have a need for involvement with the global economy. However, they differ in terms of their economic strength and future prospects. Bahrain and the United Arab Emirates have become significant offshore financial centers, and as such, are not as dependent on oil as might otherwise have been the case. With a population of 600 thousand, Bahrain has had an ongoing association with other cultures, a stable government, and good relations with the rest of the Arab world (Coopers & Lybrand 1996, 7–10).

Bahrain has been both an entrepot and a distribution center for the region. Its trade is still dominated by oil, but the government has actively promoted nonoil exports. The nation has been described as one of the most diverse economies in the region, boasting the largest collection of manufacturing industries and the biggest community of international bank branches in the Gulf (Arab World Online 1997a).

The tourist industry attracts two million visitors per year. Bahrain has been described as the Middle East's preeminent financial hub and a key player in world financial and banking circles (Arab. Net 1997). It hosts international law firms, insurance companies, accountants, and a variety of consultants in what was described earlier in Chapter 7 as a rather sophisticated service sector.

The United Arab Emirates were described in Chapter 7 as holding a unique position among offshore financial centers through their provision of significant linkages between the Arab world and the global economy. According to Ernst

& Young, "The economy is influenced by fluctuations in the international oil market because oil, gas and related petrochemical industries continue as the most important economic sector" (1990, 3).

In order to reduce the nation's oil dependency, efforts are underway to encourage foreign investment in fields thought to be of national benefit. Among such endeavors are agricultural and manufacturing projects presumed to be helpful in moving the economy toward self sufficiency. Key sectors of the economy beyond oil and gas include "utilities, communications, construction, banking and financial services, manufacturing projects and tourism" (3, 4).

Among the emirates, Dubai has been a trading center and an entrepot in the Middle East and also more recently "among markets of the Near and Far East, Europe and the United States" (5). The emirate's Department of Tourism and Commerce Marketing regards its jurisdiction as one of the world's leading trading centers. The Ministry points to pro business policies on the part of the government and one of the region's most liberal regulatory environments. Beyond that they boast no taxes on profits or incomes, no foreign exchange controls and a stable, freely convertible currency (Government of Dubai 1998). Advantages also include a sophisticated service sector, that includes major international hotels, banks, lawyers, accounting firms, advertising agencies and consultants (Government of Dubai 1998).

Qatar has relied upon oil revenues as the basis of its prosperity. However, in the face of dwindling oil reserves, the government has been showing more interest in liquefied natural gas (Arab World Online LLC 1997e). Since the nation has very large gas reserves, the change in emphasis will leave energy as the most significant sector of the economy. Unlike various other economies in the region, Qatar seems less in need of diversifying its economy. However, it will hardly be able to avoid increasing international linkages if it hopes to market its resources in exchange for needed imports.

Like Qatar, Kuwait relies upon its energy sector for its prosperity. The nation is a welfare state with one of the most comprehensive domestic social aid and extensive overseas financial aid programs in the world. In 1992, the nation had proven oil reserves of 94 billion barrels and has purchased refineries and an extensive chain of service stations in Europe (Arab World Online LLC 1997c). The nation also boasts extensive natural gas reserves although actual gas production is limited by the absence of known reserves independent of oil. The need for economic diversification seems less pressing in Kuwait than is the case with some of its neighbors. This of course presumes the ongoing health of the energy sector. Also, ongoing and perhaps increasing international linkages appear to be essential.

Among the jurisdictions under discussion in this section, Oman is the least robust economically. "In recent years the nation's public infrastructure including transportation linkages, housing and educational establishments has undergone significant expansion" (Chapter 7), and Oman has been criticized for "the establishment of an oil based rentier welfare state," which has inflated government outlays (Oman: The Taiwan of the Gulf 1995). In its most recent five-year economic plan (1996–2000), the government calls for a reduction of government spending, for the creation of more employment opportunities, and for privatization. Though oil revenues account for 85 percent of export earnings, 80 percent of government revenue, and 40 percent of GDP, they are expected to decline. This, coupled with a population of about two million, which is expected to double by 2010, presents a less than optimistic picture (Arab World Online LLC 1997d).

Clearly, the economy is in serious need of diversification and this can only be accomplished by significant increases in foreign linkages. The bulk of the nation's work force is employed in agriculture and fishing, which generates only 3 percent of its GDP. Though agricultural output has been rising, water shortages are also a problem (Oman: The Taiwan of the Gulf 1995).

The economy has also been driven by oil and gas. The government hopes to make liquefied natural gas a cornerstone for the economy as well as a significant export industry. Agriculture is heavily subsidized, but it amounts to only 2 percent of GDP and has not been able to alleviate the need to import food products (1995). The government is interested in attaining self-sufficiency in food production.

Manufacturing represents only 5 percent of GDP and is for the most part composed of light industry. The government is encouraging manufacturing activity and has invested in industrial zones (Oman: The Taiwan of the Gulf 1995). However, industrial diversification has achieved only modest success and significant further progress in that direction would appear to require expanded international business linkages.

All the economies that have been discussed are involved, in varying degrees, in supplying energy resources to international markets. Some are well supplied with energy resources and should be able to build their material well-being on that sector, assuming continuing success in world markets. Others are more in need of economic diversification.

Irrespective of their ability to rely on energy-related endeavors or their need to diversify, all five economies will have ongoing needs to maintain and improve international linkages. In pursuit of that end, various international business services may have positive roles to play. Prominent among the suppliers of such services are the major international accounting firms. Samples of the service offerings of such firms have been detailed in Chapter 7.

Any or all of the accounting firms in question have the potential for causing wide-ranging impacts in nations that host them. By providing expertise to multinational firms, the accounting firms facilitate their operations and indeed may make it possible to function in specific locations as opposed to others. By locating in specific settings, the accounting firms are also available to offer services to local businesses and public agencies. Beyond that, they may generate positive effects that can improve the efficiency of various business operations beyond their actual clientele. Those effects are not confined specifically to matters involving accounting and auditing.

Ernst & Young is a major international accounting firm with rather extensive operations in the Middle East. Their involvement appears to be self-evident. "Our decentralized organizational structure enables us to make available all the resources of an international professional services firm but apply these in a manner that is sensitive to the local business economy" (1997a).

The potential that Ernst & Young or its accounting and consulting rivals may have in assisting business and economic undertakings in the nations under discussion here appear to be almost self-evident as well. As stated earlier in Chapter 7, "Provided that the major accounting firms truly understand their host environments they are very well equipped to assist businesses in those locations with their international involvements."

SOME CONCLUDING OBSERVATIONS

In this chapter, the situation facing the various economies that have been the focus of the book has been reviewed. All of the economies in question appear to be in need of strengthening their linkages with the world at large. Some are more in need of diversification than others. Some will be able to place a certain amount of reliance on energy exports to facilitate their international needs, but even those nations would be well advised to use caution, due to the unpredictability of international energy markets.

Certain possibilities have occurred to the present authors in the course of their investigations to help these economies succeed. For example, there appear to be certain directions that planners in the larger nations of the region might well consider. It seems quite feasible for Saudi Arabia to better its economic position by more overt efforts to encourage religious visitors. By encouraging the interest of Muslims throughout the world in the holy sites and by welcoming visitors on a year-round basis, Saudi Arabia could develop a religious tourism sub sector that might well come to rival energy as a foundation of their economy.

Egypt might well benefit substantially from tourism of a less sectarian nature. The nation's rich heritage, together with the many sites that hold an international mystique, could be the basis of a very profitable tourist industry. What would be required is a somewhat more substantial tourist-oriented infrastructure and the provision of a stable, safe environment for visitors. Both Egypt and Saudi Arabia should be able to earn substantial profits, generate needed employment opportunities, and foreign exchange from a judicious nurturing of a sensibly sized and designed tourist industry.

Turkey may well be able to benefit from its considerable agricultural potential. Economists are not generally willing to recommend primary production as a basis for successful economic expansion. Nonetheless, it appears as though Turkey may have considerable potential as a major supplier of agricultural products throughout the Middle East. As tourism might in Egypt and Saudi Arabia, agriculture might well form an effective basic industry for the Turkish economy.

Both tourism and agriculture in the contexts in which they have been presented here should enlarge and hopefully improve the international linkages of the economies concerned. They are not intended as a substitute for sought after manufacturing endeavors, but instead might form a basis from which to proceed with other pursuits. Certainly economic diversification remains a goal to be recommended.

The small economies of the Persian Gulf appear to be even more dependent on successful foreign linkages for their future prosperity. Unlike their larger neighbors there are serious strictures related to their size, with respect to what developing their domestic markets may achieve. They would seem to be irreversibly dependent upon their abilities to forge places for themselves in the global economy. Some can expect ongoing strength from their oil-related activities. Others have involved themselves with offshore finance and tourism.

The small nations in question may well have much to gain from the services available from major international accounting firms. Those firms have the potential for facilitating the operations of multinational firms, including locational activity and subsequent business dealings. In jurisdictions that appear to be dependent on success in international business dealings, it would appear that the accounting firms could certainly be of service. The importance of such accounting firms in the larger nations that have been discussed is also quite substantial.

Chapter Fourteen

Some Final Reflections

In general, the nations that have been discussed in this book are dependent for their material strength and development potential upon the ongoing success of their linkages to the global economy. Those linkages are far from simple to maintain, given the political, social, cultural, and religious forces influencing them. Beyond those forces are the uncertainties associated with the necessity for balancing needed imports against extractive exports, notably oil.

Among the real or recommended policy goals that are common throughout the region is the need for economic diversification. This is especially evident in the oil-based economies. Coupled with diversification in some cases is a suggested need for privatization. The latter goal or objective may bring with it an erosion of the economic controlling power of central governments. How desirable or acceptable that may be in specific nations remains to be seen.

This book has attempted to explain the issues facing the economies in question, with specific emphasis on business environments and the way in which their parameters can influence foreign linkages and investment from abroad. In pursuing that objective, wherever possible, the real and/or potential inputs of the major international accounting firms have been considered.

As was suggested in Chapter 12, the success or failure of international linkages can be encouraged or impeded in specific jurisdictions by rules and regulations directed toward the business community. Indeed, the current authors have recommended that the nations discussed may benefit from business climates that are more receptive to foreign business interests. Those nations may do well to consider the easing of institutional constraints limiting foreign ownership, not to mention various exclusionary rules aimed at corporate operations and hurdles imposed on foreign professional personnel.

In taking such a position, the authors recognize the pervasive nature of Islam in the region and are not recommending the compromising of local customs or traditions, much less religious practices. Indeed, foreign business interests that are unwilling or unable to accommodate those concerns are hardly desirable. With that in mind, it seems prudent to emphasize that domestic laws and procedures must display some compatibility with international business interests in jurisdictions wishing to nurture such interests.

It may be tempting in some international circles to lay the blame for constraining business linkages on the forces of Islam. To do so would be to oversimplify, if not to misrepresent the role of that religion. Based on the discussion of Islam in Chapter 3, it seems clear that Islam is quite compatible with international business linkages.

The Islamic belief system is certainly compatible with a market-oriented economy based on private initiative. Indeed, certain economic practices under Islam that may give a surface appearance of retarding profit-seeking activities may actually be encouraging such activities. Two of the most widely recognized economic practices under Islam are the prohibition of interest and the annual charitable assessment known as the Zakat.

It seems clear that those practices will impact the behavior of individuals in possession of personal wealth and/or financial capital. For example, an individual in possession of financial capital will suffer a year-to-year impact from inflation, as well as from the requirement of the Zakat. It hardly takes an economist to suggest that such an individual would be well advised to invest his or her capital resources in ventures with the potential of outdistancing inflation and the year-to-year impact of the Zakat. What may be retarding economic progress in such nations is probably not Islamic in origin, but rather the result of artificial constraints or laws and regulations and the level of opportunities available.

Thus, Islam in itself is hardly a culprit guilty of constraining developmental potential in the nations that have been discussed in this book. Foreign interests contemplating involvement would be well advised to obtain an understanding of local customs and how to accommodate them. That advice would seem to apply equally well to any contemplated host destination.

Among the nations that have been discussed in this book, Islam is a pervasive force that impacts the lives of the vast majority of their residents. Ironically, Islam as a philosophy is not a supporter of authoritarian regimes, but rather is quite democratic in its social and political outlooks. Since none of the Arab nations that have been considered here are governed democratically, their rulers understand full well the necessity of affording their citizenry the philosophical space to practice their beliefs.

Indeed the Arab states in question, though authoritarian in varying degrees, dispense largess in the form of housing, medical services, and in some cases employment to their citizens. In cases where an unpredictable oil market threatens such programs, the rulers run destabilization risks. Thus, the governments in question may have very practical reasons for encouraging economic diversification.

Clearly they do have something to be gained from efficient international business and economic linkages. In pursuing such linkages, they must consider both the needs of their citizens and those of their business constituencies, both foreign and domestic.

In the preceding chapter, suggestions were made that might benefit planners in the larger nations that have been reviewed. For example, it was suggested that the economic position of Saudi Arabia might be improved if that nation were to encourage an expansion of religious tourism. The Saudi authorities could rather easily encourage foreign Muslims, who might wish to visit the holy sites on a year around basis. The infrastructure that is in place to accommodate the Hajj could easily facilitate such visitations.

If pursued judiciously a religious tourism sector might easily rival energy as a foundation for the nation's economy. Such a diversification would have obvious advantages such as added employment opportunities, an infusion of foreign exchange and of course more personalized linkages for the nation throughout the Islamic world.

The diversification of the Egyptian economy might also be encouraged through expanded support for tourism. In the case of Egypt the industry would of course be much less sectarian in nature, relying instead in the ongoing appeal of the nation's rather spectacular historical and anthropological sites. As suggested in the preceding chapter the infrastructure would require adjustments as would security measures where indicated. Of course both Saudi Arabia and Egypt would be advised to develop their tourist hosting capabilities in keeping with more general economic initiatives and cultural needs.

As mentioned in the preceding chapter, Turkey may be best served by added emphasis on agricultural exports. Difficulties with such endeavors notwithstanding, it seems clear that the nation could become a major source of agricultural products for the Middle East.

The smaller nations of the Gulf Cooperation Council that have been discussed in this volume are if anything more dependent upon substantial foreign linkages than are the three larger jurisdictions mentioned in this chapter. This is clearly the case with Bahrain and the United Arab Emirates since those jurisdictions appear to be placing so much emphasis on developing as offshore financial centers. Kuwait has extensive petroleum related business linkages with Europe through its holdings of service stations and other petroleum related enterprises. Qatar appears to be wedded to international energy markets. In the cases of Kuwait and Qatar major economic diversification seems overly optimistic but both jurisdictions are unavoidably dependent on foreign linkages for their success. Oman, which possesses many of the problems and characteristics of smaller emerging nations will rely on world markets for a wide range of goods and services that can hardly be supplied domestically.

It seems clear that all of the nations considered in this volume are dependent for their growth and prosperity upon international linkages. Such linkages appear unavoidably destined to foster philosophical and cultural encounters that will require understanding and sensitivity on the part of all concerned. Such issues can certainly be dealt with effectively, but nonetheless can be expected to require major efforts on the part of various government decision makers.

In the private sector, the major international accounting firms are in an excellent position to provide facilitative services to both businesses and government agencies in the nations concerned. To begin with, they are already performing a useful function through their provision of manuals designed to explain business climates, rules, and regulations to clients on a virtual worldwide basis. Beyond such instructional documents, the range of services that they provide should certainly assist in strengthening international business linkages and in supplying expertise to local businesses.

The firms are also in a position to advise clients on the cultural and social necessities for successful operations. In doing that, they can certainly assist in the success of business operations. Of course, they would be on questionable ground were they to elect to advise business on the avoidance of existing laws and regulations. By assuming the status of honest brokers with respect to such rules and regulations, they may be helpful if called upon to advise governments on contemplated adjustments. The potential role of these firms appears to be constrained only by what governments may permit. In some settings within these regions, such constraints may be substantial.

References and Selected Bibliography

Abdalati, Hammudah. 1993. *Islam in Focus*. Indianapolis: American Trust Publications.

Abdallah, Wagdy M. 1984. *International Accountability: An International Emphasis*. Ann Arbor, Mich.: UMI Research Press.

Abdeen, Adnan M., and Dale N. Shook. 1984. *The Saudi Financial System in the Context of Western and Islamic Finance*. New York: John Wiley & Sons.

Abi-Aad, Naji, and Michel Grenon. 1997. *Instability and Conflict in the Middle East: People, Petroleum and Security Threats*. New York: St. Martin's Press.

Abu Amara, Yosra. 1991. *Selected International Trade in Services and Development in Small Economies*. Ph.D. diss., Kent State University.

Abu-Amara McKee, Yosra, David L. McKee, and Don E. Garner. 1997. Accounting Services and Growth in the Islamic World: Some Evidence from the Mediterranean and the Middle East. In *International Business Strategies: Economic Development Issues*, Abbass F. Alkhafaji and Zakaria El-Sadek, eds., 59–63. Apollo, Pa.: Closson Press.

Accounting Standards Committee. 1983. *Statement of Standard Accounting Practice Number 16: Current Cost Accounting*. London: Accounting Standards Committee.

Agami, Abdel M., and Felix P. Kollaritsch. 1983. *Annotated International Accounting Bibliography*, 972–981. Sarasota, Fla.: American Accounting Association.

Agriculture. 1997. www.turkey.org/turkey/agric.htm

Ahmad, Shaikh Mahmud. 1952. *Economics of Islam: A Comparative Study)*. Lahore, Pakistan: Ashraf Press.

Al-Farsy, Fouad. 1986. *Saudi Arabia: A Case Study in Development*. New York: KPI Limited.

AlHashim, Dhia D., and Jeffrey S. Arpan. 1988. *International Dimensions of Accounting*. 2d ed. Boston: PWS-Kent Publishing Company.

Ali, Abdullah Yusuf. 1992. *The Meaning of the Holy Qur'án*. Brentwood, Md.: Amana Corporation.

Aliboni, Roberto, ed. 1979. *Arab Industrialization and Economic Integration*. New York: St. Martin's Press.

AlMuntheri, AlHafiz Zakiuldin. 1987. *Mukhtasar Sahih Muslim*. 6th ed. Beirut, Lebanon: Al-Maktab Al-Islami.

Al-Sabah, Dr. Y. S. F. 1980. *The Oil Economy of Kuwait*. London: Kegan Paul International.

Al-Yousuf, Ala A. 1990. *Kuwait and Saudi Arabia: From Prosperity to Retrenchment*. OIES Paper on Oil and Finance. Oxford: Oxford Institute for Energy Studies.

Amara, Yosra A. 1994a. Externally Traded Services and the Development of Small Economies. In *External Linkages and Growth in Small Economies*, David L. McKee, ed., 7–14. Westport, Conn.: Praeger.

———. 1994b. Services and Growth in Small Developing Countries, In *External Linkages and Growth in Small Economies*, David L. McKee, ed., 17–26. Westport, Conn.: Praeger.

Amara, Yosra A., Don E. Garner, and David L. McKee. 1995. A Taxonomy of Accounting Service Impacts upon Caribbean Economies. In *Business Research Yearbook: Global Business Perspectives*, Abbas F. Alkhafaji, ed., 52–56. Vol. 2. Lanham, Md.: University Press of America.

American Institute of Certified Public Accountants. 1991. *International Accounting and Auditing Standards*. New York: American Institute of Certified Public Accountants.

———. 1995. *Accounting Research Study, Number 7: Inventory of Generally Accepted Accounting Principles for Business Enterprises*. New York: American Institute of Certified Public Accountants.

Anderson, Robert E., and Albert Martinez. 1998. Supporting Private Sector Development in the Middle East and North Africa. In *Prospects for Middle Eastern and North African Economies: From Boom to Bust and Back?* Nemat Shafik, ed., 178–193. New York: St. Martin's Press.

Arab. Net. 1996. *Bahrain Business: Financial Services*. www.arab/net/bahrain/business/hn/financial.html

Arab World Online LLC. 1997a. *Country Profile: State of Bahrain*. www.awo.net/country/qverview/crbah.asp

———. 1997b. *Country Profile: The Republic of Egypt*. www.awo.net/country/overview/cregy.asp

———. 1997c. *Country Profile: State Of Kuwait*. www.awo.net/country/overview/crkuw.asp

———. 1997d. *Country Profile: Sultinate of Oman*. www.awo.net/country/overview/croman.asp

———. 1997e. *Country Profile: State of Qatar*. www.awo.net/country/overview/crqat.asp

———. 1997f. *Country Profile: United Arab Emirates*. www.awo.net/country/overview/cruae.asp

———. 1997g. *Country Profile: Kingdom of Saudi Arabia*. www.awo.net/country/overview/crsau.asp

Ariff, Mohamed. 1988. Islamic Banking. *Asian–Pacific Economic Literature* 2, no. 2: 48–64. Available on-line at www.uio.no/~stvhoy11/islbank.html

Armah, B. 1995. Trade Affected Workers in the Service Sector: 1987 and 1990. *American Journal of Economics and Sociology* 54, no. 2: 163–181.

Arpan, Jeffrey S., and Lee H. Radebaugh. 1985. *International Accounting and Multi-national Enterprises*. 2d ed. New York: John Wiley & Sons.

Arthur Andersen. 1997a. *Human Capital Services*. Istanbul, Turkey: Arthur Andersen.

———. 1997b. *Turkey, Opportunity Knocks*. Istanbul, Turkey: Arthur Andersen.

———. 1997c. *Doing Business in Turkey*. Istanbul, Turkey: Arthur Andersen.

———. 1997d. *Kuwait*. South Carolina: Arthur Andersen.

Arthur Andersen Al-Bazie & Co. 1996. *A General Guide to Kuwait Tax*. Kuwait: Andersen Worldwide.

Arthur Andersen & Company. [1963] 1984. *The Fifty Years 1913–1963*. Reprint. Chicago: Arthur Andersen.

Askari, Hossein, Maha Bazzari, and William Tyler. 1998. Policies and Economic Potential in the Countries of the Gulf Cooperation Council. In *Economic Challenges Facing Middle Eastern and North African Countries: Alternative Futures*, Nemat Shafik, ed., 225–255. New York: St. Martins Press.

Ayata, Sencer. 1993. The Rise of Islamic Fundamentalism and Its Institutional Frame-work. In *The Political and Socioeconomic Transformation of Turkey*, Atila Eralp, Muharrem Tunay, and Birol A. Yesilada, eds., 51–68. Westport, Conn.: Praeger.

Ayubi, Nazih N. 1997. *Over-Stating the Arab State: Politics and Society in the Middle East*. New York: St. Martin's Press.

Baer, W., and L. Samuelson. 1981. Toward a Service Oriented Growth Strategy. *World Development* 9, no. 6: 499–514.

Bavishi, Vinod. 1991. *International Accounting and Auditing Trends*. 2d ed. Princeton, N.J.: Center for International Analysis and Research.

Beblawi, Hazem. 1984. *The Arab Gulf Economy in a Turbulent Age*. New York: St. Martin's Press.

Beenstock, M. 1979. Corruption and Development. *World Development* 7, no. 1 (January): 15–24.

Belassa, Bela 1983. Structural Adjustment Policies in Developing Economies. *World Development* 10, no. 1 (January): 23–38.

Belkaoui, Ahmed. 1985. *International Accounting: Issues and Solutions*. Westport, Conn.: Quorum Books.

———. 1988. *The New Environment of International Accounting: Issues and Prac-tices*. Westport, Conn.: Quorum Books.

Benz, S. F. 1989. Trade Liberalization and the Global Service Economy. *Journal of World Trade Law* 19 (March–April): 95–120.

Bhaduri, Amit, Anjan Mukherji, and Ramprasad Sengupta. 1982. Problems of Long-Term Growth: A Theoretical Analysis. In *Problems and Policies in Small Economies*, Bimal Jalan, ed., 49–68. New York: St. Martin's Press.

Bhagwati, J. N. 1984. Splintering and Disembodiment of Services and Developing Nations. *World Economy* 7, no. 2: 133–143.

Bhalla, A. S. 1970. The Role of Services in Employment Expansion. *International Labor Review* 101, no. 5: 529–539.

———. 1973. A Disaggregative Approach to LDC's Tertiary Sector. *Journal of Development Studies* 10, no. 5: 529–539.

Blair, P. M. 1980. Implications of Growth in Services for Social Structure. *Social Science Quarterly* 61, no. 1: 3–22.

Bouhdiba, Abdelwahab. 1979. Arab Migrations. In *Arab Industrialization and Economic Integration*, Roberto Aliboni, ed., 134–188. New York: St. Martin's Press.

Brennan, W. John. 1979. *The Internationalization of the Accountancy Profession.* Toronto, Canada: Institute of Chartered Accountants.

Brief, Richard P. 1986. *Accounting Thought and Practice through the Years.* New York: Garland Publishing.

Bromley, Simon. 1994. *Rethinking Middle East Politics.* Austin: University of Texas Press.

Bromwich, M., and A. G. Hopwood, eds. 1983. *Accounting Standards Setting: An International Perspective.* London: Pitman.

Buckley, Peter J., and Jeremy Clegg, eds. 1991. *Multinational Enterprises in Less Developed Countries.* New York: St. Martin's Press.

Burns, Jane O. 1980. Transfer Pricing Decisions in Multinational Corporations. *Journal of International Business Studies* (Fall): 23–39.

Burns, Joseph M. 1976. *Accounting Standards and International Finance.* Washington D.C.: American Enterprise Institute of Public Policy Research.

Burton, John C., ed. 1981. *The International World of Accounting: Challenges and Opportunities.* New York: Arthur Young.

Cairns, David. 1988. Calling All National Standard Setters. *Accountancy* 104 (February): 13–14.

———. 1989. IASC's Blueprint for the Future. *Accountancy* 104 (December): 80–82.

———. 1990. Aid for the Developing World. *Accountancy* 105 (March): 82–85.

Candilis, Wary O., ed. 1988. *United States Service Industries Handbook.* New York: Praeger.

Castle, Leslie, and Christopher Findley, eds. 1988. *Pacific Trade in Services.* Sydney, Australia: Allen & Unwin.

Charles, S. 1993. Conceptualizing Services Sector Productivity. *Social and Economic Studies* 42, no. 4: 95–113.

Clark, John I., and Howard Bowen-Jones, eds. 1981. *Change and Development in the Middle East.* New York: Methuen.

Cleron, Jean Paul. 1978. *Saudi Arabia 2000: A Strategy for Growth.* New York: St. Martin's Press.

Coffey, William J., and Antoine S. Bailly. 1991. Producer Services and Flexible Production: An Exploratory Analysis. *Growth and Change* 22, no. 4: 95–117.

Collins, Stephen H. 1989. The Move to Globalization: An Interview with Ralph E. Walters. *Journal of Accountancy* 167, no. 3: 82–85.

Comor, Edward A., ed. 1994. *The Global Political Economy of Communication: Hegemony, Telecommunication and the Information Economy.* New York: St. Martin's Press.

Cook, Allan. 1989. International Business: A Chance for Change in United Kingdom Accounting. In *International Pressures for Accounting Change*, Anthony G. Hopwood, ed. Hemel Hempstead, U.K.: Prentice Hall International.

Coopers & Lybrand International. 1996. *Bahrain: A Guide for Businessmen and Investors.* Bahrain: Coopers & Lybrand Jawad Habib & Co.

———. 1997. *Coopers & Lybrand: Bahrain.* www.cooperslybrand.co..bh/

CPA Journal. 1992. International Accounting Standards: Are They Coming to America? *CPA Journal* 62, no. 10: 16–18, 21–24.

Daniel, Norman. 1993. *Islam and the West: The Making of an Image.* Oxford: Oneworld Publications.

Daniels, P. W. 1982. *Service Industries*. Cambridge: Cambridge University Press.
———. 1985. The Geography of Services. *Progress in Human Geography* 9, no. 3: 443–451.
———. 1993. *Service Industries in the World Economy*. Oxford: Blackwell Publishers.
DeBendt, J. 1996. Business Services: Markets and Transactions. *Review of Industrial Organization* 11, no. 1: 19–33.
Deloitte Touche Tohmatsu International. 1992. *Syria*. New York: Deloitte Touche Tohmatsu International.
———. 1994a. *Egypt*. New York: Deloitte Touche Tohmatsu International.
———. 1994b. *Turkey: International Tax and Business Guide*. New York: Deloitte Touche Tohmatsu International.
———. 1996. *United Arab Emirates*. New York: Deloitte Touche Tohmatsu International.
Diett, A. K., and K. Y. Lee. 1993. The Service Sector and Economic Growth: Some Cross-Sectional Evidence. *International Review of Applied Economics* 7, no. 3: 311–329.
Doyle, P., and M. Corstjens. 1983. Optimal Growth Strategies for Service Organizations. *Journal of Business* 56, no. 3: 389–405.
Dunning, J. H. 1989. Multinational Enterprises and the Growth of Services: Some Conceptual and Theoretical Issues. *The Service Industries Journal* 9: 5–34.
Eckstein, H. J., and D. M. Heier. 1985. Causes and Consequences of Service Sector Growth: The U.S. Experience. *Growth and Change* 16, no. 2: 12–17.
El-Erian, Mohamed A., and Susan Fennel. 1997. *The Economy of the Middle East and North Africa in 1997*. Washington, D.C.: International Monetary Fund.
El Mallakh, Ragasi. 1981. *The Economic Development of the United Arab Emirates*. New York: St. Martin's Press.
———. 1985. *Qatar: Energy and Development*. London: Croom Helm.
Emerson Company. 1996. *Emerson's 1996 Big Six Annual Report*. Bellevue, Wash.: Emerson Company.
———. 1996. Coopers & Lybrand: Creating "A Whole New Ball Game" for Business Assurance Services. Reprinted from *Emerson's Professional Services Review*, May–June.
Enderwick, Peter. 1991. Service Sector Multinationals and Developing Countries. In *Multinational Enterprises in Less Developed Countries*, Peter J. Buckly and Jeremy Clegg, eds., 292–309. New York: St Martin's Press.
Enderwick, Peter, ed. 1989. *Multinational Service Firms*. New York: Routledge.
Eralp, Atila. 1993. Turkey and the European Community: Prospects for a New Relationship. In *The Political and Socioeconomic Transformation of Turkey*, Atila Eralp, Muharrem Tunay, and Birol Yesilada, eds., 193–214. Westport, Conn.: Praeger.
Eralp, Atila, Muharrem Tunay, and Birol Yesilada, eds. 1993. *The Political and Socioeconomic Transformation of Turkey*. Westport, Conn.: Praeger.
Ernst & Young. 1990. *Doing Business in the United Arab Emirates*. New York: Ernst & Young International.
———. 1991. *Doing Business in Saudi Arabia*. New York: Ernst & Young International.
———. 1995–1997. *Doing Business around the World*. www.eyi.com/cgi-bin/foliocgi.../query=*/doc/{tl}/pageitems={body}?
———. 1997a. *The Middle East Practice*. www.eyi.com/mideast/meinfo.htm

————. 1997b. *Audit and Related Services.* www.eyi.com/mideast/meaudit.htm

————. 1997c. *Management Consultancy.* www.eyi.com/mideast/memcs.htm

————. 1997d. *Accounting and Financial Services.* www.eyi.com/mideast/meaccnt.htm

————. 1997e. *Taxation.* www.eyi.com/mideast/metax.htm

————. 1997f. *Middle East Taxation.* www,eyi.com/mideast/Mebbtaxb.htm

————. 1997g. *Business Community Training.* www.eyi.com/mideast/metrain.htm

Evans, Thomas G., Martin E. Taylor, and Oscar Holzmann. 1985. *International Accounting and Reporting.* New York: Macmillan.

Fakhro, Munira A. 1997. The Uprising in Bahrain: An Assessment. In *The Persian Gulf at the Millennium*, Gary G. Sick and Lawrence G. Potter, eds., 167–188. New York: St. Martin's Press.

Falk, L. H., and A. Broner. 1980. Specialization in Service Industry Employment as a State Policy. *Growth and Change* 11, no. 4: 18–23.

Falvey, R. E., and Norman Gemmell. 1995. Explaining International Differences in the Share of Services in Real Expenditure. *Economic Letters* 47, no. 1: 59–62.

Falvey, R. E., and N. A. Gemmell. 1996. Formalization and Test of the Factor Productivity Explanation of International Differences in Service Prices. *International Economic Review* 37, no. 1: 85–102.

Feketekuty, Geza. 1988. *International Trade in Services: An Overview and Blueprint for Negotiations.* Cambridge, Mass.: Ballinger.

Fenelon, K. G. 1976. *The United Arab Emirates: An Economic and Social Survey.* 2d ed. New York: Longman.

Fischer, Stanley, et al., eds. 1994. *Securing Peace in the Middle East: Project on Economic Transition.* Cambridge, Mass.: MIT Press.

Fishelson, Gideon, ed. 1989. *Economic Cooperation in the Middle East.* Boulder, Colo.: Westview Press.

Fisher, Allan G. B. 1939. *Economic Self-Sufficiency.* New York: Farrar and Rinehart.

Fitzgerald, R. D. 1981. International Harmonization of Accounting and Reporting. *International Journal of Accounting* 17 (Fall): 21–32.

Forsyth, David J. C. 1990. *Technology Policy for Small Developing Countries.* New York: St. Martin's Press.

Fox, Samuel, and Norlin G. Rueschholf. 1986. *Principles of International Accounting.* Austin, Tex.: Austin Press.

Francois, J. F. 1990. Producer Services: Scale and the Division of Labour. *Oxford Economic Papers* 42, no. 4: 715–729.

Fuchs, Victor R. 1964. *Productivity Trends in the Goods and Service Sectors, 1929–61: A Preliminary Survey.* New York: Columbia University Press.

————. 1965. The Growing Importance of the Service Industries. *Journal of Business of the University of Chicago* 38: 344–373.

————. 1968. *The Service Economy.* New York: Columbia University Press.

Fuller, Graham E. 1997. Turkey and the Middle East Northern Tier. In *The Middle East in Global Change*, Laura Guazzone, ed., 43–57. New York: St. Martin's Press.

Gambling, Trevor, and Rifaat Ahmed Abdel Karim. 1991. *Business and Accounting Ethics in Islam.* New York: Mansell.

Gause, F. Gregory III. 1997. The Political Economy of National Security in GCC States. In *The Persian Gulf at the Millennium: Essays in Politics, Economy, Security, and Religion*, Gary G. Sick and Lawrence G. Potter, eds., 61–84. New York: St. Martin's Press.

Germidis, Dimitri, and Charles Albert Michalet. 1984. *International Banks and Financial Markets in Developing Countries.* Paris: OECD Development Center Studies.

Gershuny, Jonathan. 1978. *After Industrial Society? The Emerging Self-Service Economy.* Atlantic Highlands, N.J.: Humanities Press.

Gershuny, Jonathan, and I. D. Miles. 1983. *The New Service Economy: The Transformation of Employment in Industrial Societies.* New York: Praeger.

Goe, W. R. 1991. The Growth of Producer Services Industries: Sorting through the Externalization Debate. *Growth and Change* 22, no. 4: 118–141.

Government of Dubai. 1998. *Executive Summary: Opportunities for Trade; Opportunities for Regional Offices; Opportunities for Transportation and Distribution; Opportunities for Industrial Investment.* www.dctpb.gov.ae/detpb/business/Executive-Summary.html

Hale, William. 1981. *The Political and Economic Development of Modern Turkey.* New York: St. Martin's Press.

Hameed Bin Hj, Shahul, and Mohamed Ibrahim. 1997a. *From Conventional Accounting to Islamic Accounting: A Review of the Development [of] Western Accounting Theory and Its Implications for and Differences in the Development of Islamic Accounting.* www.dundee.ac.uk/Accountancy/phd/3fr1exte.htm

———. 1997b. *A Study into the Nature of Islamic Accounting with an Empirical Investigation of Its Application in the Financing and Disclosure Practices of Islamic Financial Institutions.* www.dundee.ac.uk/Accountancy/phd/scotdoc.htm

Handoussa, Heba, and Hanaa Kheir-El-Din. 1998. A Vision for Egypt in 2012. In *Economic Challenges Facing Middle Eastern and North African Countries: Alternative Futures*, Nemat Shafik, ed., 53–77. New York: St. Martin's Press.

Harker, Patrick T., ed. 1995. *The Service Productivity and Quality Challenge.* Boston: Kluwer.

Harrington, James W., Alan D. MacPherson, and John R. Lombard. 1991. Interregional Trade in Producer Services: Review and Synthesis. *Growth and Change* 22, no. 4: 75–93.

Havrylyshyn, Oleh. 1997. *A Global Integration Strategy for the Mediterranean Countries: Open Trade and Market Reforms.* Washington, D.C.: International Monetary Fund.

Heely, James A., and Roy L. Nersesian. 1993. *Global Management Accounting: A Guide for Executives of International Corporations.* Westport, Conn.: Quorum Books.

Higgins, Benjamin. 1983. From Growth Poles to Systems of Interactions in Space. *Growth and Change* 14, no. 4: 2–13.

Hitchens, D. M. W. N., P. N. O'Farrell, and C. Conway. 1994. Business Service Use by Manufacturing Firms in Mid Wales. *Environment and Planning A* 26, no.1: 95–106.

Holmes, Sir Frank, ed. 1987. *Economic Adjustment: Policies and Problems.* Washington, D.C.: International Monetary Fund.

Hopwood, Anthony G., ed. 1989. *International Pressures for Accounting Change.* Hemel Hempstead, U.K.: Prentice Hall International.

Ibrahim, Shahul Hameed Bin Hj. Mohamed. 1997. *From Conventional to Islamic Accounting: A Review of the Development of Western Accounting Theory and Its Implications for and Differences in the Development of Islamic Accounting.* www.dundee.ac.uk/Accountancy/phd/3fr1exte.htm

International Monetary Fund. 1997. *Financial Systems and Labor Markets in the Gulf Cooperation Council Countries.* Washington, D.C.: International Monetary Fund.

Ismail, Azman. 1997. *Insurance and Shari'a'.* www.islam.org.au/articles/19/insurance.htm

Jalan, Bimal, ed. 1982. *Problems and Policies in Small Economies.* New York: St. Martin's Press.

Jameson, Kenneth P. 1977. The Development of the Service Industry: An Empirical Investigation. *Quarterly Review of Economics and Business* 17, no. 10: 31–40.

Jbili, Abdelali, Vincente Galbis, and Amer Bisat. 1997. Financial Systems and Reform in the Gulf Cooperation Council Countries. In *Financial Systems and Labor Markets in the Gulf Cooperation Council Countries*, by International Monetary Fund, 1–24. Washington, D.C.: International Monetary Fund.

Johany, Ali D., Michel Berne, and J. Wilson Mixon, Jr. 1986. *The Saudi Arabian Economy.* Baltimore, Md.: Johns Hopkins University Press.

Johns, R. A., and C. M. LeMarchant. 1993. *Finance Centres: British Isles Offshore Development since 1979.* London: Pinter.

Jussawalla, Meheroo, Tadayuki Okama, and Toshihiro Araki, eds. 1989. *Information Technology and Global Interdependence.* Westport, Conn.: Greenwood Press.

Kedourie, Elie, and Sylvia G. Haim, eds. 1988. *Essays on the Economic History of the Middle East.* London: Frank Cass.

Kilmarx, Robert A., and Yonah Alexander, eds. 1982. *Business and the Middle East: Threats and Prospects.* New York: Pergamon Press.

Knauerhase, Ramon. 1975. *The Saudi Arabian Economy.* New York: Praeger.

Kotb, Sayed. 1970. *Social Justice in Islam.* Translated from Arabic to English by John B. Hardie. New York: Octagon Books.

KPMG Fakhro. 1997. *List of Services Provided by KPMG Fakhro.* php.indiana.edu/~hqasem/kpmg/kpmgserv.html

KPMG International. 1997a. *Industry.* www.kpmg.com/indust.html

———. 1997b. *Services.* www.kpmg.com/services.html

———. 1997c. *Statistics.* www.kpmg.com/stats.html

———. 1997d. *World Wide Presence.* www.kpmg.com/wwpres.html

———. 1997e. *KPMG International Contact Partners.* www.kpmg.com/mideast.html

KPMG Peat Marwick LLP. 1997f. *Annual Report 1997.* New York: KPMG Peat Marwick LLP.

Kubursi, Afti A. 1984. *Oil, Industrialization and Development in the Arab Gulf States.* London: Croom Helm.

Kuran, Timur. 1997. The Genesis of Islamic Economics: A Chapter in the Politics of Muslim Identity. *Social Research* 64, no. 2: 301–338.

Levitt, T. 1986. *The Marketing Imagination.* New York: The Free Press.

Leyshon, A., P. W. Daniels, and N. S. Thrift. 1987. Internationalization of Professional Producer Services: The Case of Large Accountancy Firms. *Working Papers on Producer Services*, no. 3 (March). St. David's University, Lampeter and University of Liverpool.

Library of Congress. 1997a. *Egypt—A Country Study.* lcweb2.loc.gov/frd/cs/egtoc.html

———. 1997b. *Jordan—A Country Study.* lcweb2.loc.gov/frd/cs/jotoc.html

———. 1997c. *Saudi Arabia—A Country Study.* leweb2.loc.gov/frd/es/satoc.html

Lloyd, P. J., and R. M. Sundrum. 1982. Characteristics of Small Economies. In *Problems and Policies in Small Economies*, Bimal Jalan, ed., 17–38. New York: St. Martin's Press.

Looney, Robert E. 1982. *Saudi Arabia's Development Potential.* Lexington, Mass.: D. C. Heath and Company.

Mawdudi, Sayyid Abul A'la. 1992. *Let Us Be Muslims.* Khurram Murad, trans. and ed. Leicester, U.K.: The Islamic Foundation.

McKee, David L. 1988. *Growth, Development and the Service Economy in the Third World.* New York: Praeger.

McKee, David L., ed. 1994. *External Linkages and Growth in Small Economies.* Westport, Conn.: Praeger.

McKee, David L., Yosra A. Amara, and Don E. Garner. 1995. International Services As Facilitators. *Foreign Trade Review* 29, no. 4: 254–264.

McKee, David L., Yosra Abu-Amara McKee, and Don E. Garner. 1997a. Some Reflections on Accounting Services in the Global Economy. In *Business Research Yearbook: Global Business Perspectives*, Jerry Biberman and Abbass Alkhafaji, eds., 35–39. Vol. 4.

———. 1998. Some Foundations and Facilitators of Business Expansion in Saudi Arabia. In *Business Research Yearbook: Global Business Perspectives*, Jerry Biberman and Abbass Alkhafaji, eds., 385–389. Vol. 5

———. 1997b. The Positive Functions of Offshore Financial Centers. *Journal of Global Competitiveness* 5, no. 1: 406–413.

McKee, David L., and Don E. Garner. 1992. *Accounting Services, the International Economy, and Third World Development.* Westport, Conn.: Praeger.

———. 1996. *Accounting Services, Growth, and Change in the Pacific Basin.* Westport, Conn.: Quorum Books.

McKee, David L., Don E. Garner, and Yosra AbuAmara McKee. 1998. *Accounting Services and Growth in Small Economies: Evidence from the Caribbean Basin.* Westport, Conn.: Quorum Books.

Melvin, J. R. 1995. History and Measurement in the Service Sector: A Review. *Income and Wealth* 41, no. 4: 481–494.

MFA. 1997a. *Banking in Turkey.* www.mfa.gov.tr/grupc/c5.htm

———. 1997b. *Development of Infrastructure.* www.mfa.gov.tr/grupc/clb.htm

———. 1997c. *Energy Sector in Turkey.* www.mfa.gov.tr/grupc/industry/energy.htm

———. 1997d. *External Payments and Debts.* www.mfa.gov.tr/grupc/cld.htm

———. 1997e. *Industrial Analysis by Sectors.* www.mfa.gov.tr/grupc/cle.htm

———. 1997f. *Industry.* www.mfa.gov.tr/grupc/Indus96.htm

———. 1997g. *Overview of Turkish Economic Development.* www.mfa.gov.tr/grupc/cla.htm

Moliver, Donald M., and Paul J. Abbondante. 1980. *The Economy of Saudi Arabia.* New York: Praeger.

Most, Kenneth S. 1988. *Advances in International Accounting.* Vol. 2. Greenwich, Conn.: JAI Press.

Mottahedeh, Roy P., and Mamoun Fandy. 1997. The Islamic Movement: The Case for Democratic Inclusion. In *The Persian Gulf at the Millennium: Essays in Politics, Economy, Security, and Religion*, Gary G. Sick and Lawrence G. Potter, eds., 297–318. New York: St. Martin's Press.

Mueller, Gerhard G., Helen Gernon, and Gary Meek. 1991. *Accounting: An International Perspective*. Homewood, Ill.: Irwin.

Nafi, Zuhair Ahmed. 1983. *Economic and Social Development in Qatar*. London: Frances Pinter.

Nando.net and Reuter Information Service. 1997. *Saudi Arabia Takes First Steps to Join WTO*. www.nando.net/newsroom/ntn/world/052696/world16-833html

Nell, Edward. 1988. *Prosperity and Public Spending: Transformational Growth and the Role of Government*. Boston: Unwin Hyman.

Nobes, C. W., and R. H. Parker, eds. 1991. *Comparative International Accounting*. 3d ed. Oxford: Irwin.

Nonneman, Gerd. 1988. *Development, Administration and Aid in the Middle East*. New York: Routledge, Chapman Hall.

Norton, Augustus Richard. 1997. Political Reform in the Middle East. In *The Middle East in Global Change*, Laura Guazzone, ed. New York: St. Martin's Press.

Noyelle, Thierry J., and Anna B. Dutka. 1988. *International Trade in Business Services*. Cambridge: Ballinger.

Nugent, Jeffery B., and Theodore H. Thomas, eds. 1985. *Bahrain and the Gulf: Past Perspectives and Alternative Futures*. New York: St. Martin's Press.

Nurkse, Ragner. 1967. *Problems of Capital Formation in Underdeveloped Countries and Patterns of Trade and Development*. New York: Oxford University Press.

Nusbaumer, Jaques. 1987. *Services in the Global Market*. Boston, Mass.: Kluwer Academic.

O'Farrell, P.N. 1994. Manufacturing Demand for Business Services. *Cambridge Journal of Economics* 19, no. 4: 523–543.

O'Farrell, P. N., and L. A. R. Moffat. 1995. Business Services and Their Impact upon Client Performance: An Exploratory Interregional Analysis. *Regional Studies* 29, no. 2: 111–124.

O'Farrell, P. N., L. A. R. Moffat, and P. A. Wood. 1995. Internationalization of Business Services: A Methodological Critique of Foreign-Market Entry-Mode Choice. *Environment and Planning A* 27, no. 5: 683–697.

Ohmae, Kenichi. 1990. *The Borderless World: Power and Strategy in the Interlinked Economy*. New York: McKinsey & Company.

O'Malley, Shaun F. 1992. Accounting Across Borders. *Financial Executive* 8, no. 2: 28–31.

Oman. 1997. www.ita.doc.gov/mena/projoman.txt

Oman: The Taiwan of the Gulf. 1995. *Gulf States Newsletter* 502 (16 January). www.ex.ac.uk/ags/502.htm

Organization for Economic Cooperation and Development. 1980a. Accounting Standards for International Business. *OECD Observer* 104 (May): 28–29.

———. 1980b. *Accounting Practices in OECD Countries*. Paris: OECD.

———. 1986. *Financial Resources for Developing Countries: 1985 and Recent Trends*. Paris: OECD.

Orsine, Larry L., and Lawrence R. Hudack. 1992. EEC Financial Reporting: Another Source of Harmonization of Accounting Principles. *CPA Journal* 62, no. 10: 20.

Oweiss, Ibrahim M. 1982. Egypt: Strategic, Economic, and Political Assessment. In *Business and the Middle East: Threats and Prospects*, Robert A. Kilmarx and Yonah Alexander, eds., 57–90. New York: Pergamon.

Pakravan, Karim. 1997. The Emerging Private Sector: New Demands on an Old System. In *The Persian Gulf at the Millennium: Essays in Politics, Economy, Security, and Religion*, Gary G. Sick and Lawrence G. Potter, eds., 115–126. New York: St. Martin's Press.

Parry, Thomas G. 1973. The International Firm and National Economic Policy. *The Economic Journal* 84, no. 332: 1201–1221.

Patrikis, Ernest T. 1996. *Islamic Finance in the United States—The Regulatory Framework.* www.ny.frb.org/phiome/news/speeches/ep960523.html

Peavy, Dennis E., and Stuart K. Webster. 1990. Is GAAP the Gap to International Markets? *Management Accounting* 72, no. 2: 31–35.

Porter, Michael E. 1990. *The Competitive Advantage of Nations.* New York: The Free Press.

Price Waterhouse. 1991. *Doing Business in Saudi Arabia.* New York: World Firm Limited.

———. 1993. *Doing Business in Turkey.* New York: World Firm Limited.

———. 1995. *Doing Business in Egypt.* New York: World Firm Limited.

———. 1996a. *Doing Business in Qatar.* New York: World Firm Limited.

———. 1996b. *Doing Business in the United Arab Emirates.* New York: World Firm Limited.

———. 1997a. *Audit and Business Advisory Services.* www.pw.com/abs/

———. 1997b. *Business Processes.* www.pw.com/mes/sv-bus-proc.htm

———. 1997c. *Doing Business in Bahrain.* New York: World Firm Limited.

———. 1997d. *Energy: Products and Services.* www.pw.com/energy/products.htm

———. 1997e. *Information Technology.* www.pw.com/mcs/sv-info-tech.htm

———. 1997f. *Managing Change.* www.pw.com/mcs/sv-change.htm

———. 1997g. *Petroleum.* www.pw.com/energy/petro.htm

———. 1997h. *Services.* www.pw.com/wo/services.htm

———. 1997i. *Tax and Legal Services.* www.pw.com/tl/

———. 1997j. *Utilities.* www.pw.com/energy/utility.htm

Pridham, B. R., ed. 1985. *Economy, Society and Culture in Contemporary Yemen.* London: Croom Helm.

Prieto, F. J. 1986. Services: A Disquieting Link between America and the World Economy. *Cepal Review*, no. 30: 117–136.

Rahmon, M. Z., and J. E. Finnerty. 1986. International Accounting Standards and Transnational Corporations. *Revista Internationale di Scienze Economiche e Commercial* 33, no. 6–7: 697–714.

RAND Corporation. 1995. *Oman: A Unique Foreign Policy Produces a Key Player in Middle Eastern and Global Diplomacy.* www.rand.org/publications/RB/RB2501/RB2501.html

Riahi-Belkaoui, Ahmed. 1994. *Accounting in the Developing Countries.* Westport, Conn.: Quorum Books.

Riddle, D. I. 1986. *Service-Led Growth: The Role of the Service Sector in World Development.* New York: Praeger.

Robinson, E. A. G. 1963. *Economic Consequences of the Size of Nations.* New York: St. Martin's Press.

Robinson, Richard D. 1988. *The International Transfer of Technology: Theory Issues and Practice.* Cambridge, Mass.: Ballinger.

Romanoff, E., and S. H. Levine. 1993. Information Industry Dynamics and the Service Industries. *Environment and Planning A* 25, no. 3: 305–316.

Roth, Gabriel. 1982. *The Private Provision of Public Services in Developing Countries.* New York: Oxford University Press.

Sabagn, Georges, ed. 1989. *The Modern Economic and Social History of the Middle East in Its World Context.* New York: Cambridge University Press.

Salem, Paul E. 1997. Arab Political Currents, Arab–European Relations and Mediterraneanism. In *The Middle East in Global Change*, Laura Guazzone, ed., 23–42. New York: St. Martin's Press.

Samuels, J. M., and J. Oliga. 1982. Accounting Standards in Developing Countries. *International Journal of Accounting* 18 (Fall): 67–88.

Samuels, J. M., and A. G. Piper. 1985. *International Accounting: A Survey.* New York: St. Martin's Press.

Sassanpour, Cyrus, Ghazi Joharji, Alexei Kireyev, and Martin Petri. 1997. Labor Market Challenges and Policies in the Gulf Cooperation Council Countries. In *Financial Systems and Labor Markets in the Gulf Cooperation Council Countries*, International Monetary Fund, 25–50. Washington, D.C.: International Monetary Fund.

Saunders, Robert J., Jeremy J. Warford, and Wellenius Bjorn. 1984. *Telecommunications and Economic Development.* 2d ed. Baltimore, Md.: Johns Hopkins University Press for the World Bank.

Segal-Horn, Susan. 1993. The Internationalization of Service Firms. *Advances in Strategic Management* 9: 31–55.

Seznec, Jean-Francois. 1987. *The Financial Markets of the Arabian Gulf.* New York: Croom Helm.

Shafik, Nemat, ed. 1998a. *Economic Challenges Facing Middle Eastern and North African Countries: Alternative Futures.* New York: St. Martin's Press.

———. 1998b. *Prospects for Middle Eastern and North African Economies: From Boom to Bust and Back?* New York: St. Martin's Press.

Shari'a'te Accounting: An Ethical Construction of Accounting Knowledge. 1997. les.man.ac.uk/cpa96/txt/triyuwon.txt

Shelp, Ronald Kent. 1981. *Beyond Industrialization: Ascendancy of the Global Service Economy.* New York: Praeger.

Sick, Gary G., and Lawrence G. Potter, eds. 1997. *The Persian Gulf at the Millennium.* New York: St. Martin's Press.

Sletmo, Gunnar K., and Gaven Boyd, eds. 1993. *Pacific Service Enterprises and Pacific Cooperation.* Boulder, Colo.: Westview Press.

Soufi, Wahib Abdulfattah, and Richard T. Mayer. 1991. *Saudi Arabian Industrial Investment: An Analysis of Government–Business Relationships.* New York: Quorum Books.

Spero, Joan E. 1989. The Information Revolution and Fianancial Services: A New North–South Issue? In *Information Technology and Global Interdependence*, Meheroo Jussawalla, Tadayuki Okama, and Toshihiro Araki, eds., 109–117. Westport, Conn.: Greenwood Press.

Stanback, Thomas M., Jr., Peter J. Bearse, Thierry J. Noyelle, and Robert A. Karasek. 1981. *Services: The New Economy.* Totowa, N.J.: Allanheld, Osmun & Co.

Stern, Robert M., and Bernard M. Hoekmen. 1988. Issues in International Trade in Services. In *Pacific Trade in Services*, Leslie Castle and Christopher Findlay, eds., 19–63. Sydney, Australia: Allen & Unwin.

Stevens, Paul J. 1997. Oil and the Gulf: Alternative Futures. In *The Persian Gulf at the Millennium: Essays in Politics, Economy, Security, and Religion*, Gary G. Sick and Lawrence G. Potter, eds., 85–114. New York: St. Martin's Press.

Stigler, George J. 1956. *Trends in Employment in the Service Industries*. Princeton, N.J.: Princeton University Press.

Technology Development Program. 1995. *TDP Projects and Activities*. its-idsc.gov.eg/tdp/doc/more.htm

Tisdell, C. A. 1990. *Natural Resources, Growth and Development: Economics, Ecology and Resource-Scarcity*. New York: Praeger.

Tisdell, Clem. 1993. Small Island Economies in a World of Economic Change. *Mimeograph*. University of Queensland, Australia.

Tisdell, Clem A., and I. J. Fairbairn. 1984. Labor Supply Constraints on Industrialization, and Production Deficiencies in Traditional Sharing Societies. *Journal of Economic Development* 9: 7–24.

Togan, Subidey. 1998. Determinents of Economic Growth in Turkey. In *Economic Challenges Facing Middle Eastern and North African Countries: Alternative Futures*, Nemat Shafik, ed., 159–177. New York: St. Martin's Press.

Tordoir, Pieter. 1995. *The Professional Knowledge Economy: The Management and Integration of Professional Services in Business Organizations*. Boston: Kluwer Academic.

Tucker, Ken, and Mark Sundberg. 1988. *International Trade in Services*. New York: Routledge.

Turel, Oktar. 1993. The Development of Turkish Manufacturing Industry during 1976–1987: An Overview. In *The Political and Socioeconomic Transformation of Turkey*, Atila Eralp, Muharrem Tunay, and Birol A. Yesilada, eds., 69–97. Westport, Conn.: Praeger.

United Nations Center on Transnational Corporations. 1982. *Towards International Standardization of Corporate Accounting and Reporting*. New York: United Nations Center on Transnational Corporations.

———. 1983. *Transnational Corporations in World Development: Third Survey*. New York: United Nations Center on Transnational Corporations.

———. 1987. *Foreign Direct Investment, the Service Sector and International Banking*. New York: United Nations Center on Transnational Corporations.

United Nations Economic Commission for Western Asia. 1985. *Economic Integration in Western Asia*. New York: St. Martin's Press.

United States Energy Information Administration. 1997. *Qatar*. www.eia.doe.gov/emeu/cabs/qatar.html

U.S.–Saudi Arabian Business Council. 1997a. *About the Business Council*. www.us-saudi-business.org/abcinfo.htm

———. 1997b. *The Saudi Arabian Economy*. www.us-saudi-business.org/economy.htm

———. 1997c. *Doing Business in Saudi Arabia*. www.us-saudi-business.org/business.htm

University of Missouri at St. Louis. 1997. *International Business Practices in Oman*. www.smartliz.com/sbs/arts/bpr58.htm

Vogel, Frank E. 1997. Islamic Governance in the Gulf: A Framework for Analysis, Comparison, and Prediction. In *The Persian Gulf at the Millenium: Essays in Politics, Economy, Security, and Religion*, Gary G. Sick and Lawrence G. Potter, eds., 249–295. New York: St. Martin's Press.

Waeczorek, J. 1995. Sectoral Trends in World Employment and the Shift towards Services. *International Labor Review* 134, no. 2: 205–226.

Waite, Charles A. 1988. Service Sector: Its Importance and Prospects for the Future. In *United States Service Industries Handbook*, Wray O. Candilis, ed., 1–22. New York: Praeger.

Wallace, R. S. Olusegun, John M. Samuels, and Richard J. Briston. 1990. *Research in Third World Accounting*. Vol. 1. London: JAI Press.

Warf, B. 1996. International Engineering Services, 1982–92. *Environment and Planning* 28, no. 4: 667–686.

Wilson, Robert. 1983. *Banking and Finance in the Arab Middle East*. New York: St. Martin's Press.

World Bank. 1997. *World Development Report: The State in a Changing World*. New York: Oxford University Press.

Wu, Fredrick, and Donald W. Hackett. 1977. The Internationalization of U.S. Public Accounting Firms. *International Journal of Accounting* 12 (Spring): 81–91.

Wyatt, Arthur. 1989. International Accounting Standards: A New Perspective. *Accounting Horizons* 3 (September): 105–108.

Wyatt, Arthur R. 1992. Seeking Credibility in a Global Economy. *New Accountant* 8, no. 1: 4–6, 51–52.

Yesilada, Birol A. 1993. Turkish Foreign Policy toward the Middle East. In *The Political and Socioeconomic Transformation of Turkey*, Atila Eralp, Muharrem Tunay, and Birol Yesilada, eds., 169–192. Westport, Conn.: Praeger.

Index

ABOUT THE AUTHORS

David L. McKee is Professor of Economics in the Graduate School of Management of Kent State University, where he specializes in development economics and economic change. Among his publications are *Urban Environments in Emerging Economies* (Praeger, 1994); *Energy, the Environment and Public Policy: Issues for the 1990s* (Praeger, 1991); and *Growth, Development, and the Service Economy in the Third World* (Praeger, 1988).

Don E. Garner is Professor and Chair of the Department of Accounting at California State University, Stanislaus. He is a certified public accountant and a certified internal auditor as well as a specialist in auditing and accounting. Among his publications are *Accounting Services, the International Economy, and Third World Development* (Praeger, 1992); *Accounting Services, Growth, and Change in the Pacific Basin* (Quorum, 1996); both with David L. McKee; and *Accounting Services and Growth in Small Economies* (Quorum, 1998); with David L. McKee and Yosra AbuAmara McKee.

Yosra AbuAmara McKee is a private consultant, specializing in trade and development issues. Her work on international trade and services, economic integration and regional development has been aired in various professional publications and presentations. She is co-author of *Beyond Edge Cities* (1997) and *Accounting Services and Growth in Small Economies: Evidence from the Caribbean Basin* (Quorum, 1998) with Don E. Garner and David L. McKee.

ISBN 1-56720-139-3

EAN

9 781567 201390

90000>

HARDCOVER BAR CODE